RUNAWAYS

LIVE FAST

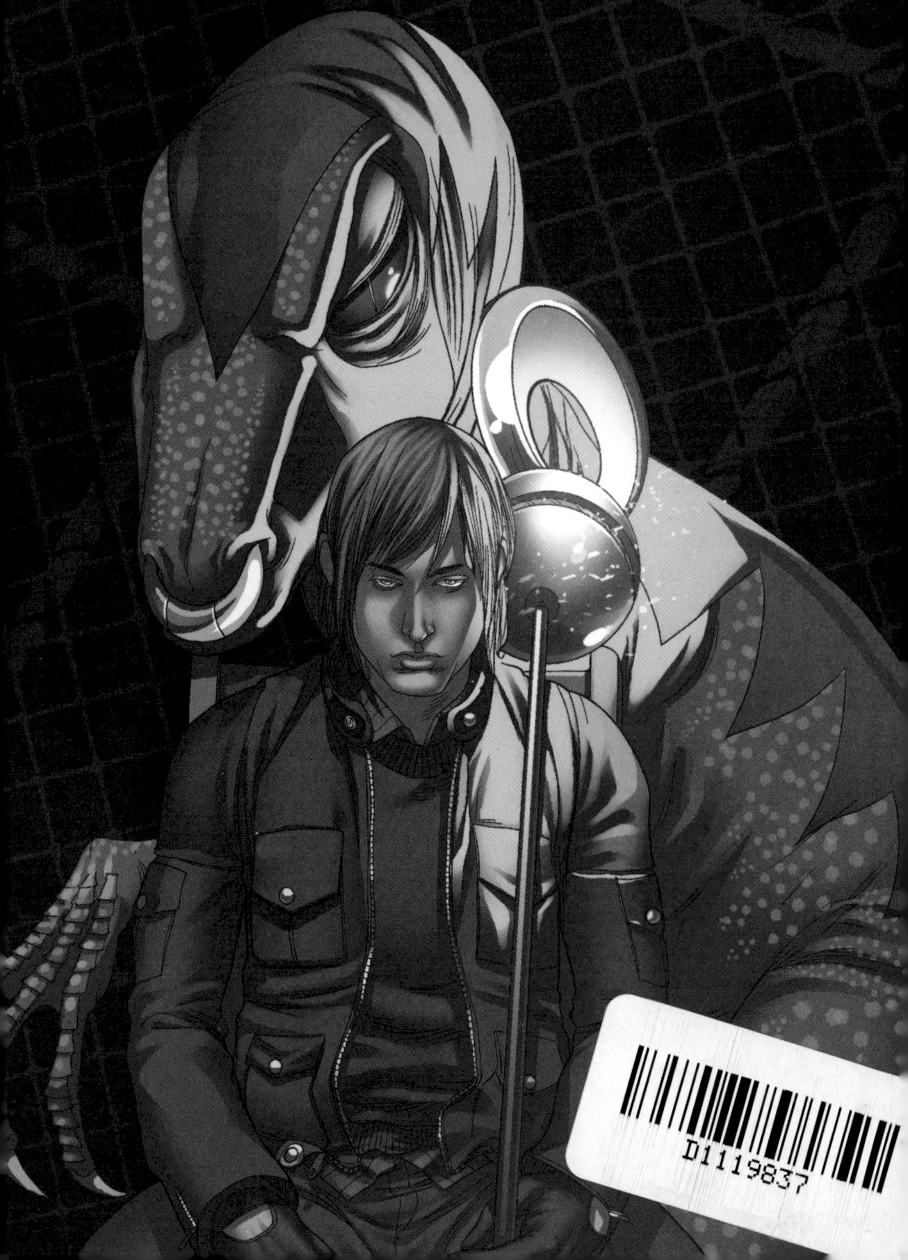

RUNAWAYS →

LIVE FAST

Writer: **Brian K. Vaughan**
Pencilers: **Adrian Alphona and Mike Norton (Issues #19-21)**
Inker: **Craig Yeung**
Colorist: **Christina Strain**
Letterer: **Virtual Calligraphy's Randy Gentile**
Cover Art: **Jo Chen**
Assistant Editors: **Daniel Ketchum, Sean Ryan & Nathan Cosby**
Editor: **Nick Lowe**
Special thanks to **C.B. Cebulski & MacKenzie Cadenhead**

Runaways created by **Brian K. Vaughan & Adrian Alphona**

Collection Editor: **Jennifer Grünwald**
Assistant Editors: **Michael Short & Cory Levine**
Associate Editor: **Mark D. Beazley**
Senior Editor, Special Projects: **Jeff Youngquist**
Senior Vice President of Sales: **David Gabriel**
Vice President of Creative: **Tom Marvelli**

Editor in Chief: **Joe Quesada**
Publisher: **Dan Buckley**

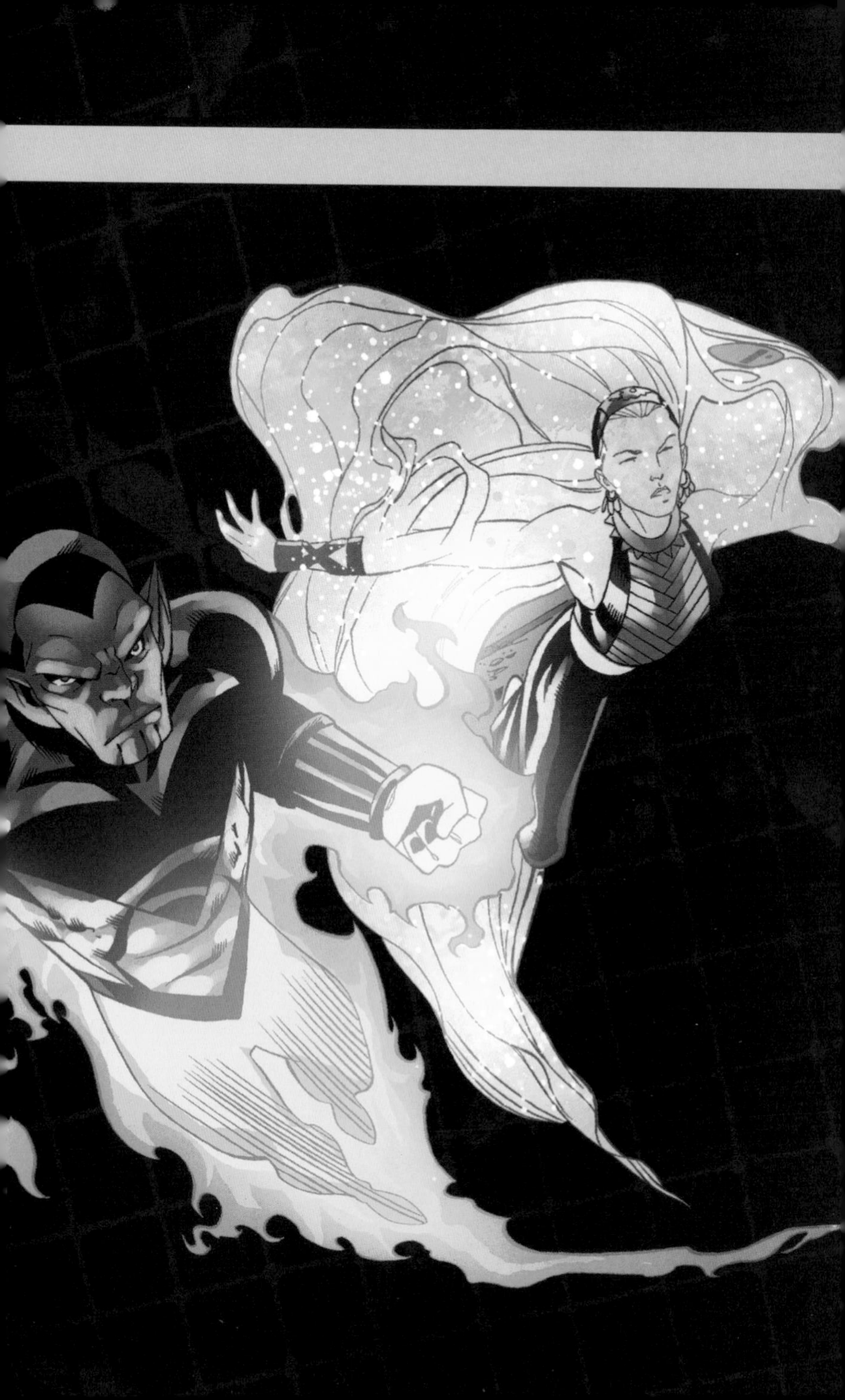

PREVIOUSLY:

At some point in their lives, all kids think they have the most evil parents in the world, but Nico Minoru and her friends really did.

Discovering that they were the children of a group of super-villains known as The Pride the teenagers stole weapons and resources from these criminals, before running away from home and eventually defeating their parents. But that was just the beginning. Together, the teenage runaways now hope to atone for their parents' crimes by taking on the new threats trying to fill The Pride's void.

After a ferocious battle with an all-new Pride led by a temporally displaced Geoffrey Wilder (father of the late Alex Wilder, the Runaways' traitorous leader), Gert Yorkes died in the arms of her boyfriend. With her final breath, Gert "willed" control of her telepathic dinosaur to Chase Stein, just before the devastated young man stole a decoder ring and Wilder's copy of the Abstract, a mystical tome containing powerful secrets.

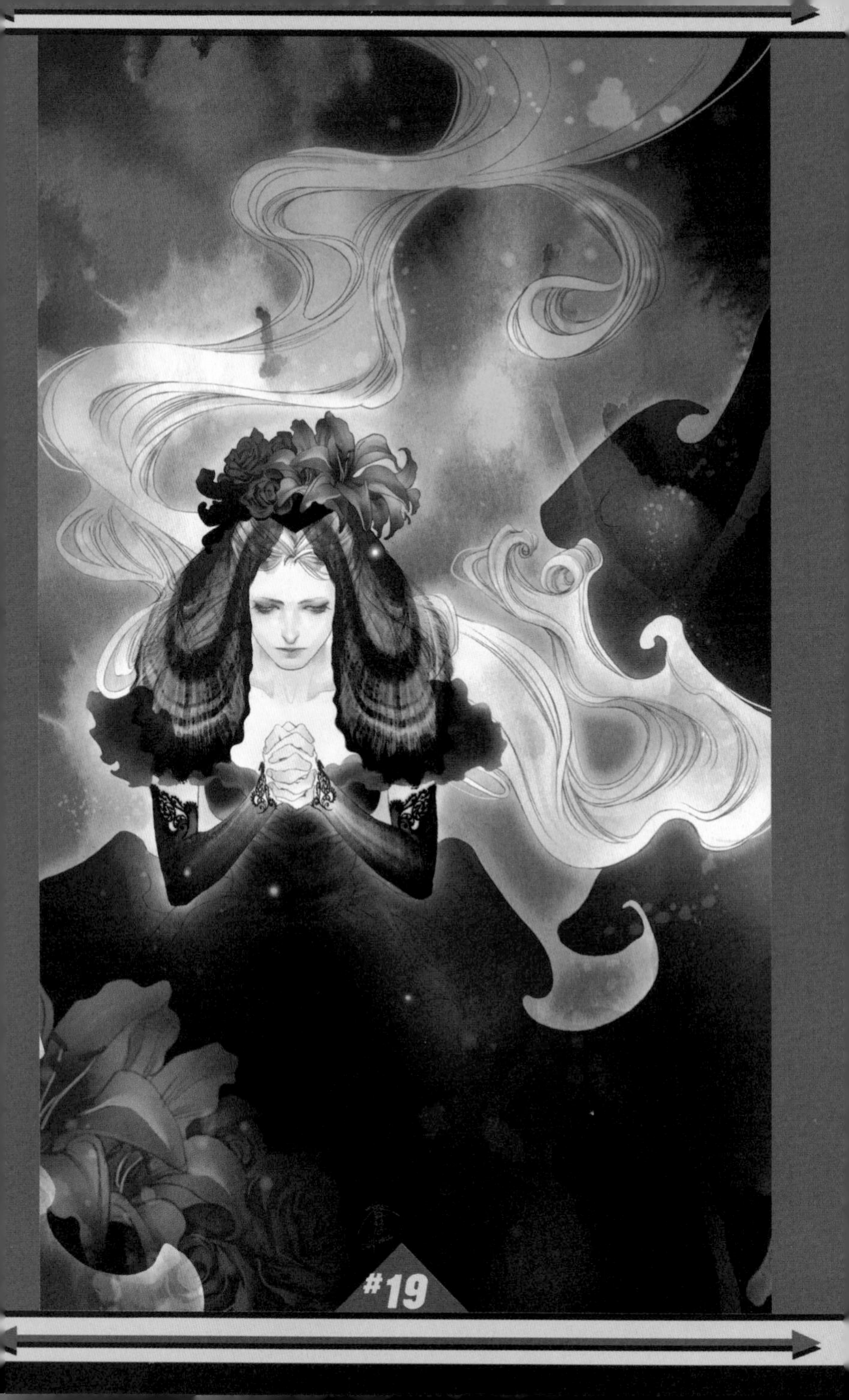
#19

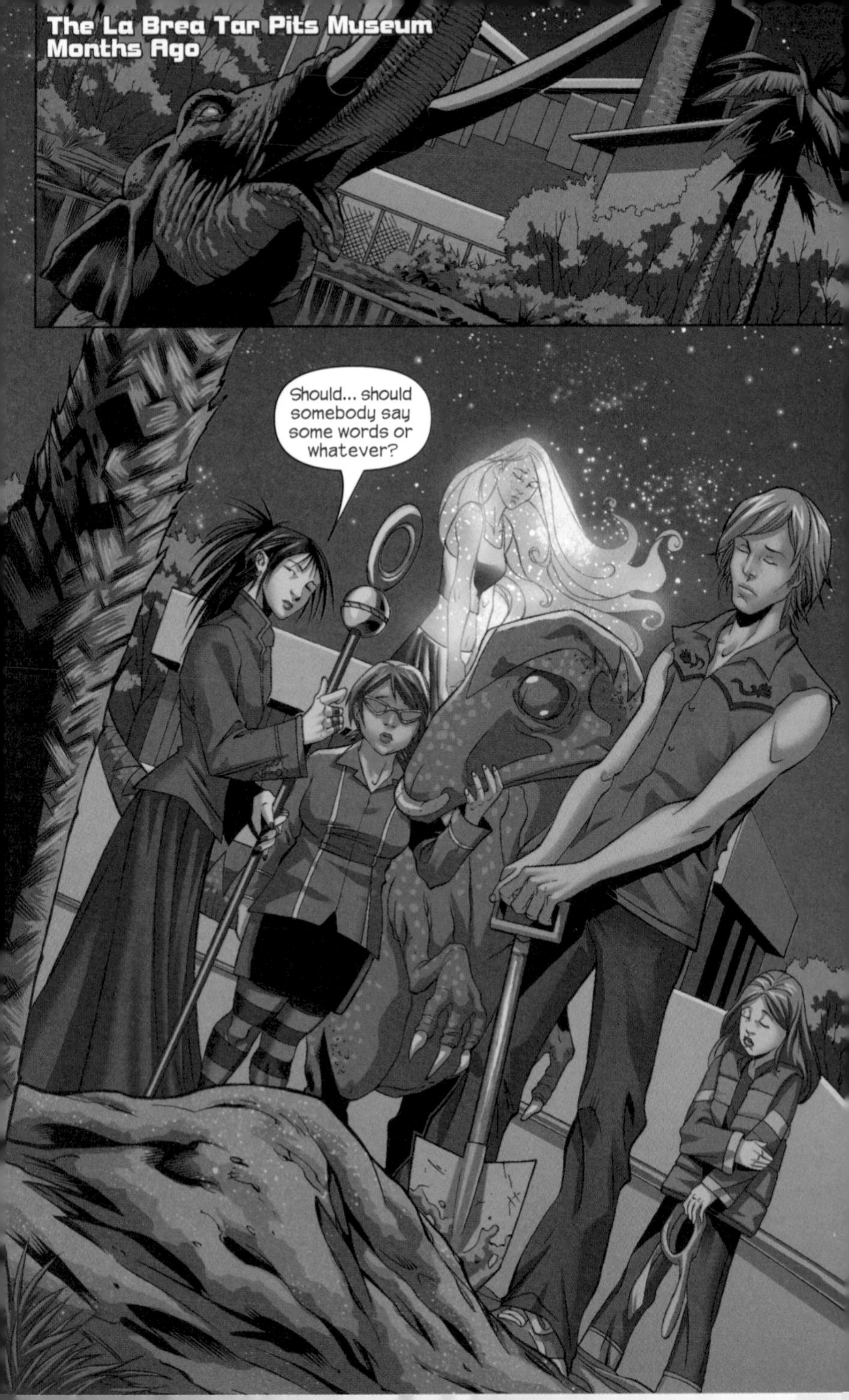
The La Brea Tar Pits Museum
Months Ago
Should... should somebody say some words or whatever?

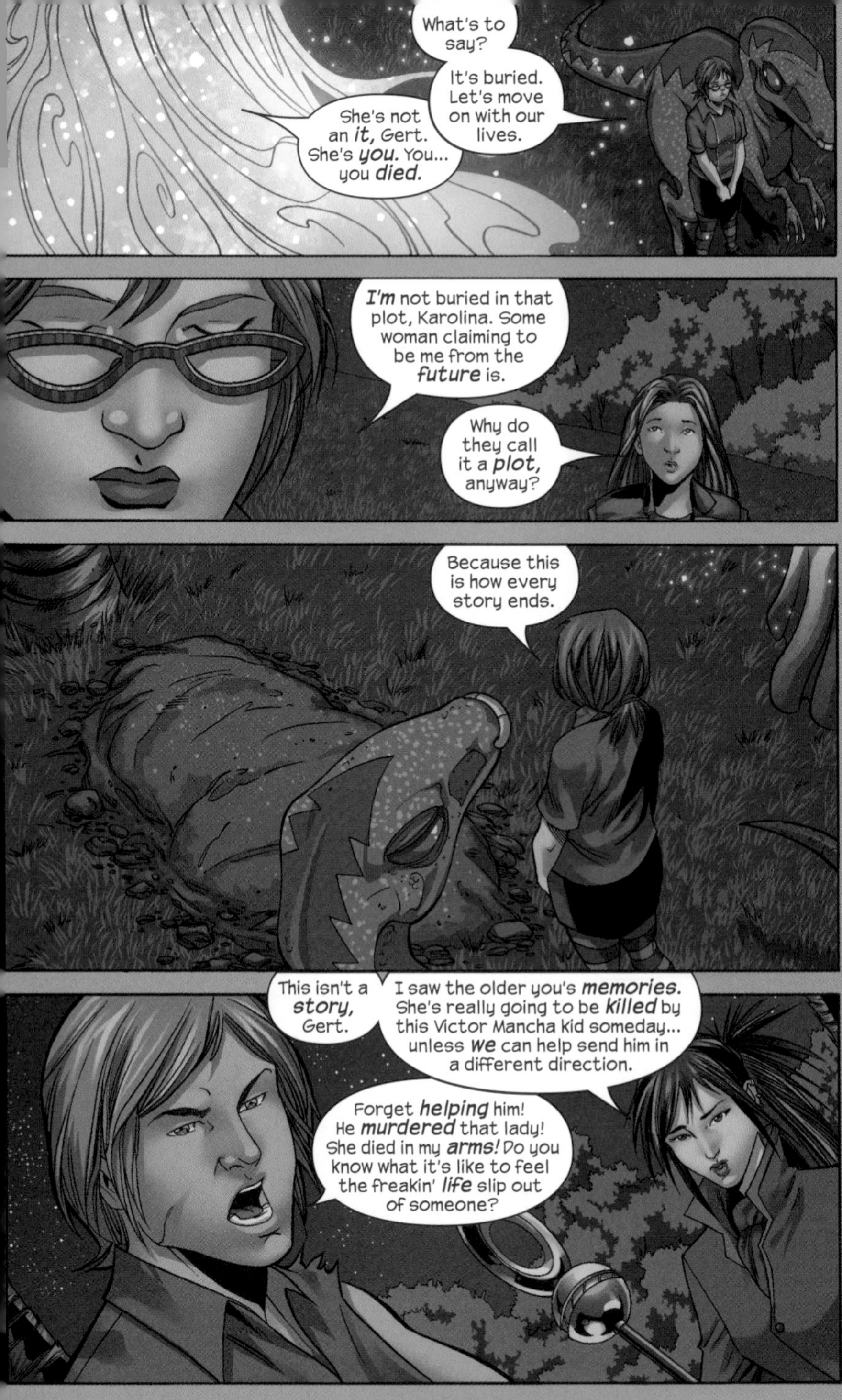
What's to say?
It's buried. Let's move on with our lives.
She's not an *it,* Gert. She's ***you.*** You... you ***died.***
I'm not buried in that plot, Karolina. Some woman claiming to be me from the ***future*** is.
Why do they call it a ***plot,*** anyway?
Because this is how every story ends.
This isn't a ***story,*** Gert.
I saw the older you's ***memories.*** She's really going to be ***killed*** by this Victor Mancha kid someday... unless ***we*** can help send him in a different direction.
Forget ***helping*** him! He ***murdered*** that lady! She died in my ***arms!*** Do you know what it's like to feel the freakin' ***life*** slip out of someone?

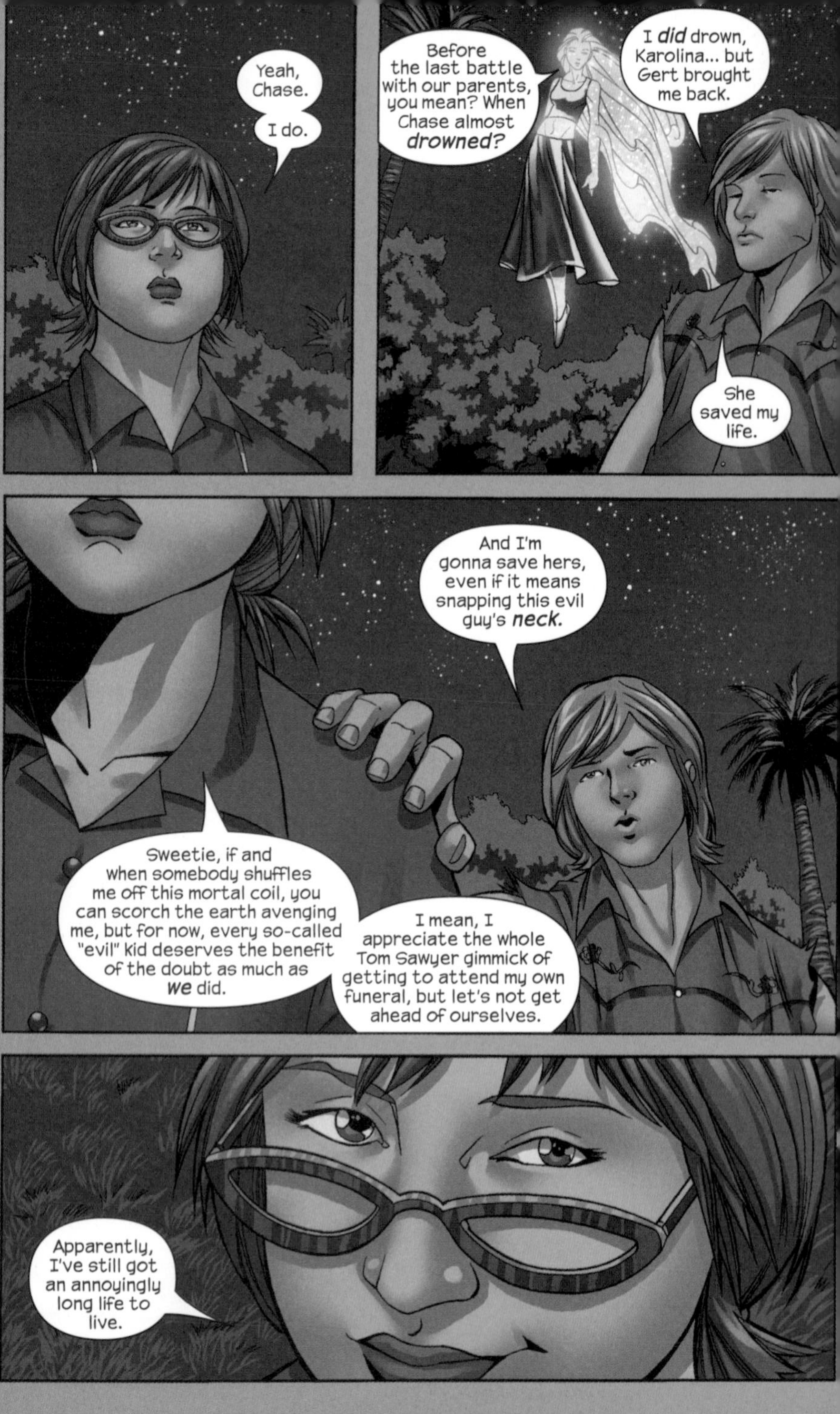
Yeah, Chase.
I do.
Before the last battle with our parents, you mean? When Chase almost *drowned*?
I *did* drown, Karolina... but Gert brought me back.
She saved my life.
And I'm gonna save hers, even if it means snapping this evil guy's *neck.*
Sweetie, if and when somebody shuffles me off this mortal coil, you can scorch the earth avenging me, but for now, every so-called "evil" kid deserves the benefit of the doubt as much as *we* did.
I mean, I appreciate the whole Tom Sawyer gimmick of getting to attend my own funeral, but let's not get ahead of ourselves.
Apparently, I've still got an annoyingly long life to live.

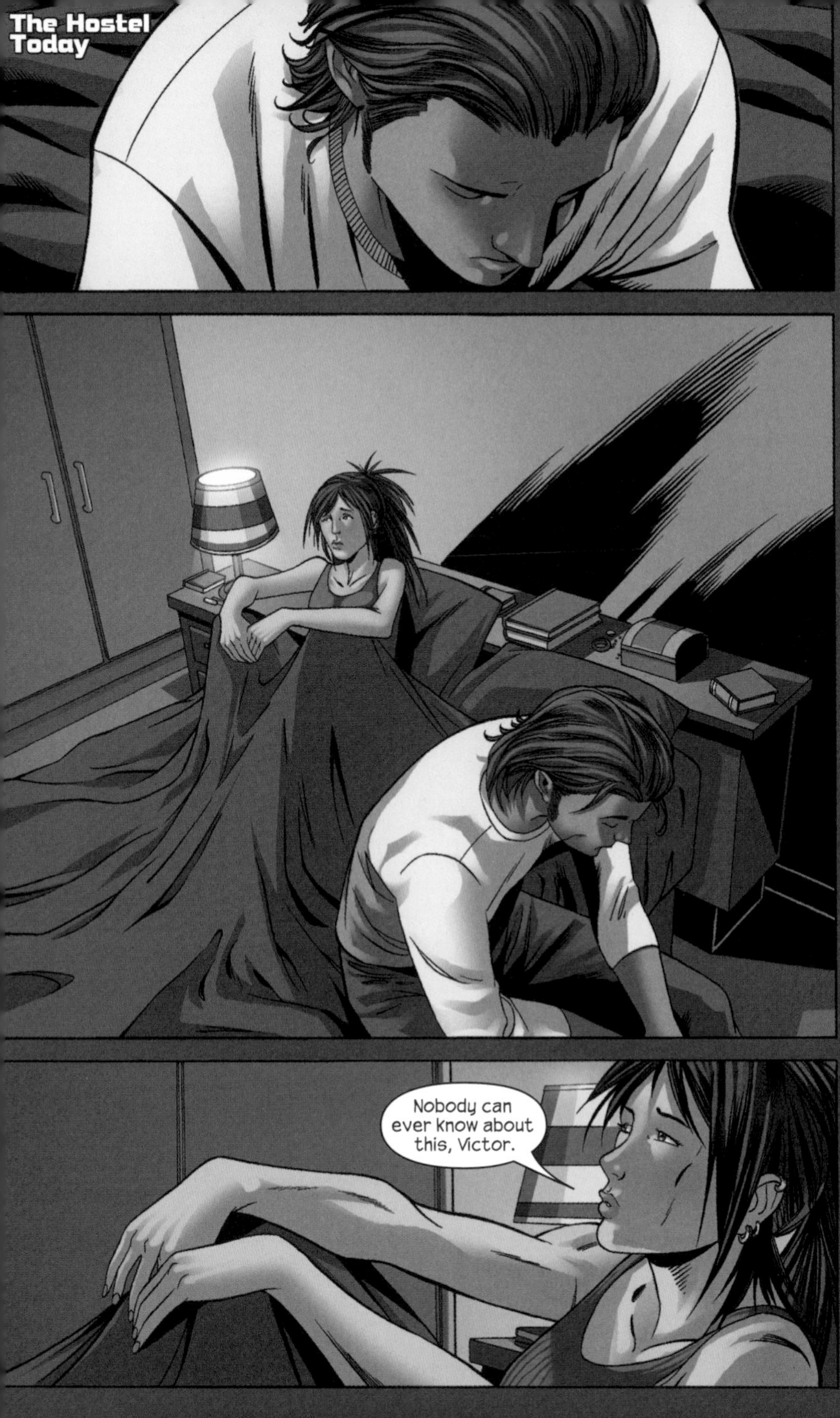
The Hostel
Today
Nobody can ever know about this, Victor.

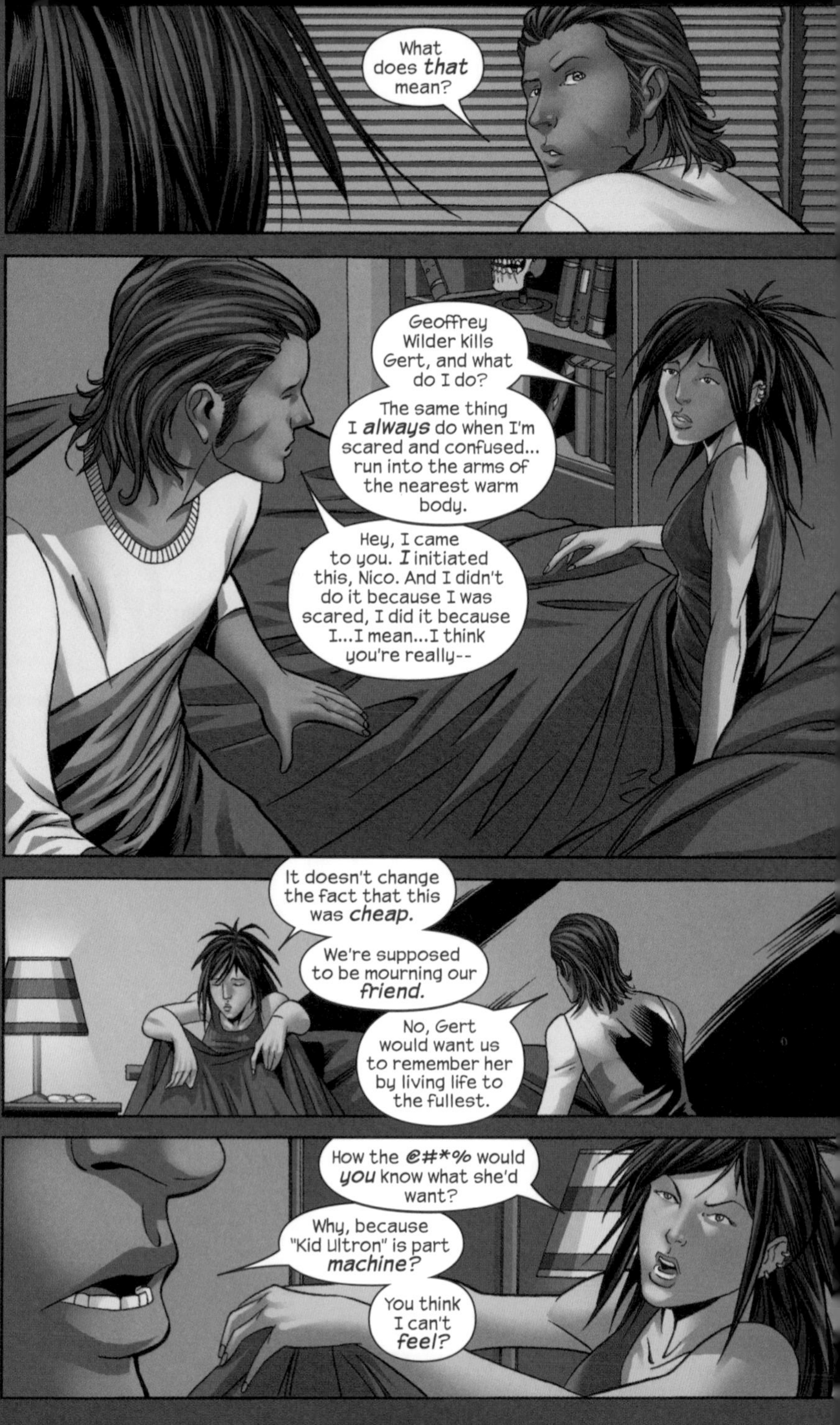
What does *that* mean?
Geoffrey Wilder kills Gert, and what do I do?
The same thing I *always* do when I'm scared and confused... run into the arms of the nearest warm body.
Hey, I came to you. *I* initiated this, Nico. And I didn't do it because I was scared, I did it because I...I mean...I think you're really--
It doesn't change the fact that this was *cheap.*
We're supposed to be mourning our *friend.*
No, Gert would want us to remember her by living life to the fullest.
How the @#*% would *you* know what she'd want?
Why, because "Kid Ultron" is part *machine?*
You think I can't *feel?*

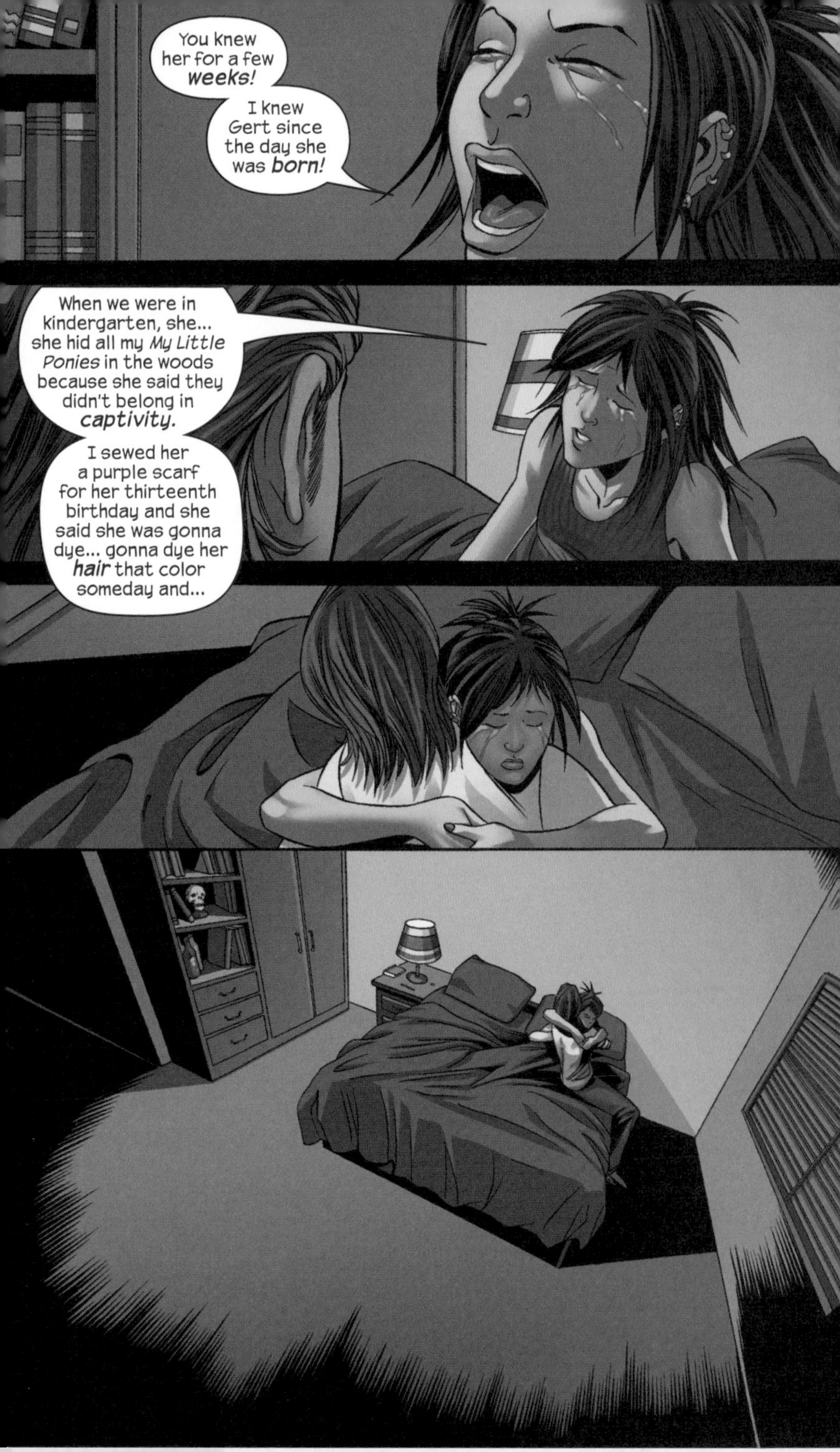

You knew her for a few *weeks!*
I knew Gert since the day she was *born!*
When we were in kindergarten, she... she hid all my *My Little Ponies* in the woods because she said they didn't belong in *captivity.*
I sewed her a purple scarf for her thirteenth birthday and she said she was gonna dye... gonna dye her *hair* that color someday and...

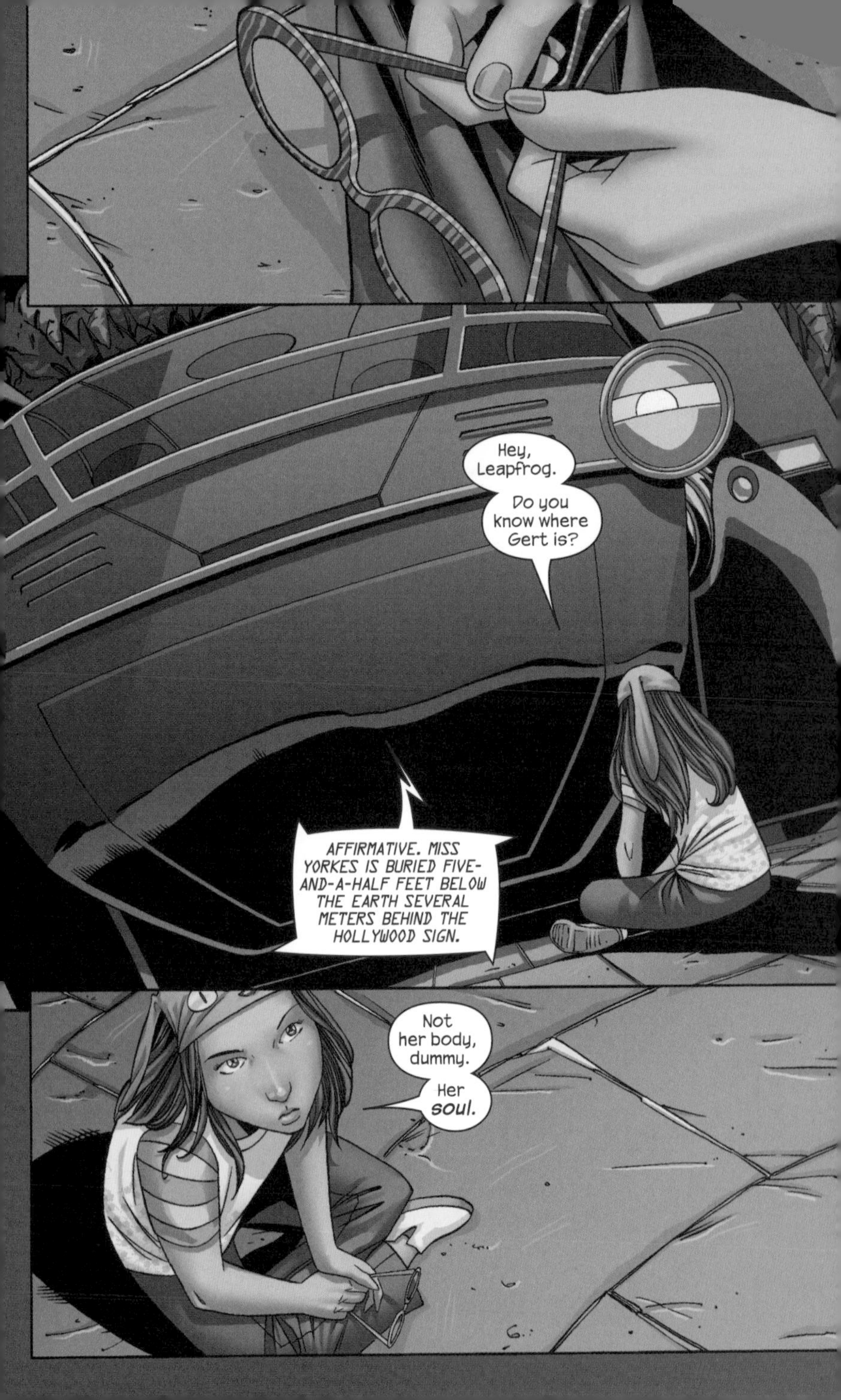

Hey, Leapfrog.
Do you know where Gert is?
AFFIRMATIVE. MISS YORKES IS BURIED FIVE-AND-A-HALF FEET BELOW THE EARTH SEVERAL METERS BEHIND THE HOLLYWOOD SIGN.
Not her body, dummy.
Her *soul.*

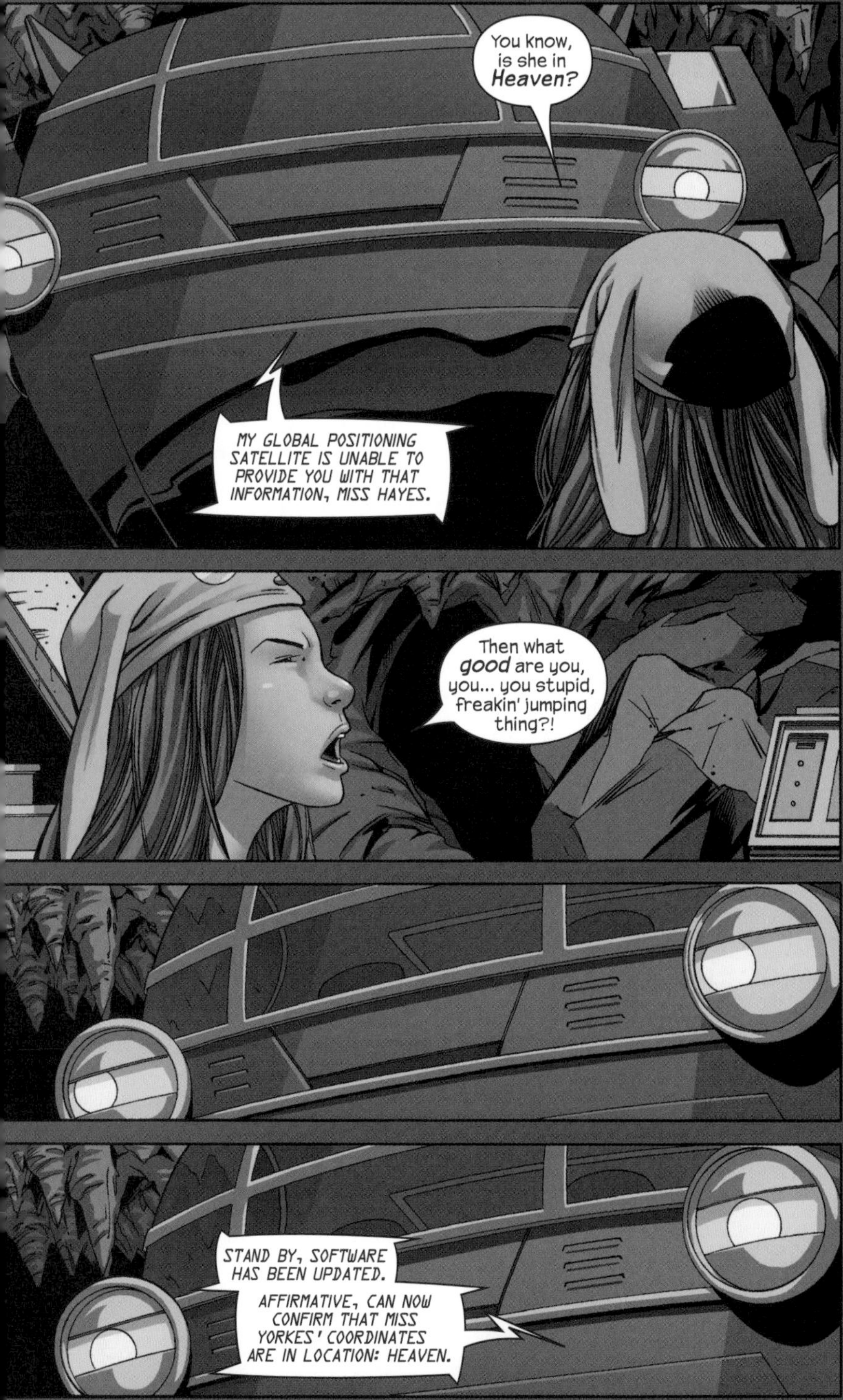
You know, is she in *Heaven*?
MY GLOBAL POSITIONING SATELLITE IS UNABLE TO PROVIDE YOU WITH THAT INFORMATION, MISS HAYES.
Then what *good* are you, you... you stupid, freakin' jumping thing?!
STAND BY, SOFTWARE HAS BEEN UPDATED.
AFFIRMATIVE, CAN NOW CONFIRM THAT MISS YORKES' COORDINATES ARE IN LOCATION: HEAVEN.

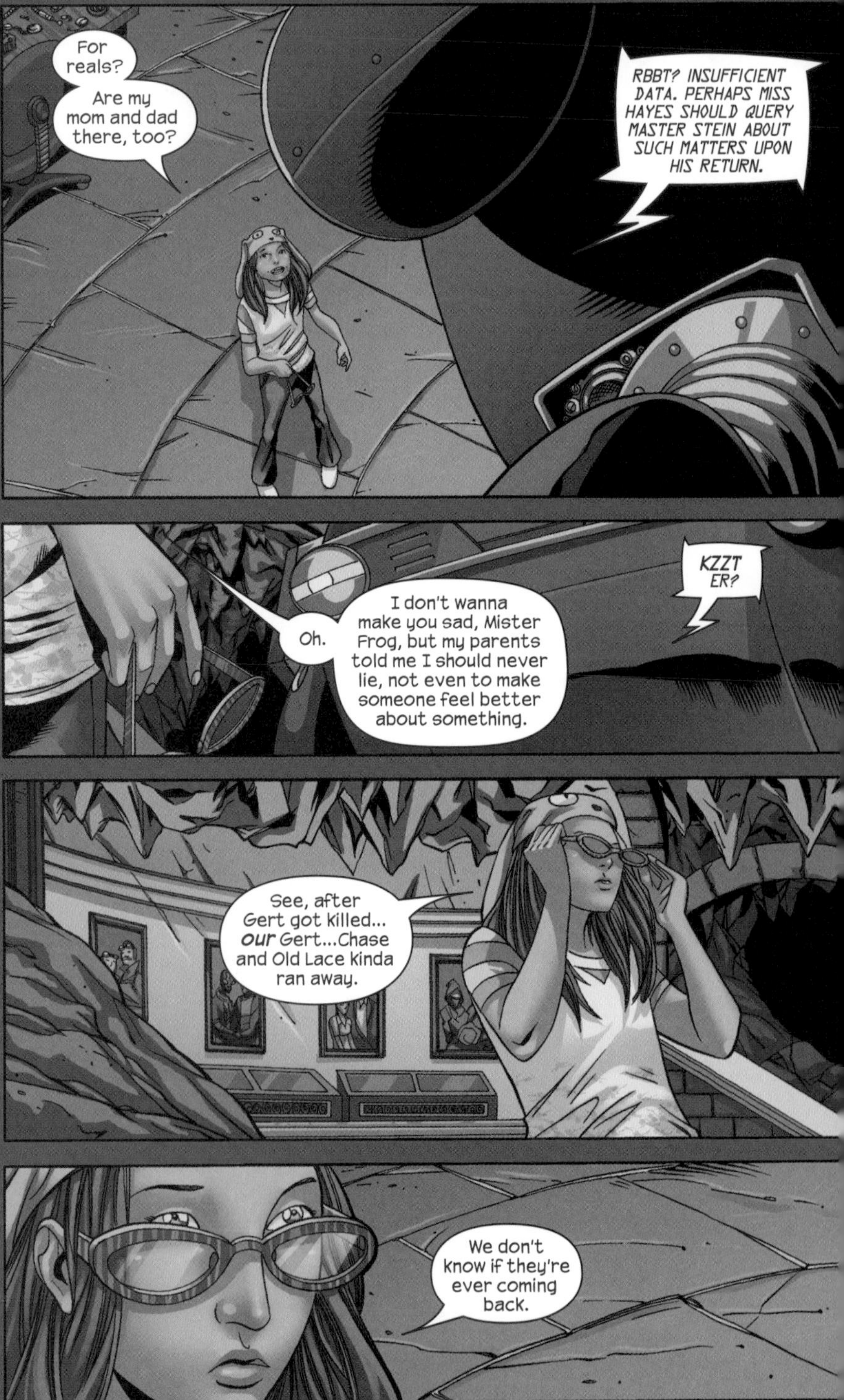
For reals?
Are my mom and dad there, too?
RBBT? INSUFFICIENT DATA. PERHAPS MISS HAYES SHOULD QUERY MASTER STEIN ABOUT SUCH MATTERS UPON HIS RETURN.
Oh.
I don't wanna make you sad, Mister Frog, but my parents told me I should never lie, not even to make someone feel better about something.
KZZT ER?
See, after Gert got killed... *our* Gert...Chase and Old Lace kinda ran away.
We don't know if they're ever coming back.

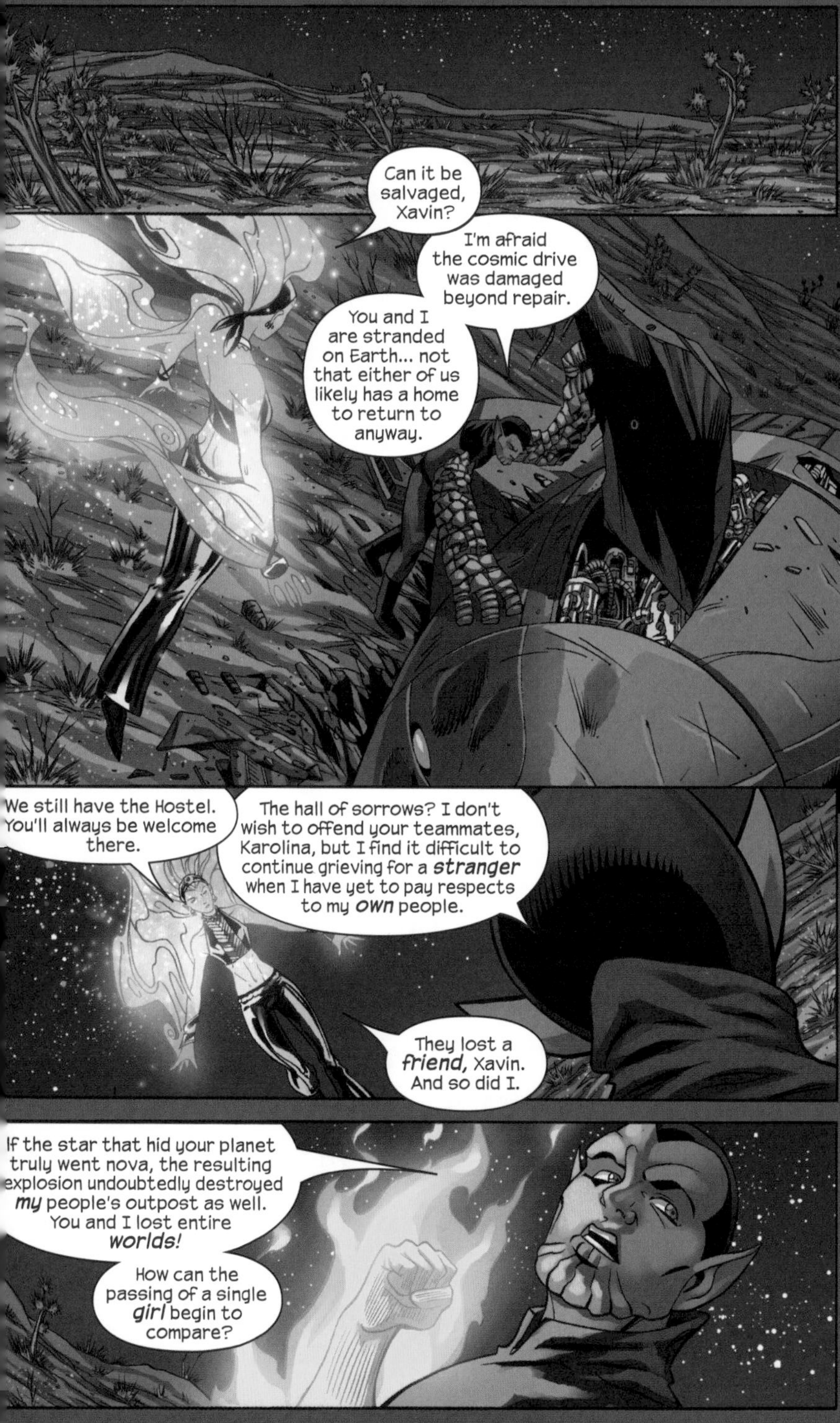
Can it be salvaged, Xavin?
I'm afraid the cosmic drive was damaged beyond repair.
You and I are stranded on Earth... not that either of us likely has a home to return to anyway.
We still have the Hostel. You'll always be welcome there.
The hall of sorrows? I don't wish to offend your teammates, Karolina, but I find it difficult to continue grieving for a stranger when I have yet to pay respects to my own people.
They lost a friend, Xavin. And so did I.
If the star that hid your planet truly went nova, the resulting explosion undoubtedly destroyed my people's outpost as well. You and I lost entire worlds!
How can the passing of a single girl begin to compare?

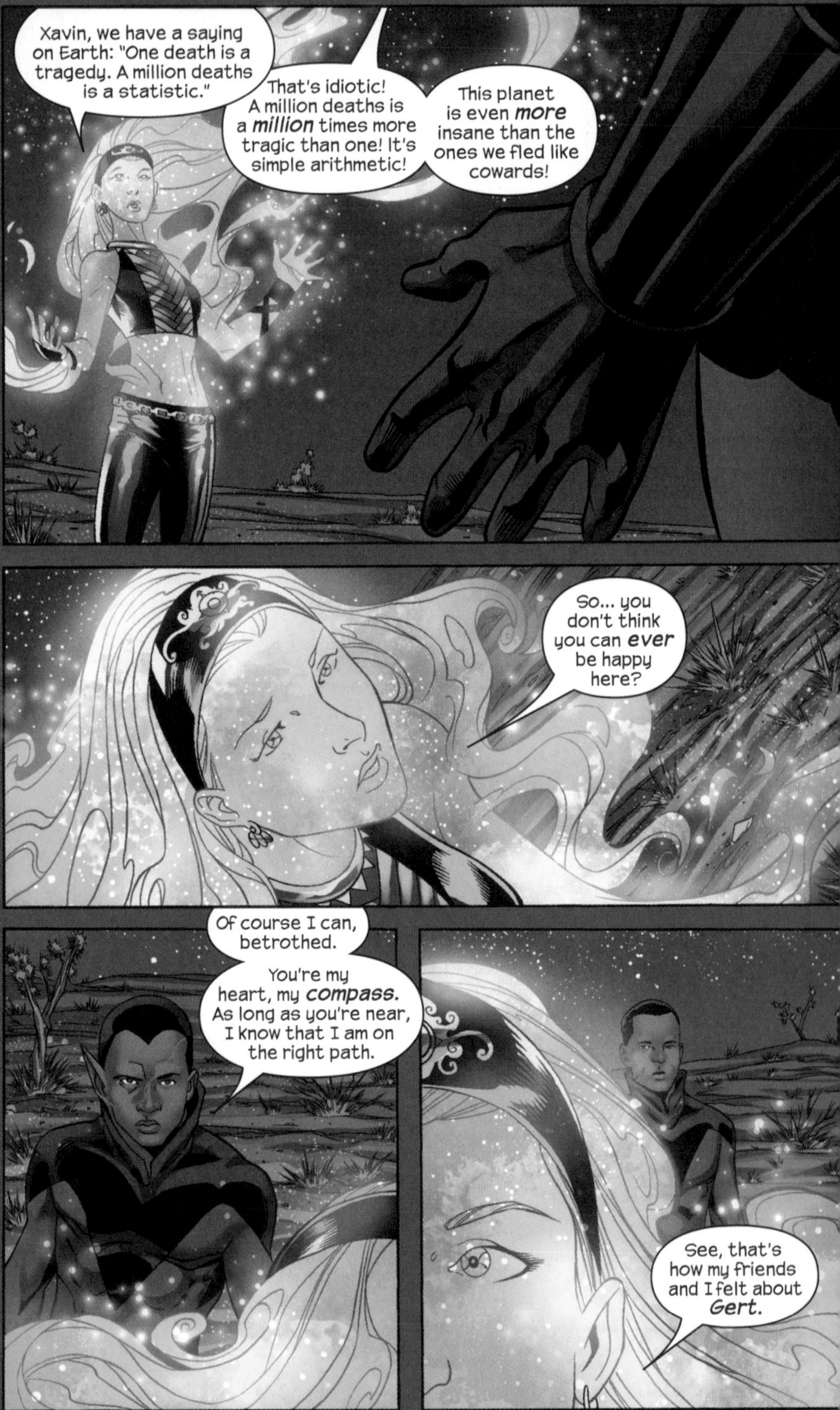
Xavin, we have a saying on Earth: "One death is a tragedy. A million deaths is a statistic."
That's idiotic! A million deaths is a *million* times more tragic than one! It's simple arithmetic!
This planet is even *more* insane than the ones we fled like cowards!
So... you don't think you can *ever* be happy here?
Of course I can, betrothed.
You're my heart, my *compass.* As long as you're near, I know that I am on the right path.
See, that's how my friends and I felt about *Gert.*

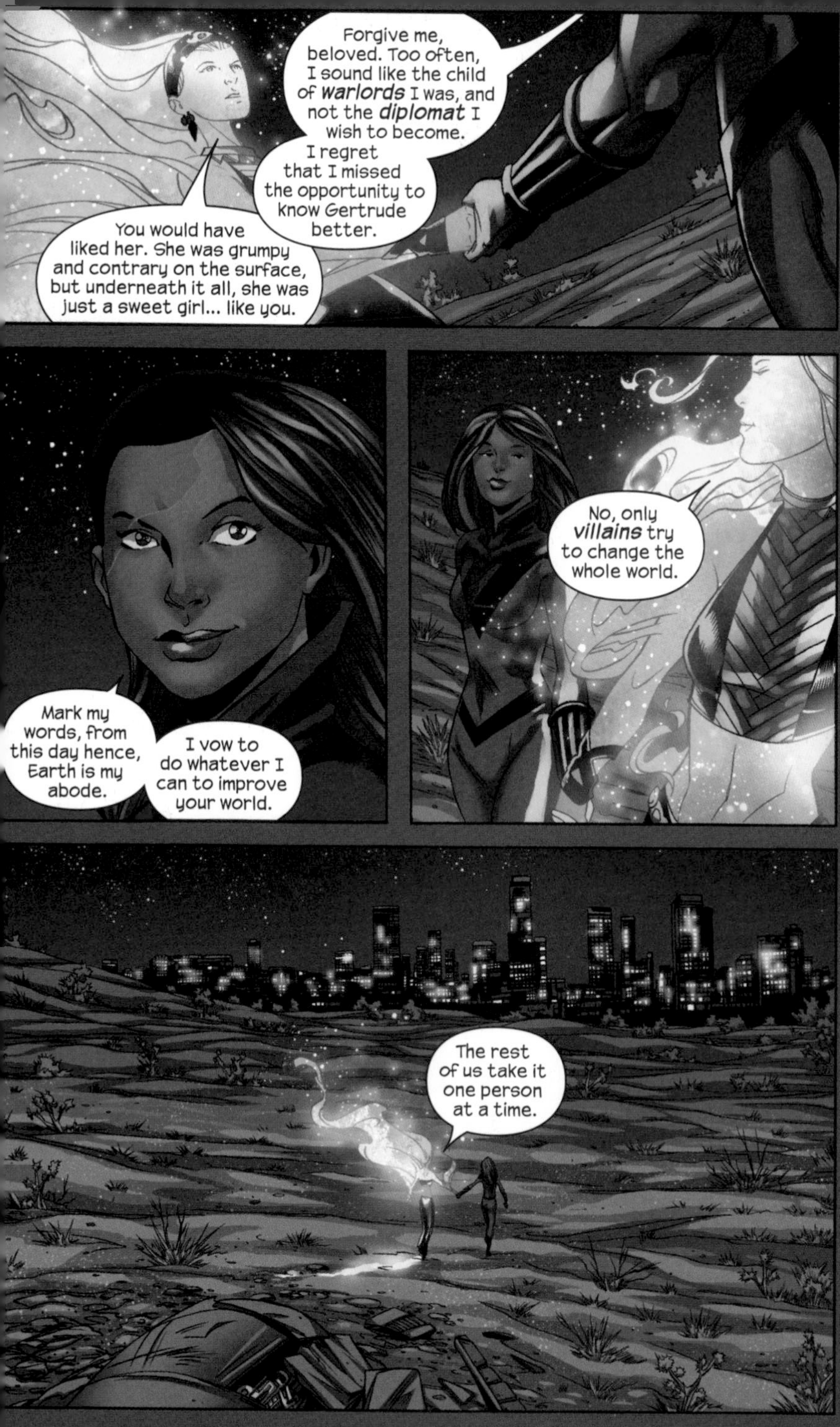
Forgive me, beloved. Too often, I sound like the child of *warlords* I was, and not the *diplomat* I wish to become.
I regret that I missed the opportunity to know Gertrude better.
You would have liked her. She was grumpy and contrary on the surface, but underneath it all, she was just a sweet girl... like you.
Mark my words, from this day hence, Earth is my abode.
I vow to do whatever I can to improve your world.
No, only *villains* try to change the whole world.
The rest of us take it one person at a time.

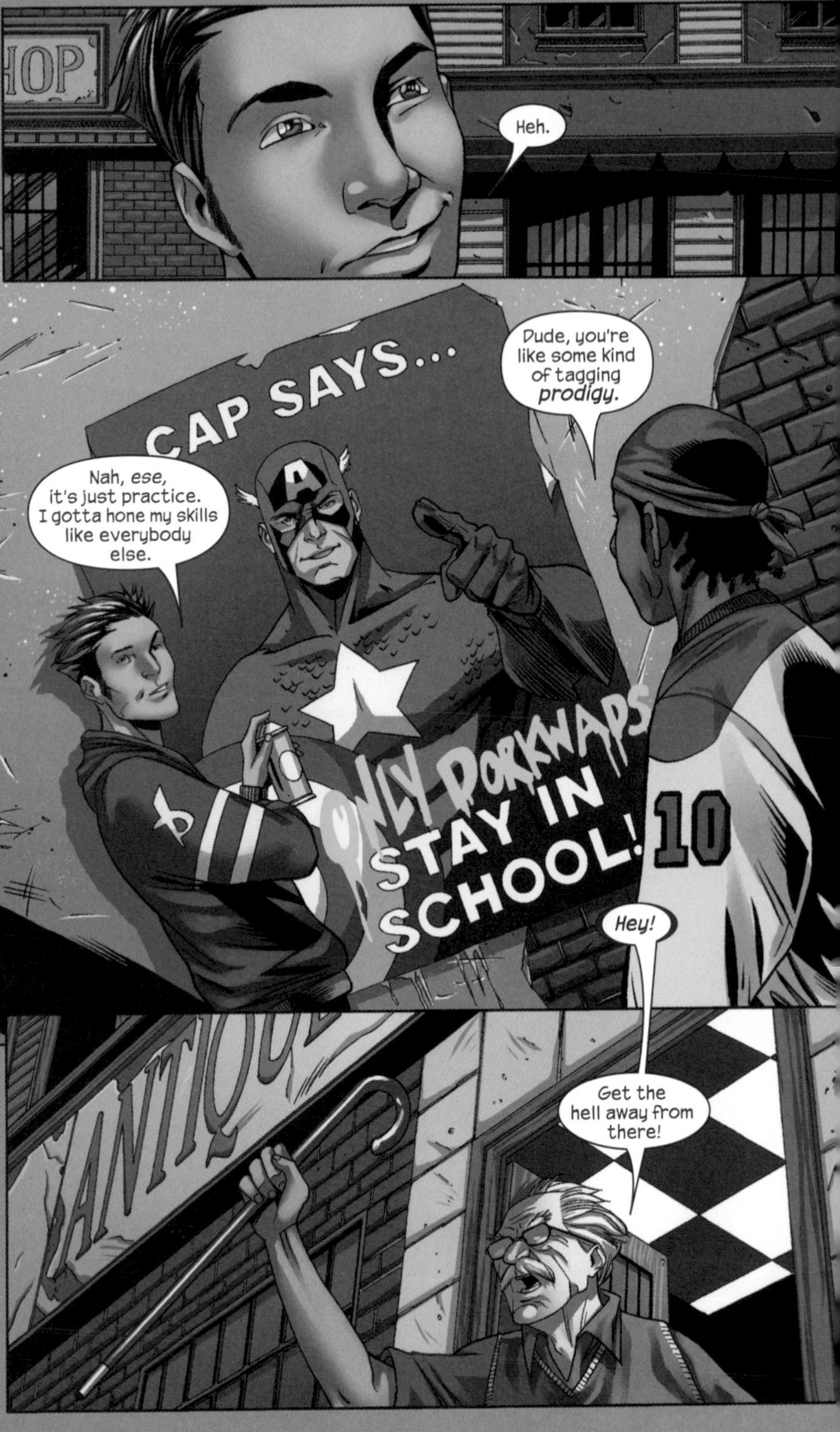

HOP
Heh.
CAP SAYS...
Dude, you're like some kind of tagging *prodigy*.
Nah, *ese*, it's just practice. I gotta hone my skills like everybody else.
ONLY DORKWADS STAY IN SCHOOL!
10
Hey!
ANTIQUE
Get the hell away from there!

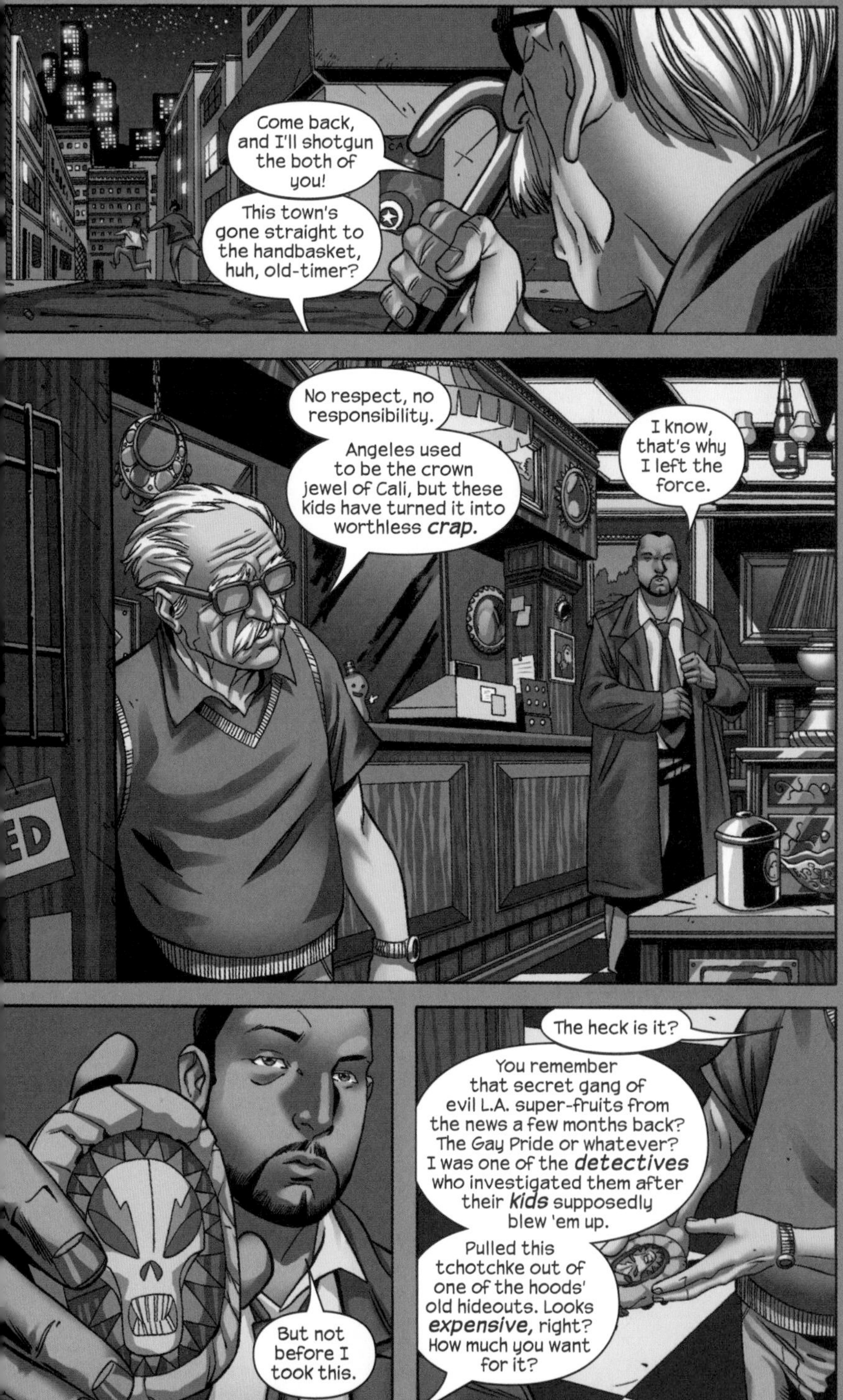
Come back, and I'll shotgun the both of you!
This town's gone straight to the handbasket, huh, old-timer?
No respect, no responsibility.
Angeles used to be the crown jewel of Cali, but these kids have turned it into worthless *crap.*
I know, that's why I left the force.
ED
But not before I took this.
The heck is it?
You remember that secret gang of evil L.A. super-fruits from the news a few months back? The Gay Pride or whatever? I was one of the *detectives* who investigated them after their *kids* supposedly blew 'em up.
Pulled this tchotchke out of one of the hoods' old hideouts. Looks *expensive,* right? How much you want for it?

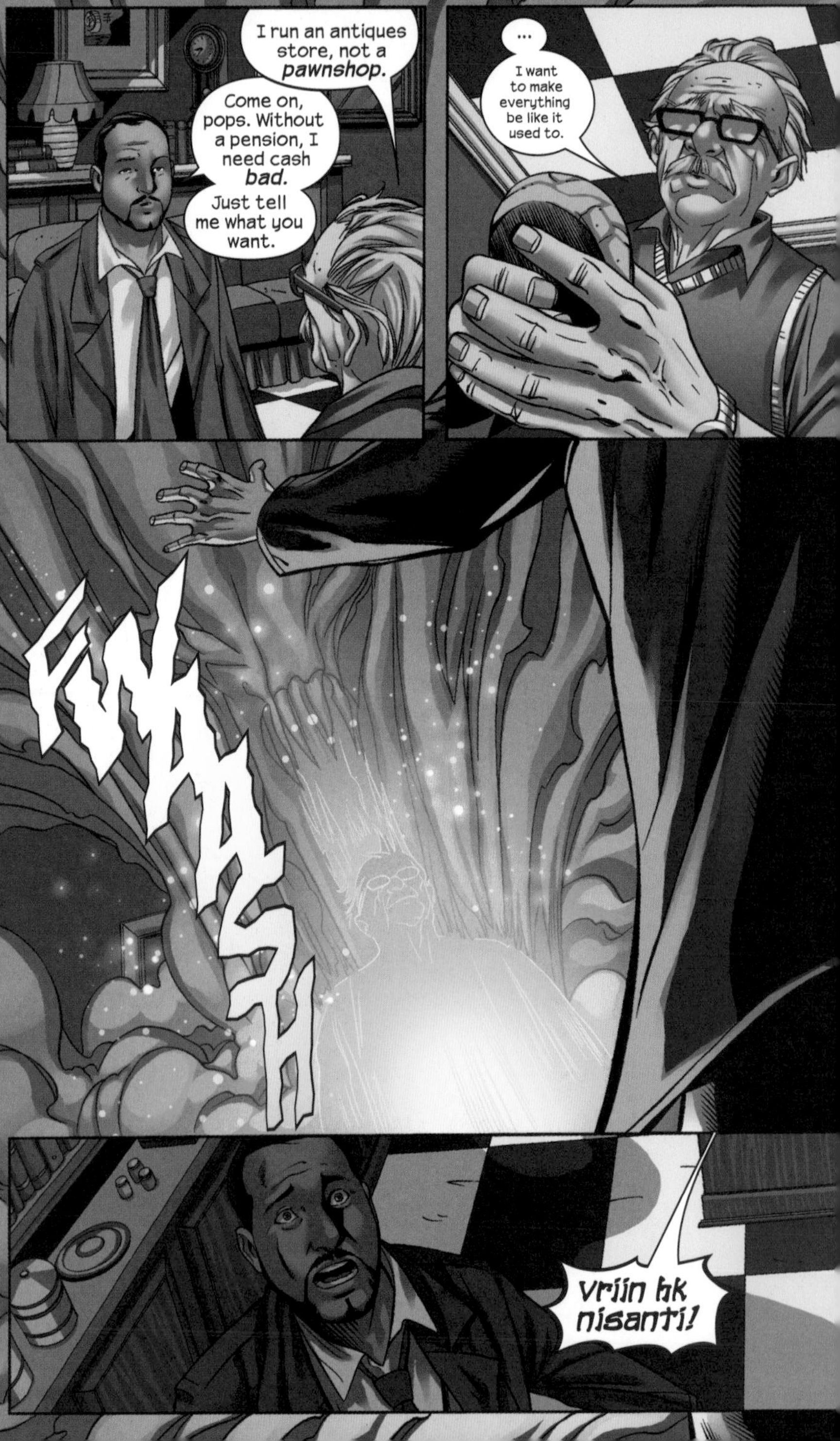

I run an antiques store, not a pawnshop.
Come on, pops. Without a pension, I need cash bad.
Just tell me what you want.
...
I want to make everything be like it used to.
FWASH
Vriin hk nisanti!

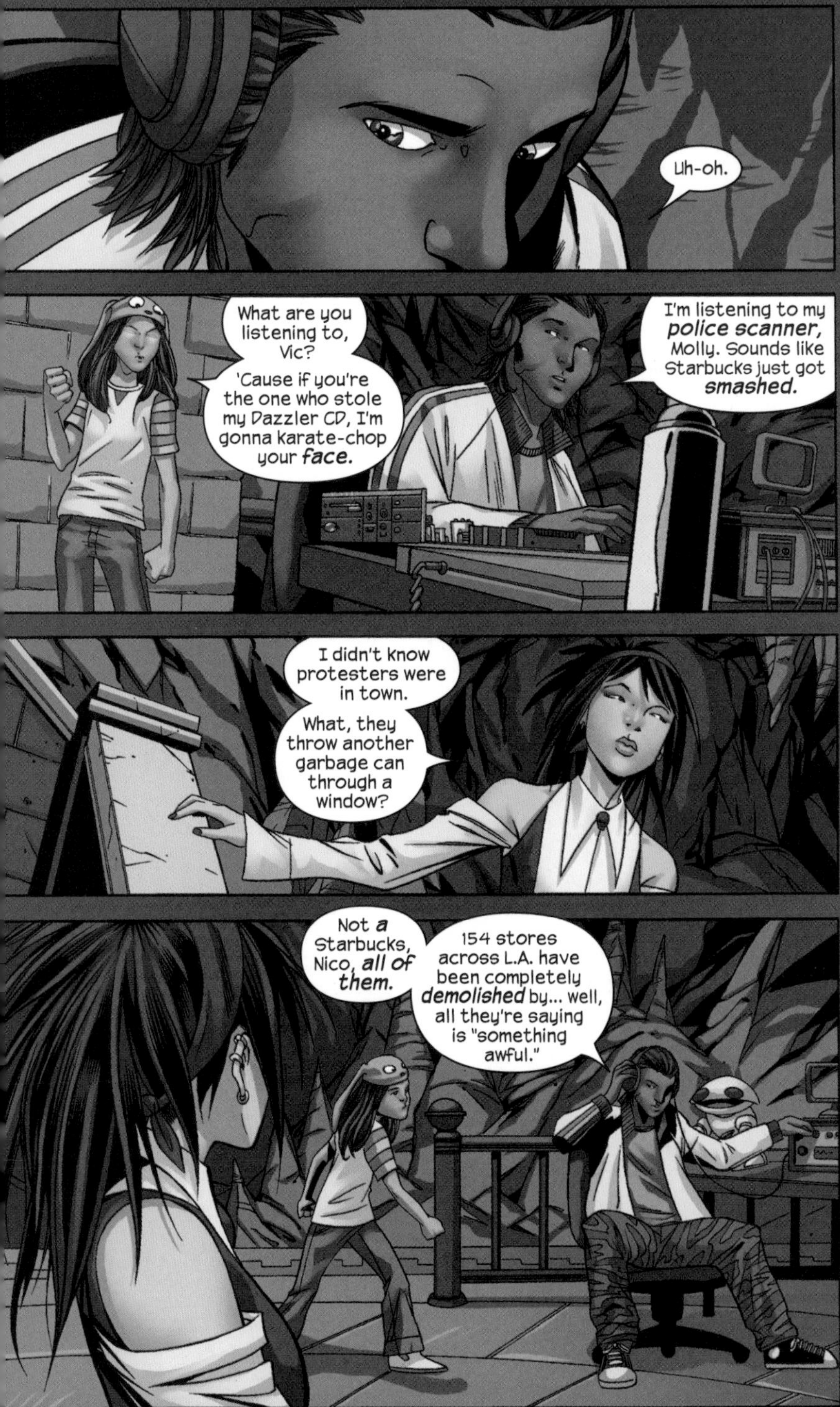
Uh-oh.
What are you listening to, Vic?
'Cause if you're the one who stole my Dazzler CD, I'm gonna karate-chop your *face.*
I'm listening to my *police scanner,* Molly. Sounds like Starbucks just got *smashed.*
I didn't know protesters were in town.
What, they throw another garbage can through a window?
Not *a* Starbucks, Nico, *all of them.*
154 stores across L.A. have been completely *demolished* by... well, all they're saying is "something awful."

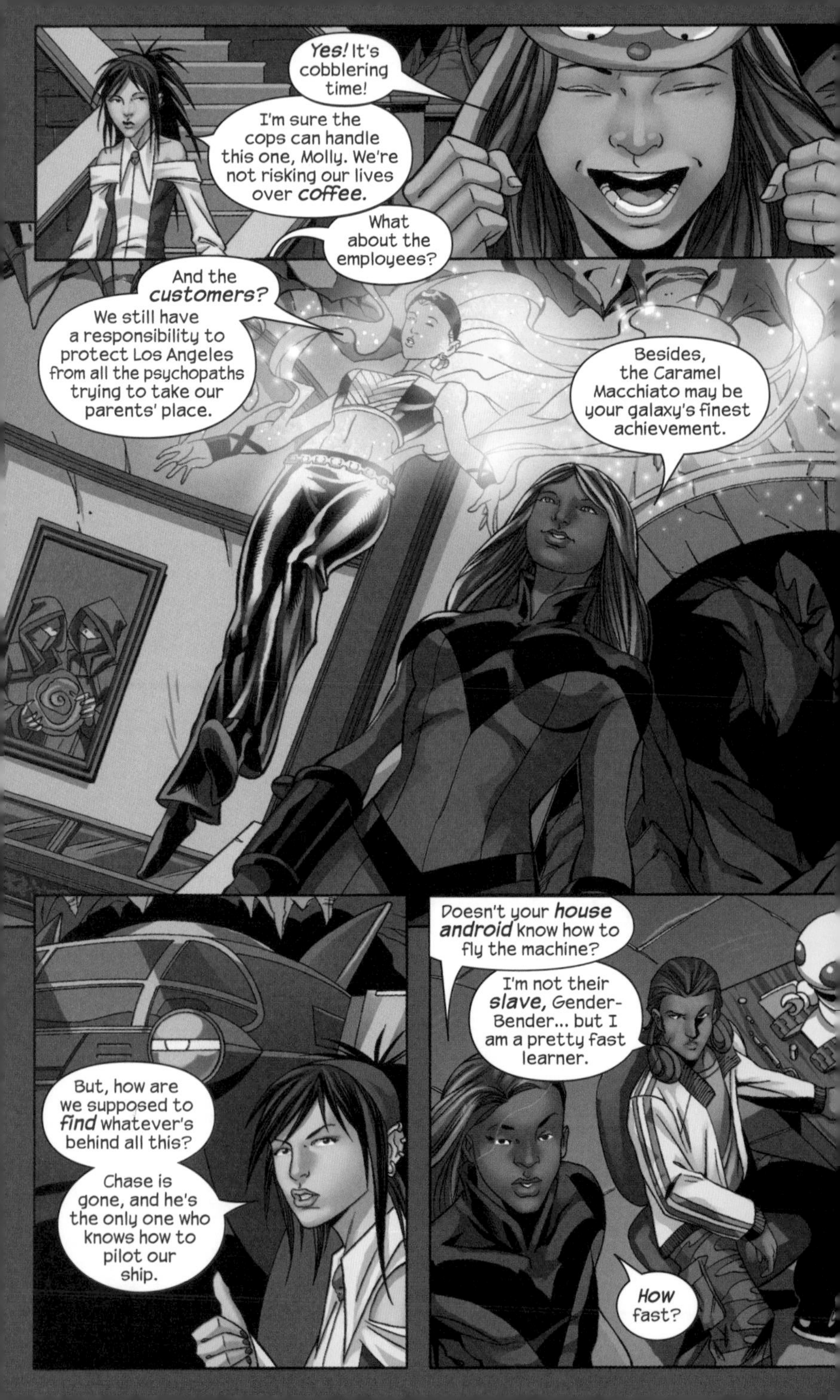

Yes! It's cobblering time!
I'm sure the cops can handle this one, Molly. We're not risking our lives over coffee.
What about the employees?
And the customers? We still have a responsibility to protect Los Angeles from all the psychopaths trying to take our parents' place.
Besides, the Caramel Macchiato may be your galaxy's finest achievement.
But, how are we supposed to find whatever's behind all this?
Chase is gone, and he's the only one who knows how to pilot our ship.
Doesn't your house android know how to fly the machine?
I'm not their slave, Gender-Bender... but I am a pretty fast learner.
How fast?

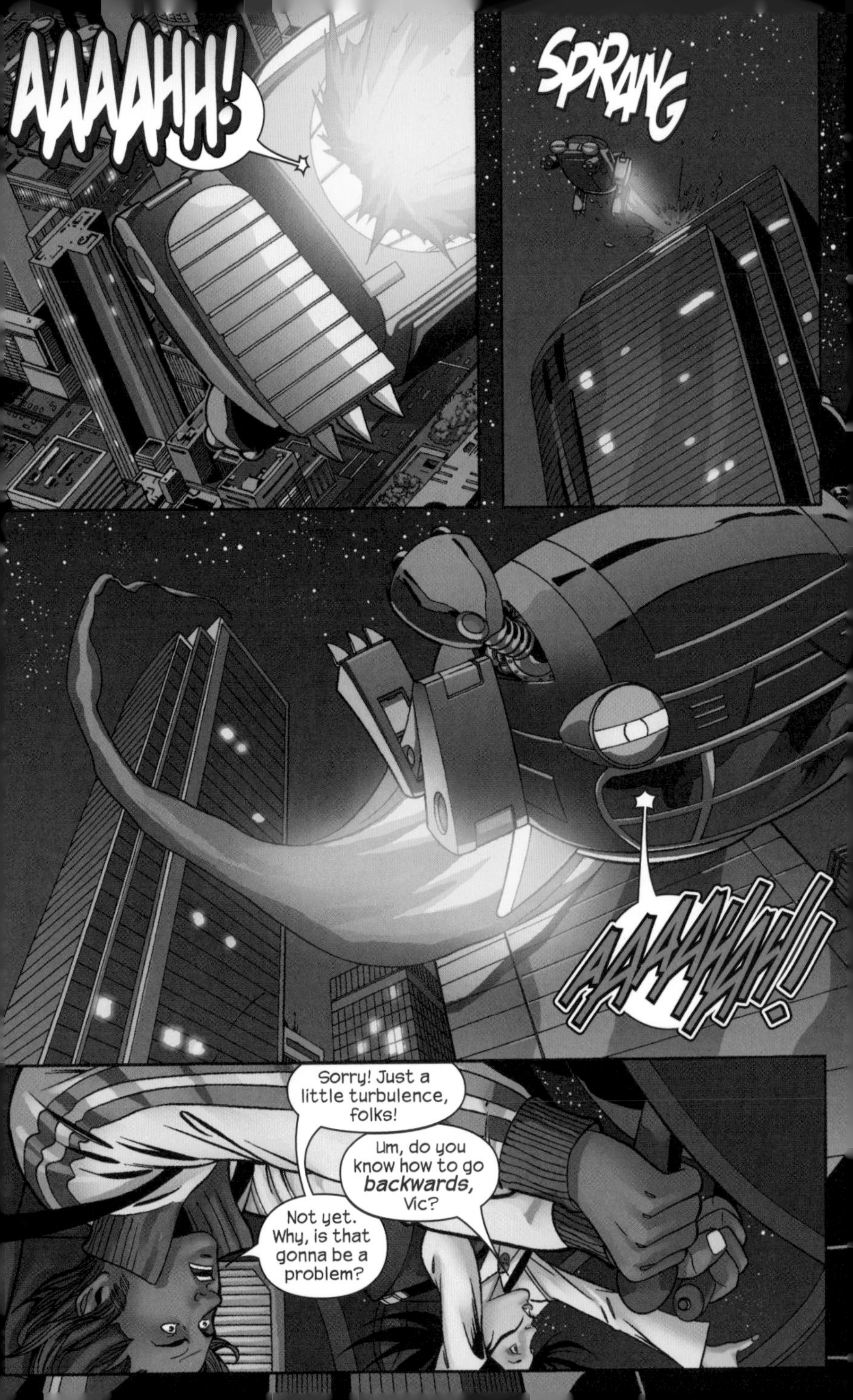
AAAAHH!
SPRANG
AAAAAAAH!
Sorry! Just a little turbulence, folks!
Um, do you know how to go *backwards,* Vic?
Not yet. Why, is that gonna be a problem?

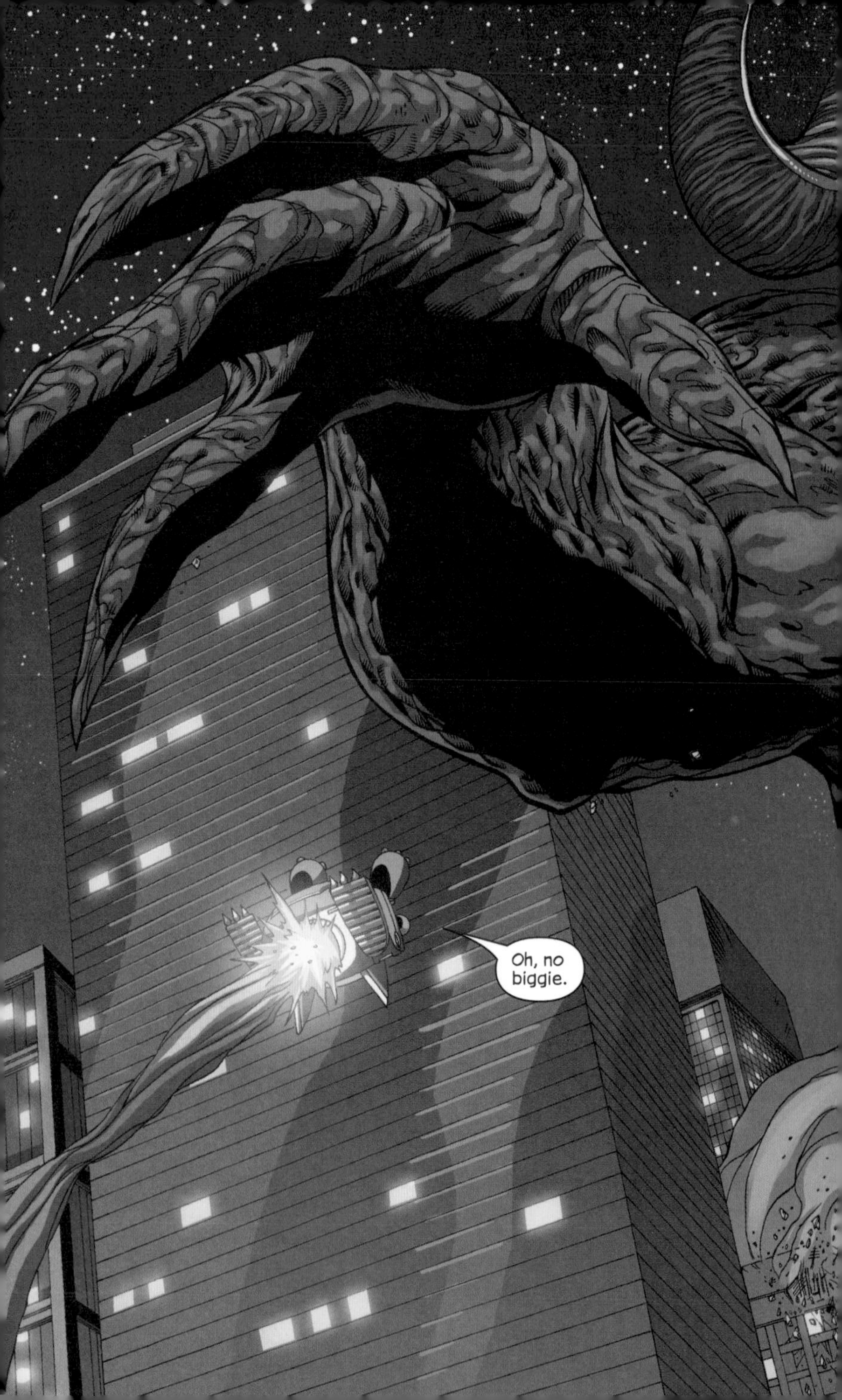
Oh, no biggie.

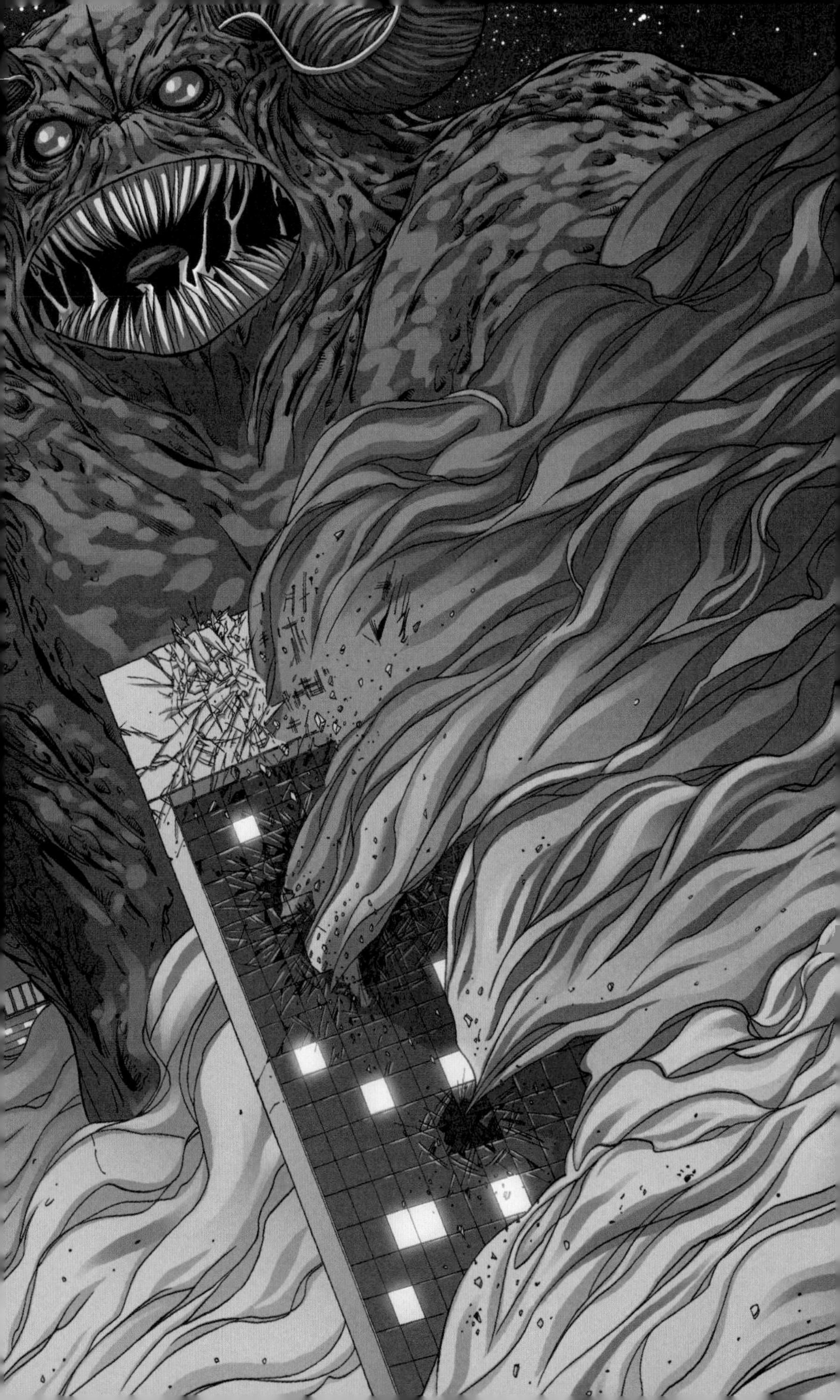

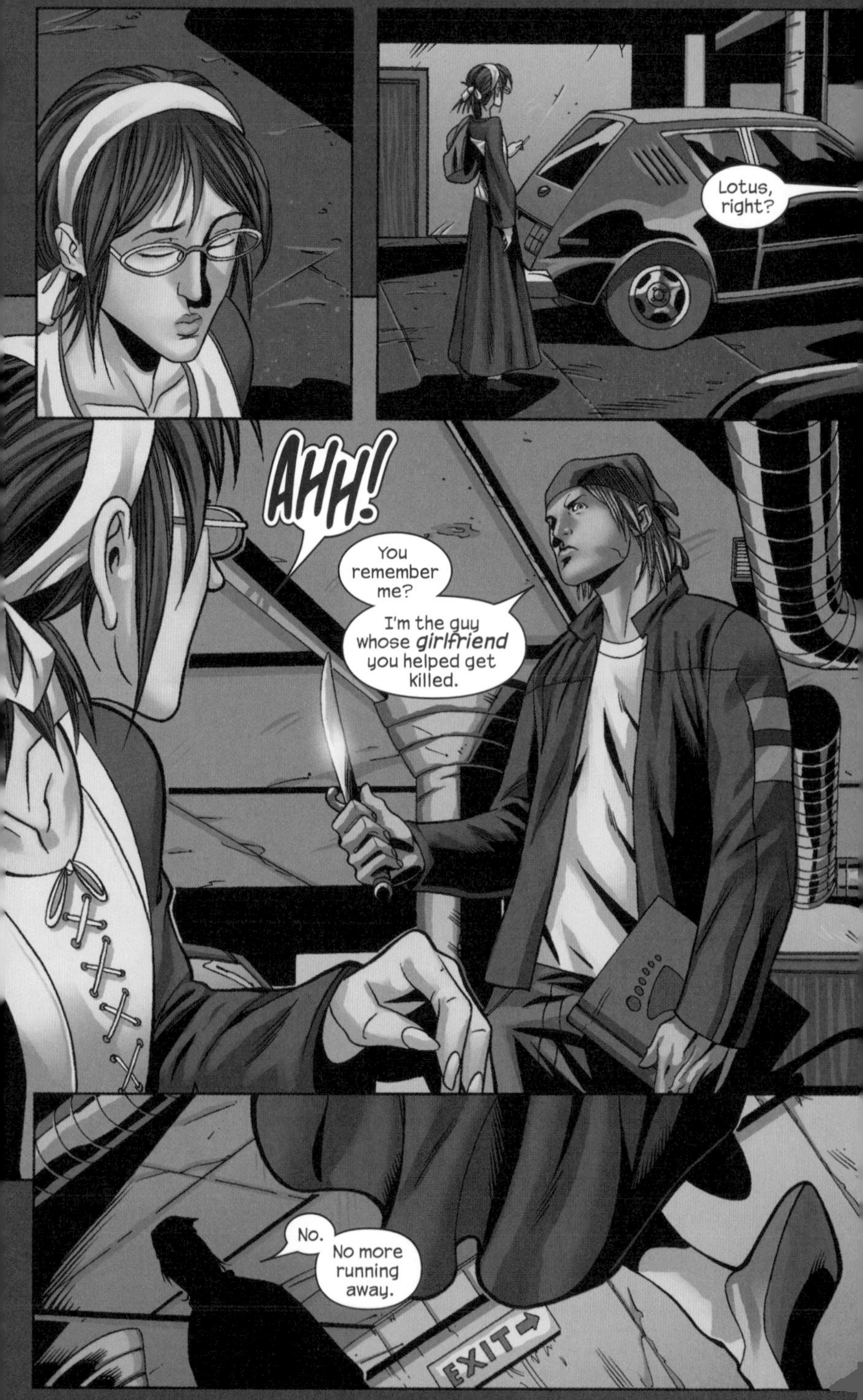

Lotus, right?
AHH!
You remember me?
I'm the guy whose girlfriend you helped get killed.
No.
No more running away.
EXIT

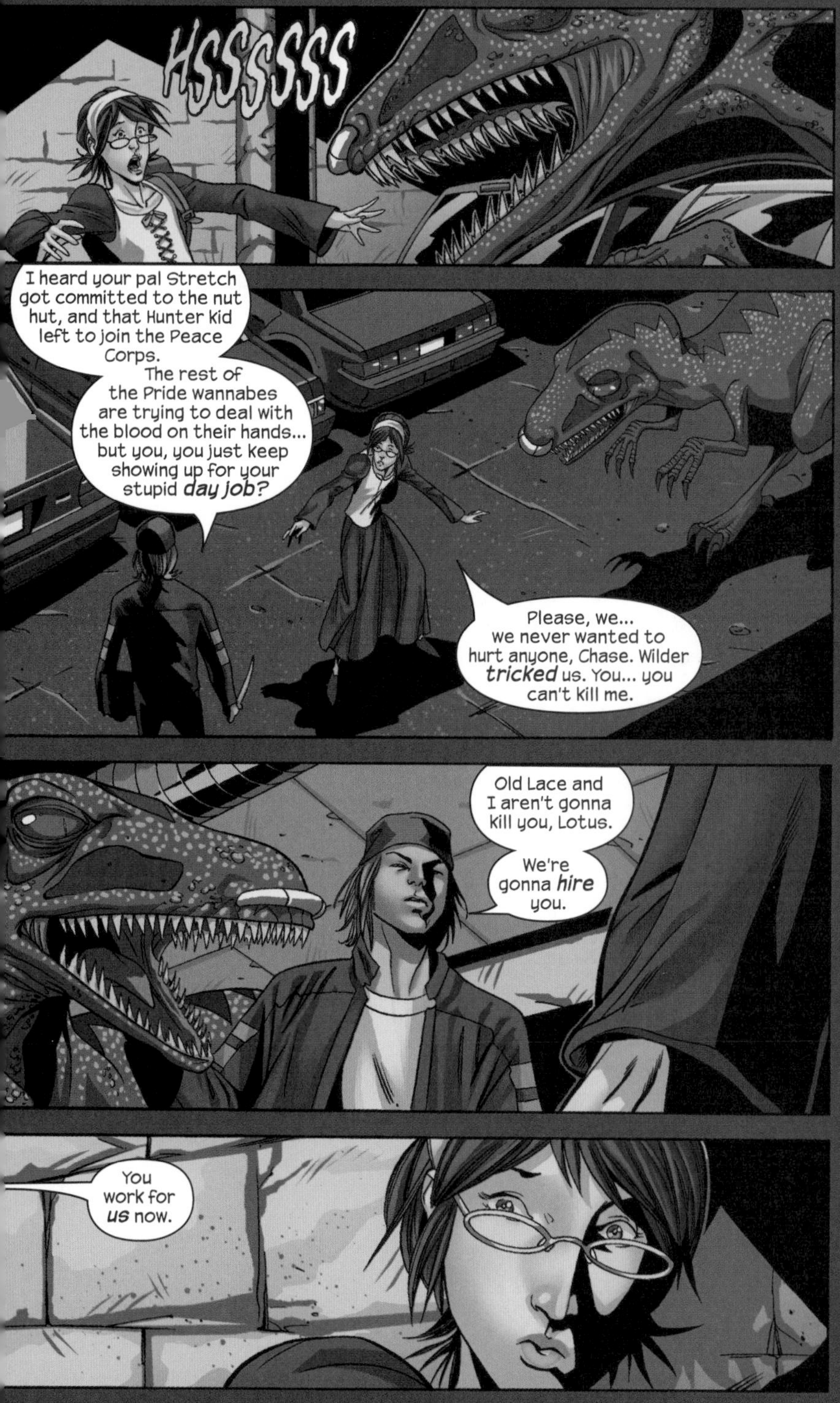
HSSSSSS
I heard your pal Stretch got committed to the nut hut, and that Hunter kid left to join the Peace Corps.
The rest of the Pride wannabes are trying to deal with the blood on their hands... but you, you just keep showing up for your stupid *day job?*
Please, we... we never wanted to hurt anyone, Chase. Wilder *tricked* us. You... you can't kill me.
Old Lace and I aren't gonna kill you, Lotus.
We're gonna *hire* you.
You work for *us* now.

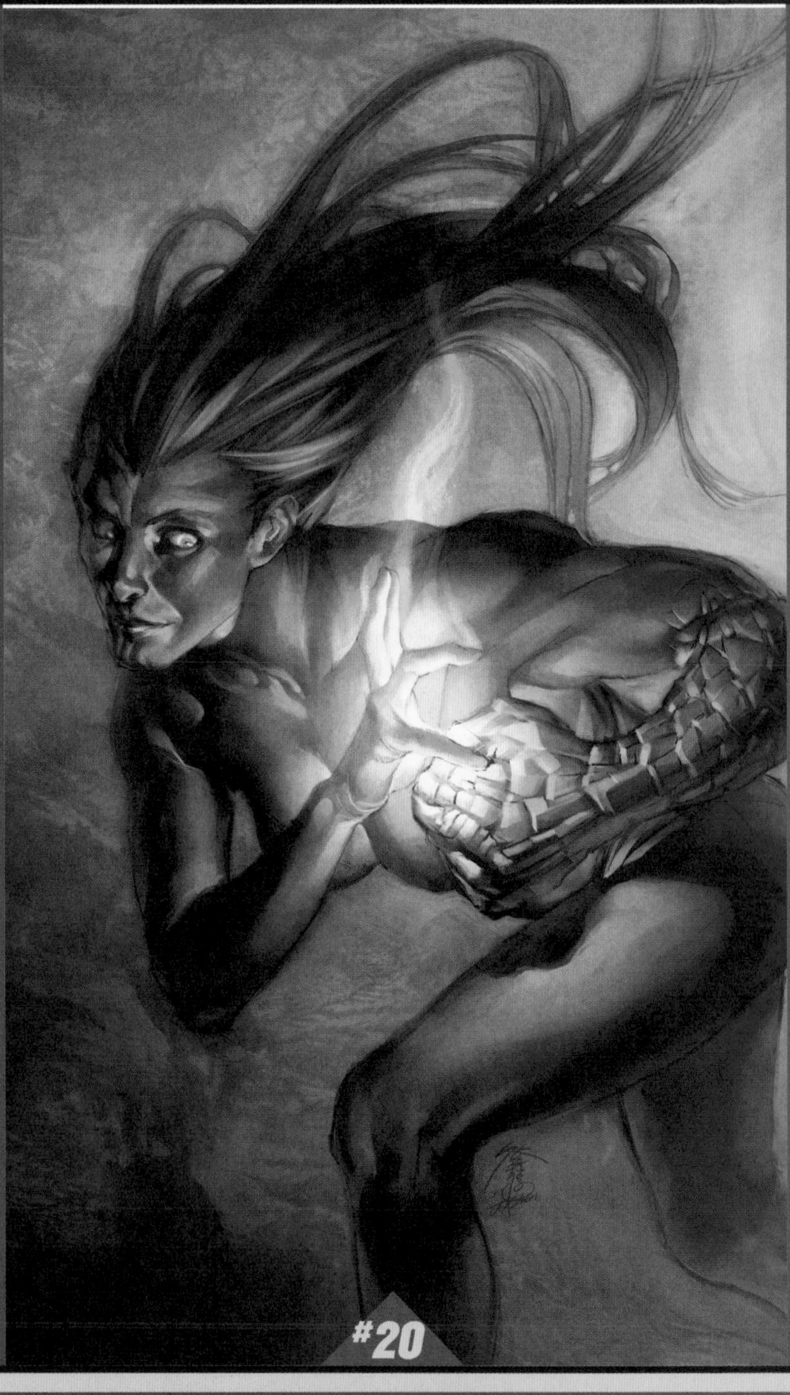
#20

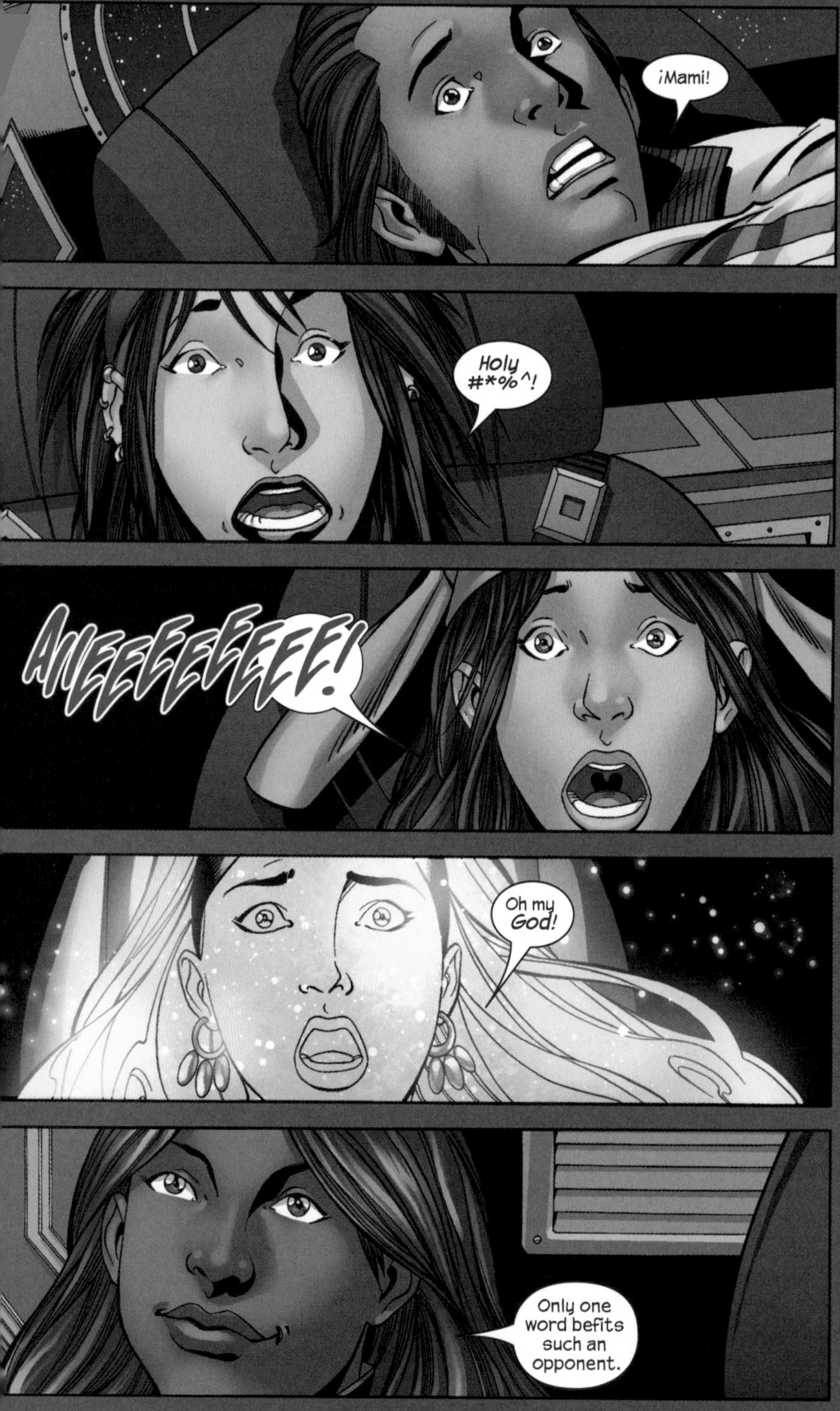
¡Mami!
Holy #*%^!
AIIEEEEEEEEE!
Oh my God!
Only one word befits such an opponent.

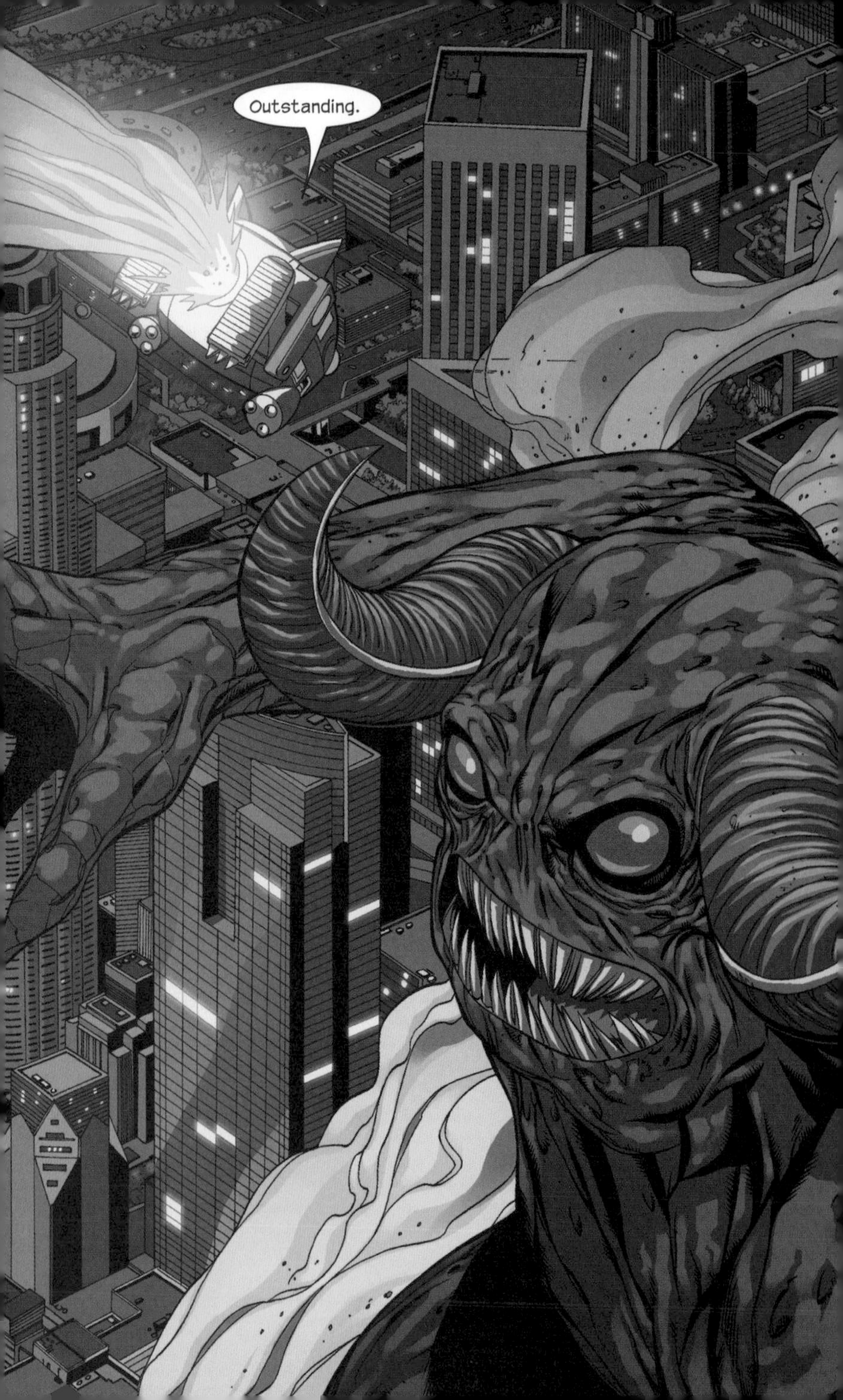
Outstanding.

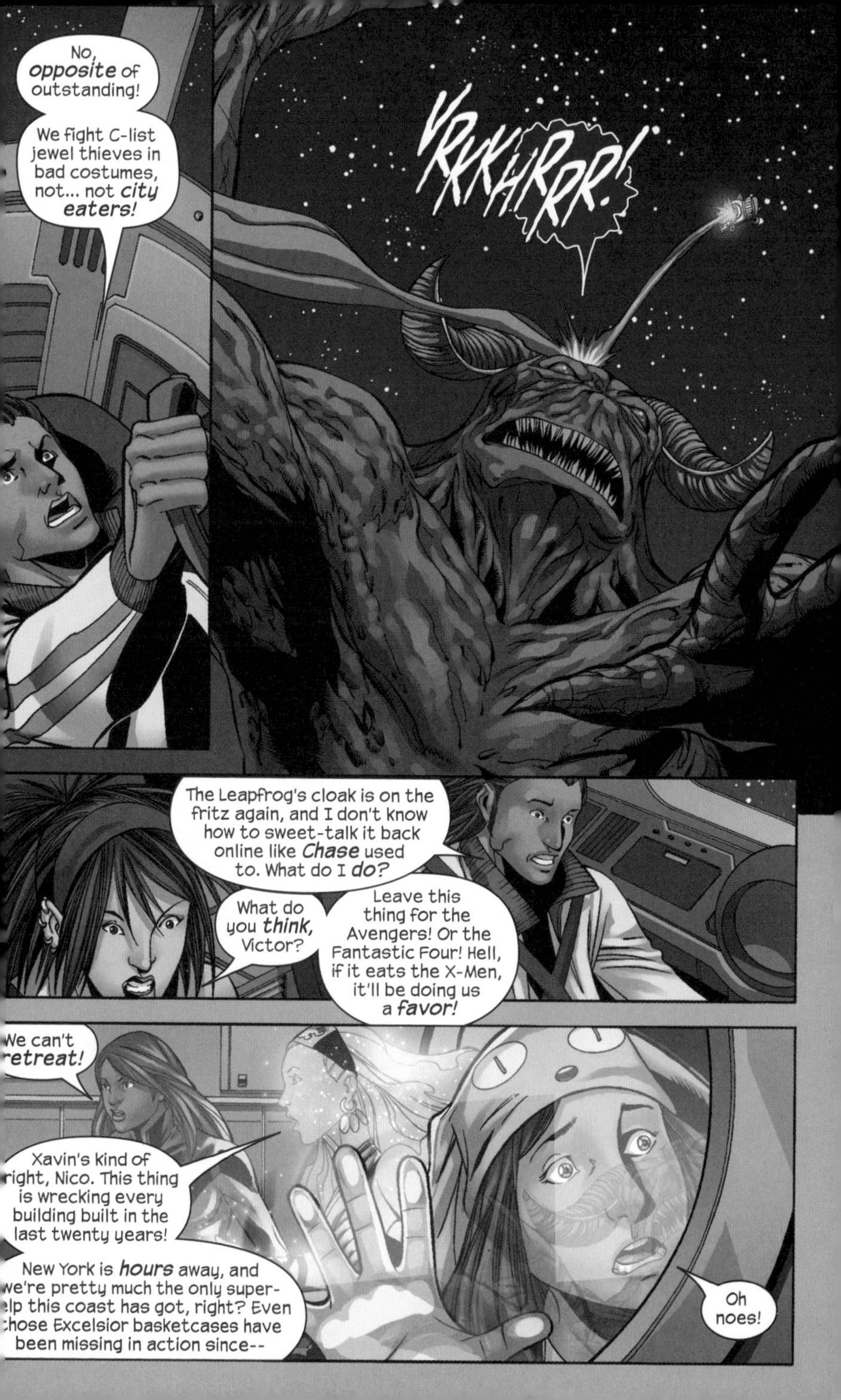
No, opposite of outstanding!
We fight C-list jewel thieves in bad costumes, not... not city eaters!
VRKKHRRR!
The Leapfrog's cloak is on the fritz again, and I don't know how to sweet-talk it back online like Chase used to. What do I do?
What do you think, Victor?
Leave this thing for the Avengers! Or the Fantastic Four! Hell, if it eats the X-Men, it'll be doing us a favor!
We can't retreat!
Xavin's kind of right, Nico. This thing is wrecking every building built in the last twenty years!
New York is hours away, and we're pretty much the only super-
lp this coast has got, right? Even
hose Excelsior basketcases have been missing in action since--
Oh noes!

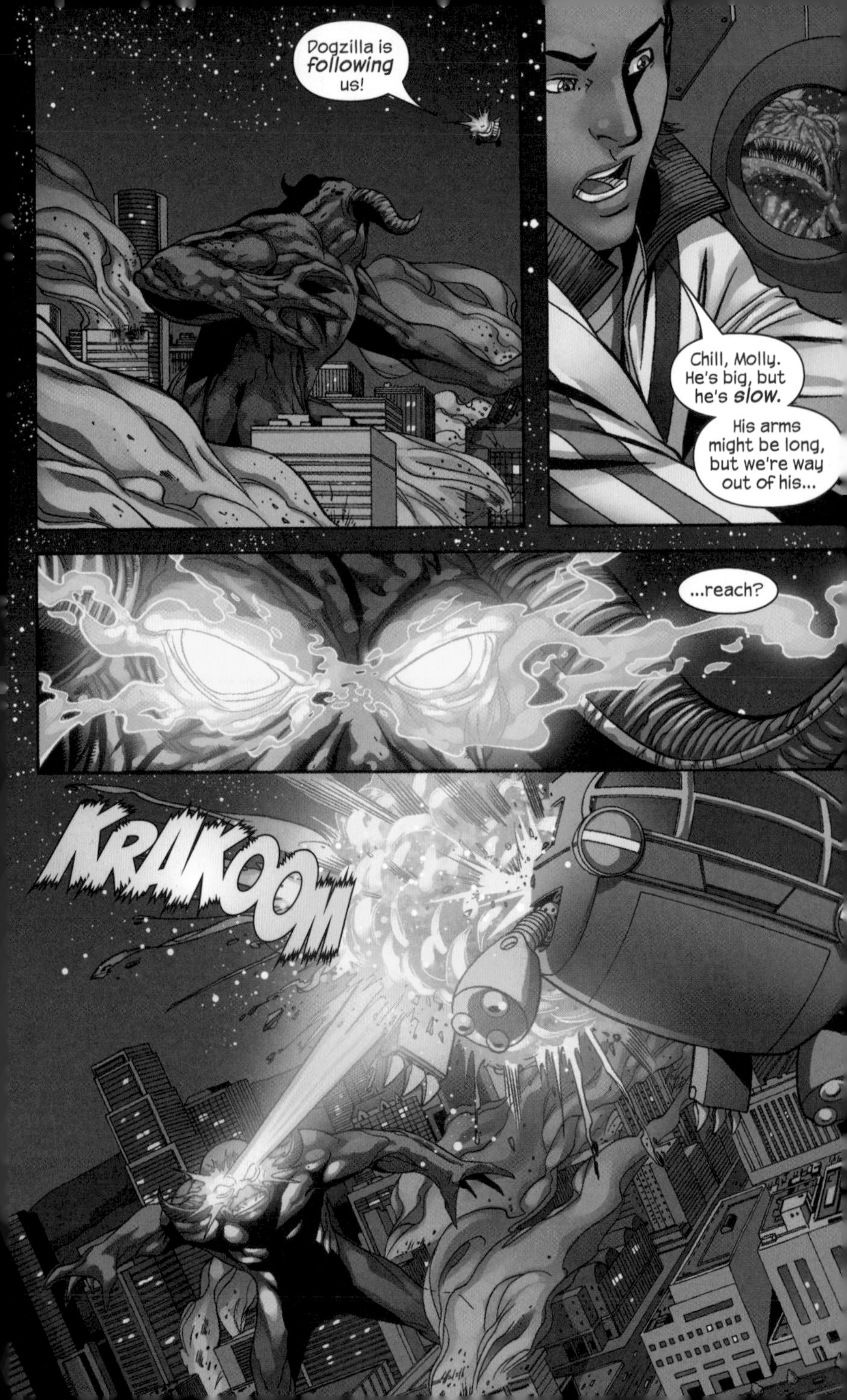
Dogzilla is following us!
Chill, Molly. He's big, but he's slow.
His arms might be long, but we're way out of his...
...reach?
KRAKOOM

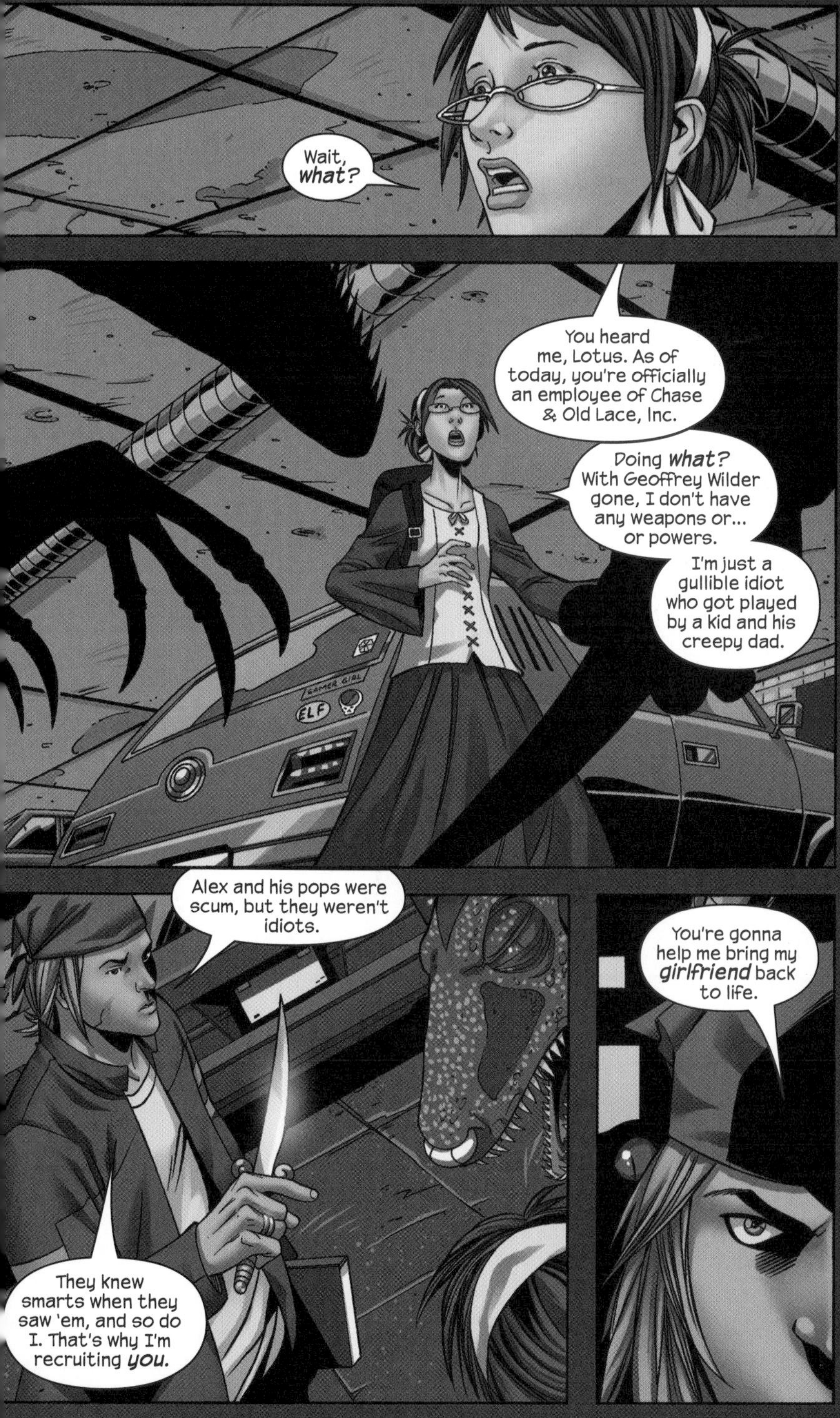
Wait, *what?*
You heard me, Lotus. As of today, you're officially an employee of Chase & Old Lace, Inc.
Doing *what?* With Geoffrey Wilder gone, I don't have any weapons or... or powers.
I'm just a gullible idiot who got played by a kid and his creepy dad.
GAMER GIRL
ELF
Alex and his pops were scum, but they weren't idiots.
They knew smarts when they saw 'em, and so do I. That's why I'm recruiting *you.*
You're gonna help me bring my *girlfriend* back to life.

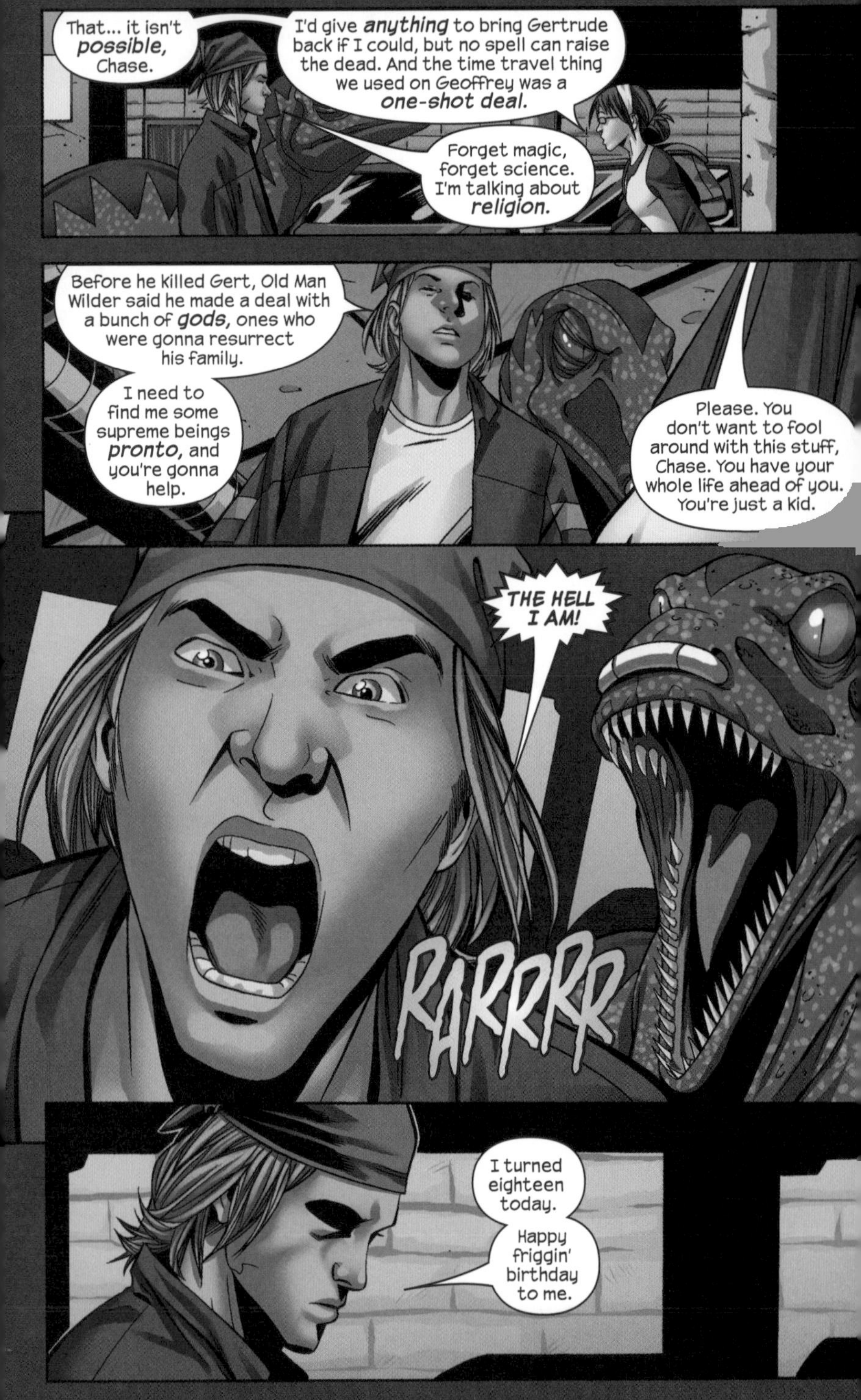
That... it isn't *possible,* Chase.
I'd give ***anything*** to bring Gertrude back if I could, but no spell can raise the dead. And the time travel thing we used on Geoffrey was a ***one-shot deal.***
Forget magic, forget science. I'm talking about ***religion.***
Before he killed Gert, Old Man Wilder said he made a deal with a bunch of ***gods,*** ones who were gonna resurrect his family.
I need to find me some supreme beings ***pronto,*** and you're gonna help.
Please. You don't want to fool around with this stuff, Chase. You have your whole life ahead of you. You're just a kid.
THE HELL I AM!
RARRRR
I turned eighteen today.
Happy friggin' birthday to me.

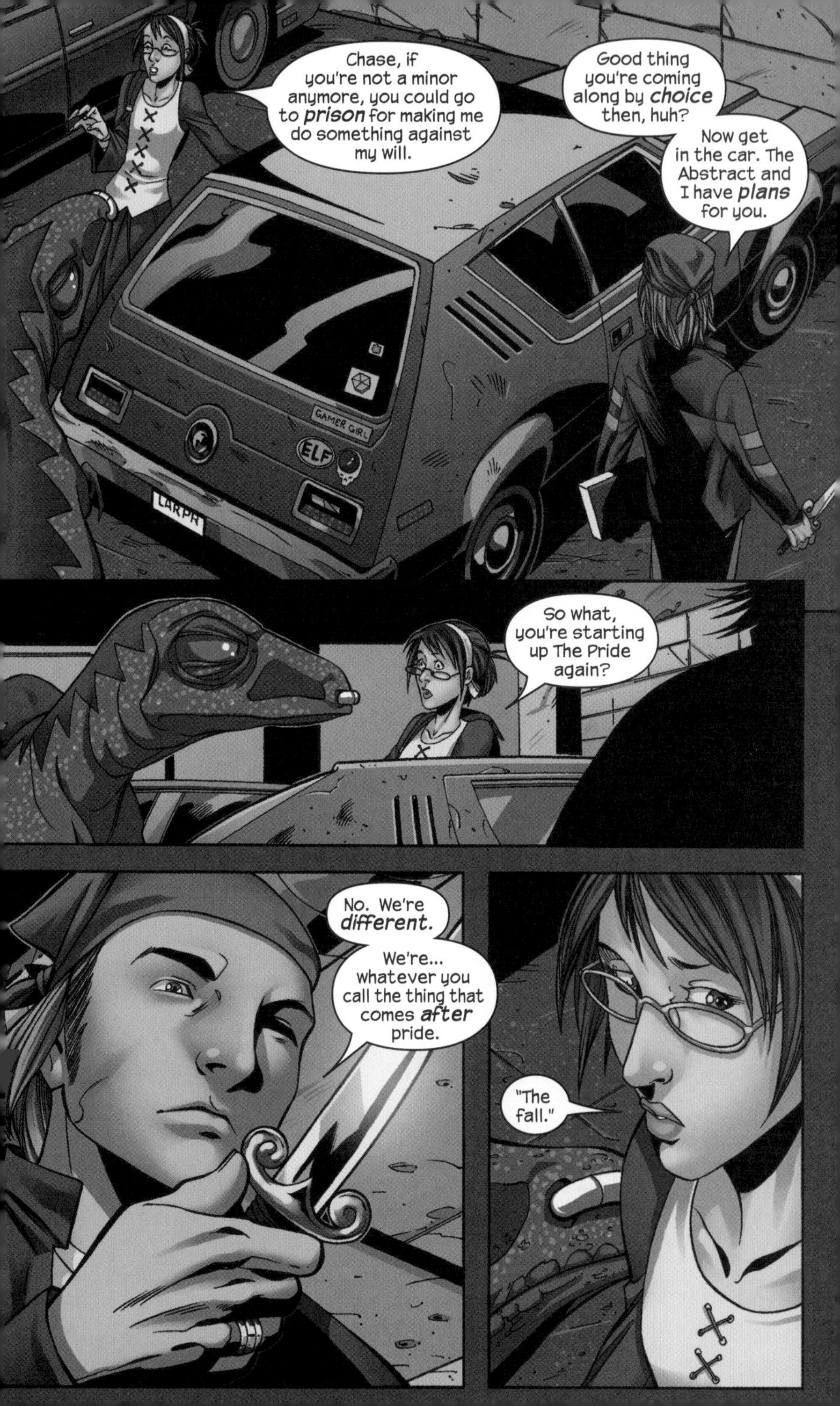
Chase, if you're not a minor anymore, you could go to *prison* for making me do something against my will.
Good thing you're coming along by *choice* then, huh?
Now get in the car. The Abstract and I have *plans* for you.
GAMER GIRL
ELF
LARPR
So what, you're starting up The Pride again?
No. We're *different.*
We're... whatever you call the thing that comes *after* pride.
"The fall."

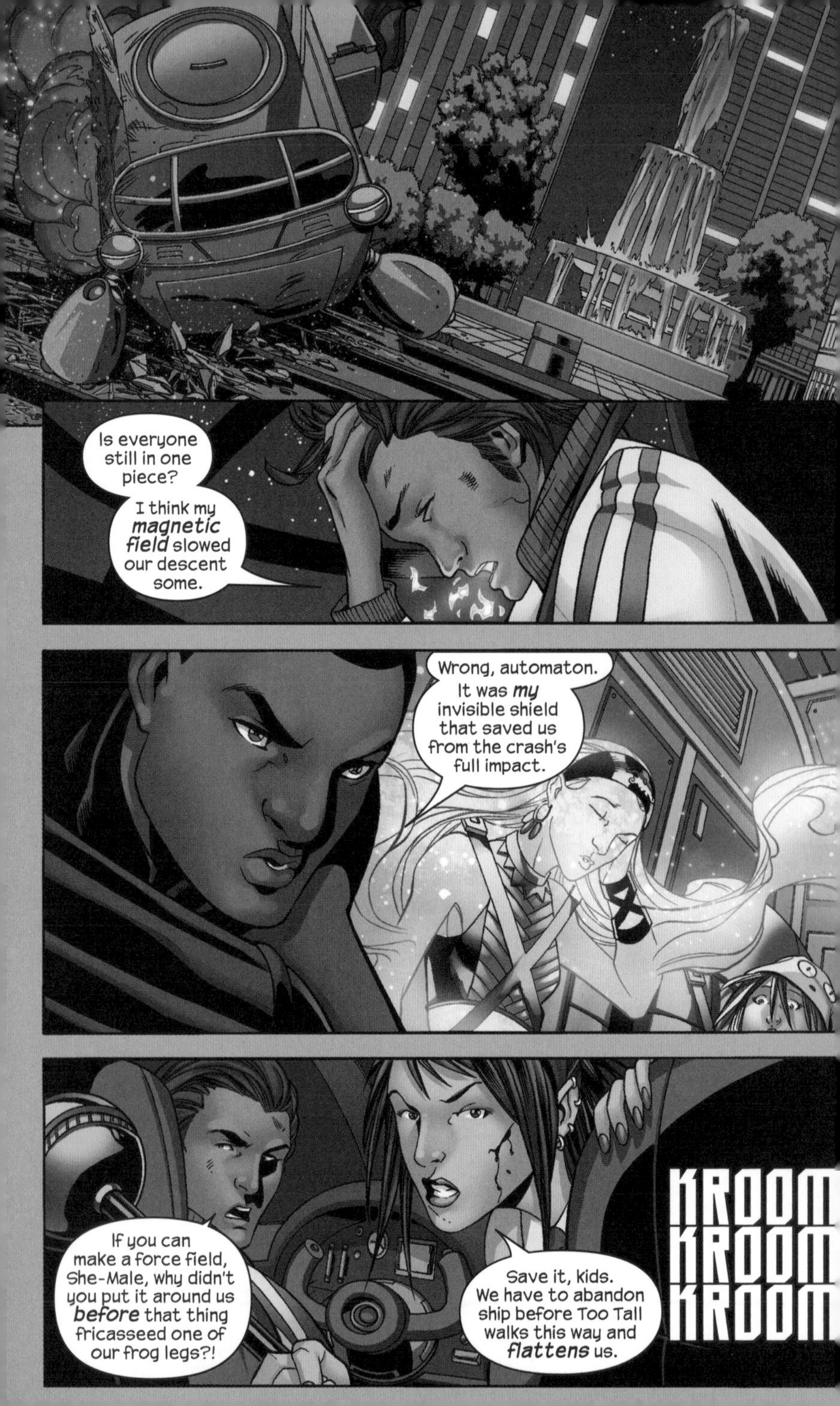
Is everyone still in one piece?
I think my *magnetic field* slowed our descent some.
Wrong, automaton. It was *my* invisible shield that saved us from the crash's full impact.
If you can make a force field, She-Male, why didn't you put it around us *before* that thing fricasseed one of our frog legs?!
Save it, kids. We have to abandon ship before Too Tall walks this way and *flattens* us.
KROOM KROOM KROOM

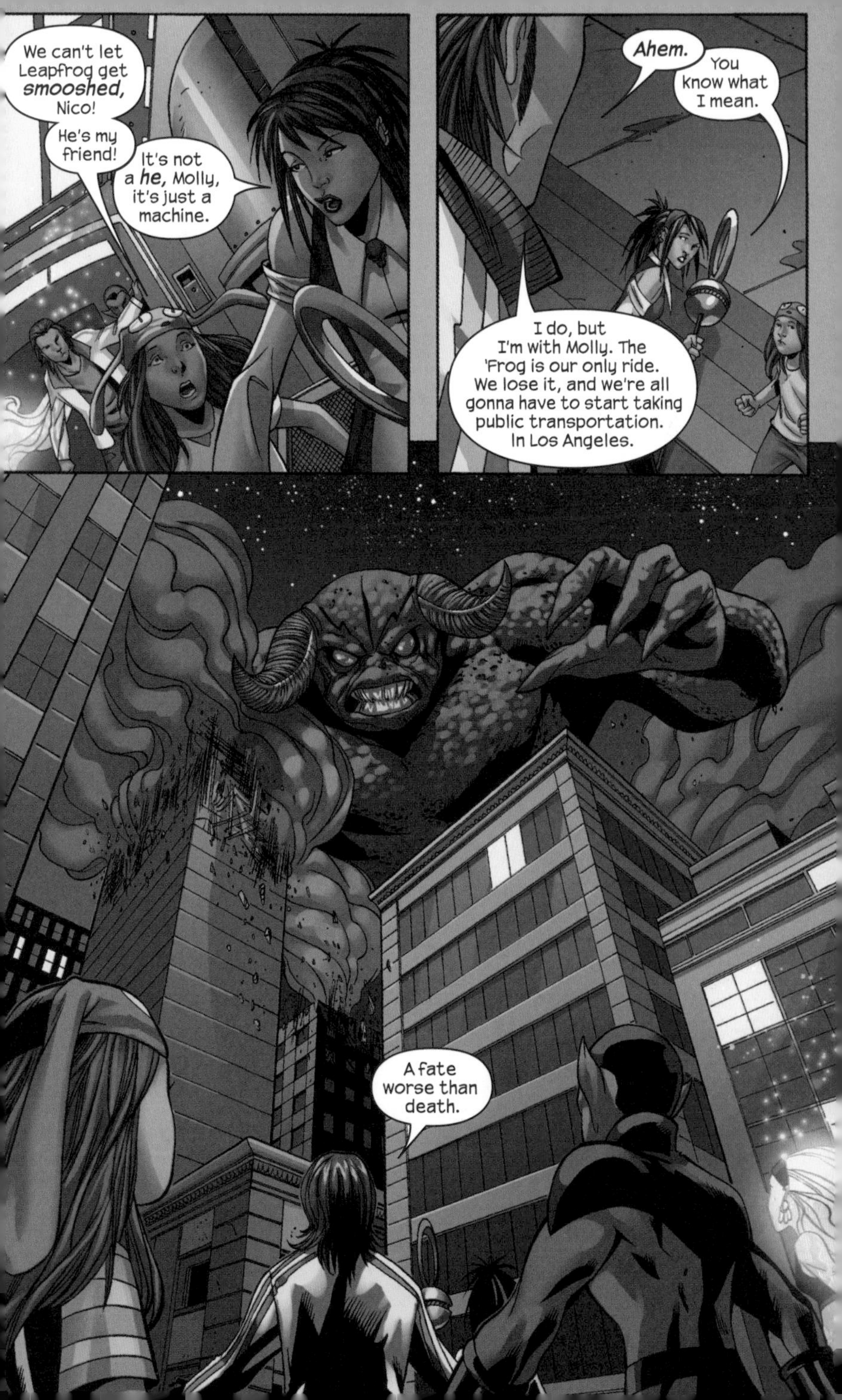
We can't let Leapfrog get *smooshed,* Nico!
He's my friend!
It's not a *he,* Molly, it's just a machine.
Ahem.
You know what I mean.
I do, but I'm with Molly. The 'Frog is our only ride. We lose it, and we're all gonna have to start taking public transportation. In Los Angeles.
A fate worse than death.

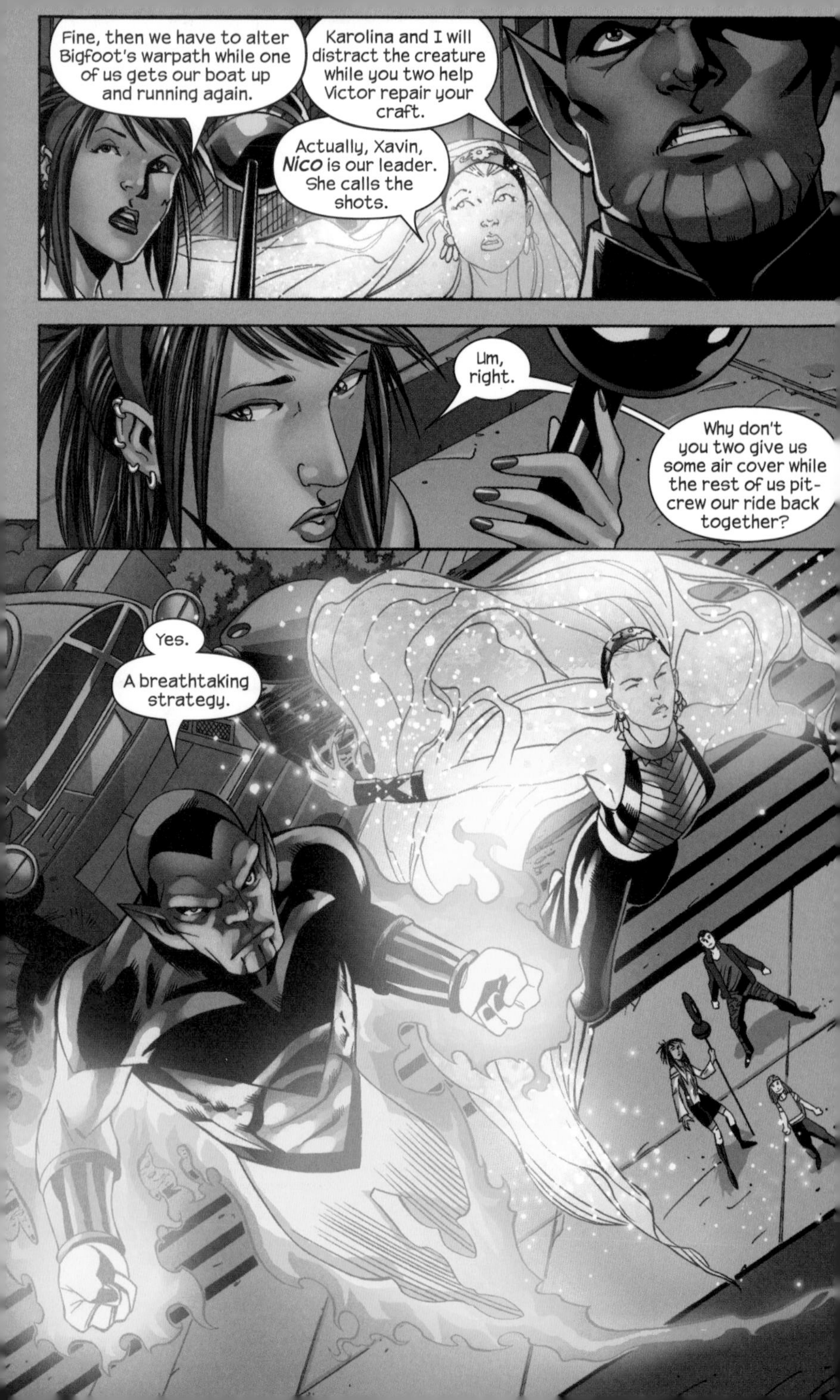
Fine, then we have to alter Bigfoot's warpath while one of us gets our boat up and running again.
Karolina and I will distract the creature while you two help Victor repair your craft.
Actually, Xavin, *Nico* is our leader. She calls the shots.
Um, right.
Why don't you two give us some air cover while the rest of us pit-crew our ride back together?
Yes.
A breathtaking strategy.

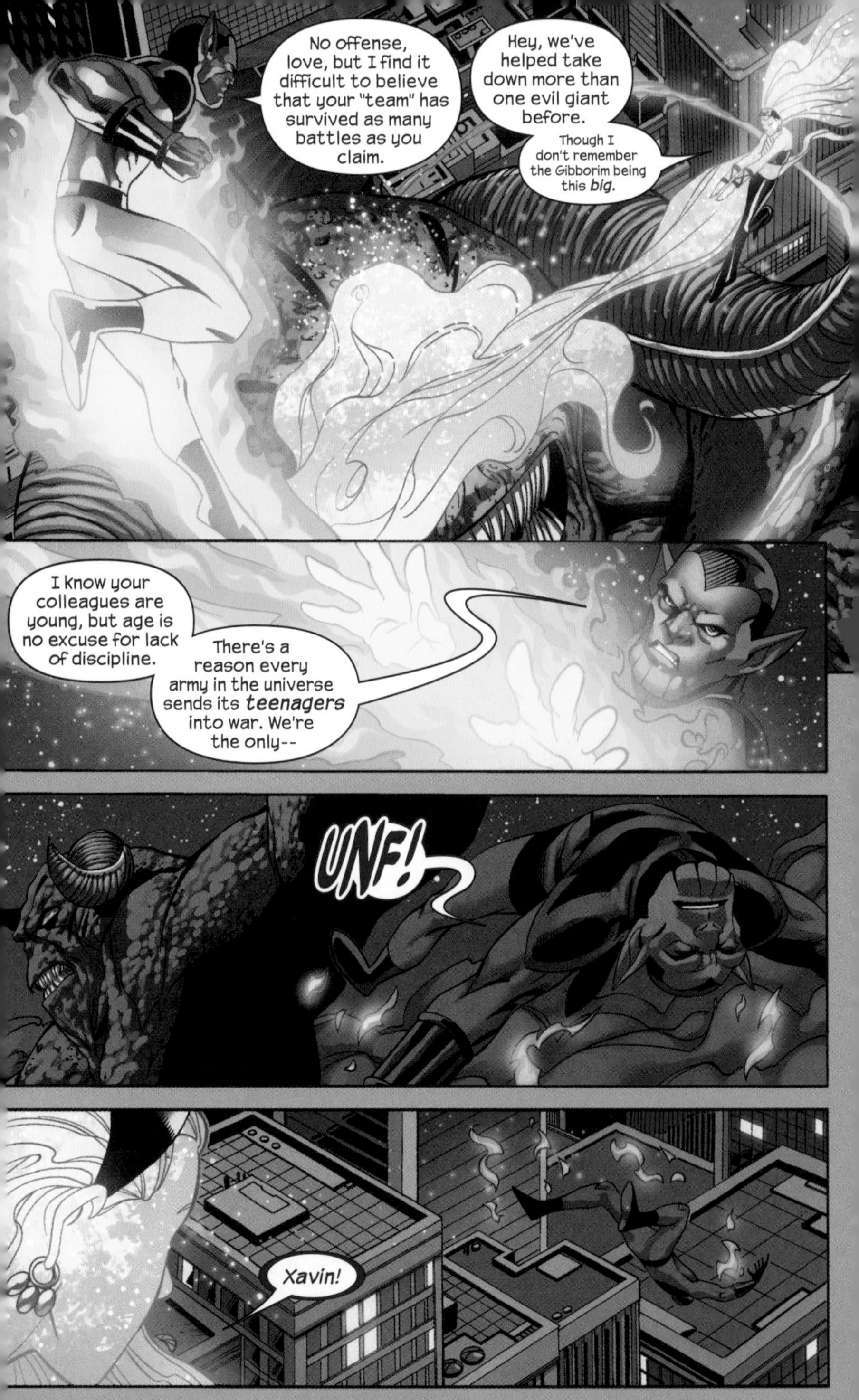
No offense, love, but I find it difficult to believe that your "team" has survived as many battles as you claim.
Hey, we've helped take down more than one evil giant before.
Though I don't remember the Gibborim being this *big*.
I know your colleagues are young, but age is no excuse for lack of discipline.
There's a reason every army in the universe sends its *teenagers* into war. We're the only--
UNF!
Xavin!

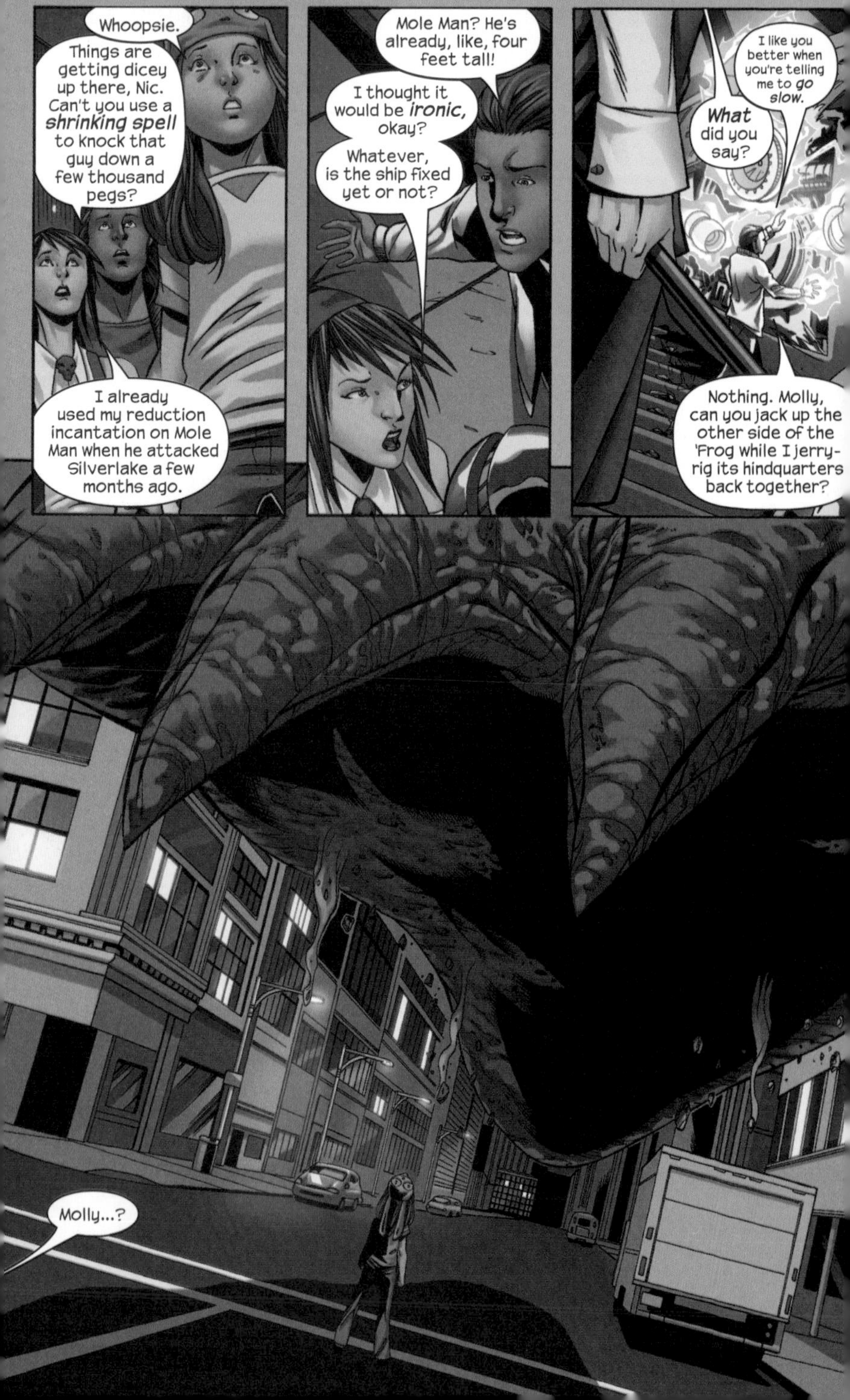
Whoopsie.
Things are getting dicey up there, Nic. Can't you use a shrinking spell to knock that guy down a few thousand pegs?
I already used my reduction incantation on Mole Man when he attacked Silverlake a few months ago.
Mole Man? He's already, like, four feet tall!
I thought it would be ironic, okay?
Whatever, is the ship fixed yet or not?
What did you say?
I like you better when you're telling me to go slow.
Nothing. Molly, can you jack up the other side of the 'Frog while I jerry-rig its hindquarters back together?
Molly...?

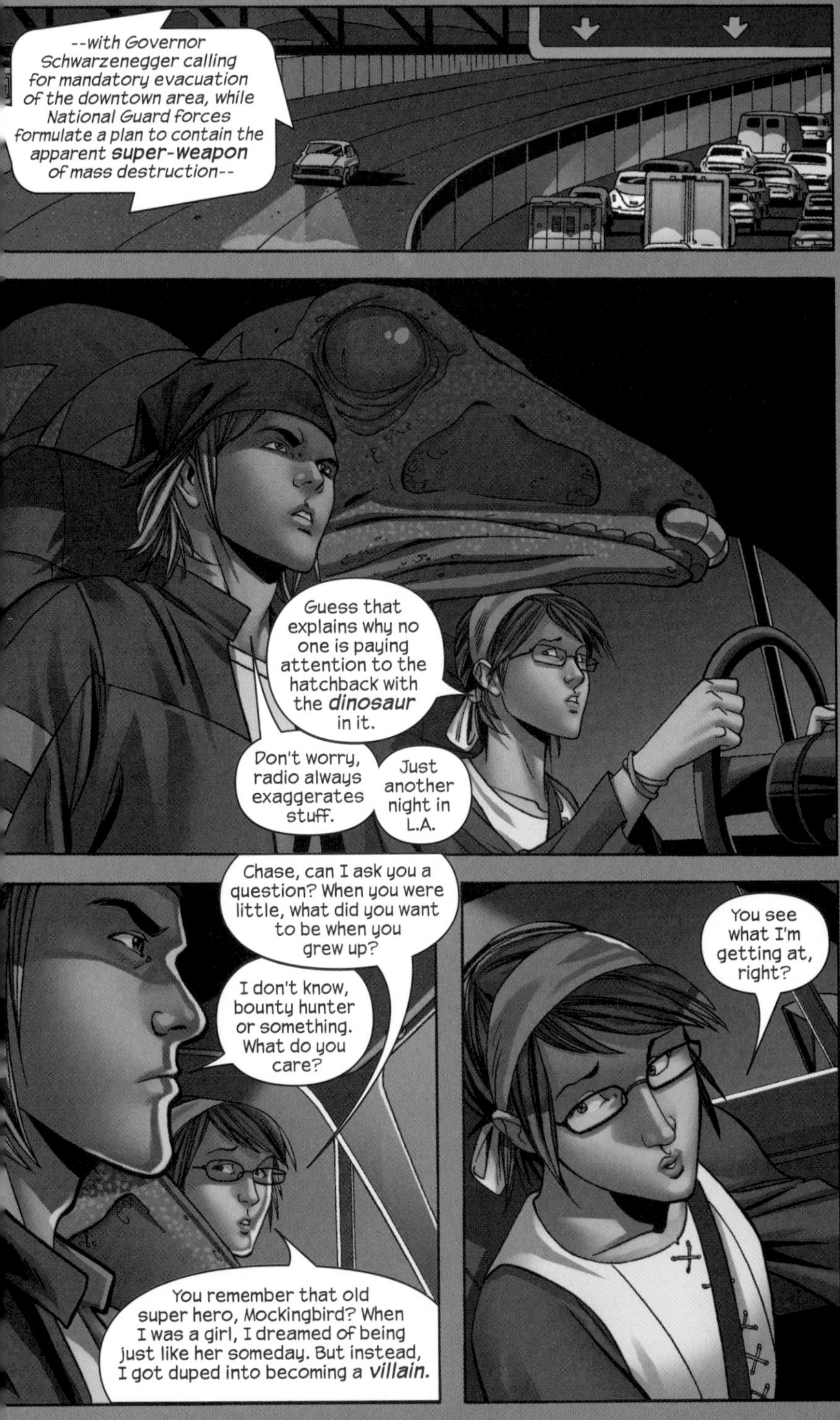
--with Governor Schwarzenegger calling for mandatory evacuation of the downtown area, while National Guard forces formulate a plan to contain the apparent **super-weapon** of mass destruction--
Guess that explains why no one is paying attention to the hatchback with the ***dinosaur*** in it.
Don't worry, radio always exaggerates stuff.
Just another night in L.A.
Chase, can I ask you a question? When you were little, what did you want to be when you grew up?
I don't know, bounty hunter or something. What do you care?
You remember that old super hero, Mockingbird? When I was a girl, I dreamed of being just like her someday. But instead, I got duped into becoming a ***villain.***
You see what I'm getting at, right?

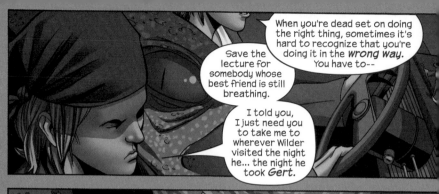

When you're dead set on doing the right thing, sometimes it's hard to recognize that you're doing it in the *wrong way*. You have to--

Save the lecture for somebody whose best friend is still breathing.

I told you, I just need you to take me to wherever Wilder visited the night he... the night he took *Gert*.

DONUTS

Well, this is the place.

Believe it or not, I guess.

I'll, uh, just keep the motor running while you do whatever it is you have to do here.

Nice try, Hippie Chick.

But our date is just getting started.

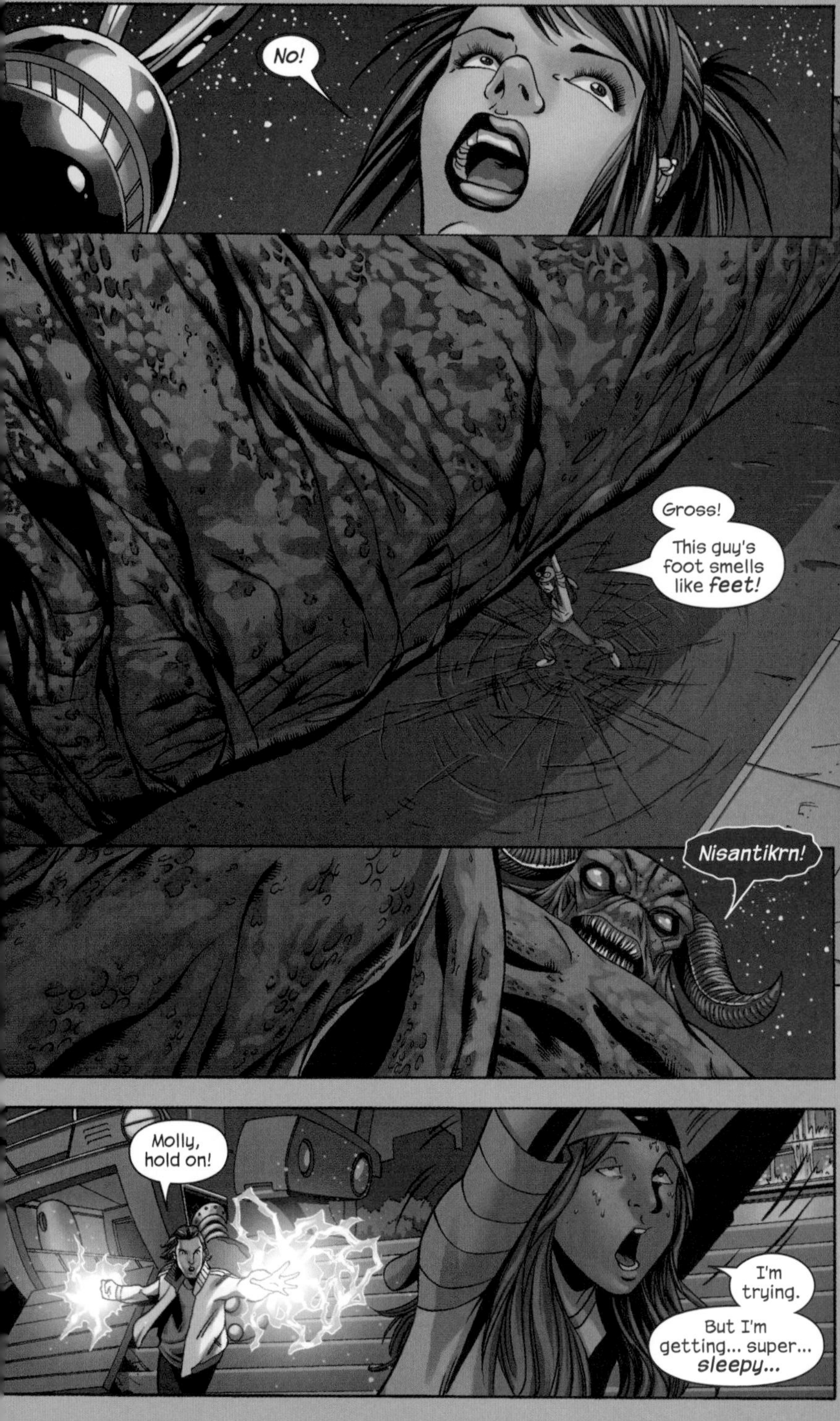
No!
Gross!
This guy's foot smells like *feet!*
Nisantikrn!
Molly, hold on!
I'm trying.
But I'm getting... super... *sleepy...*

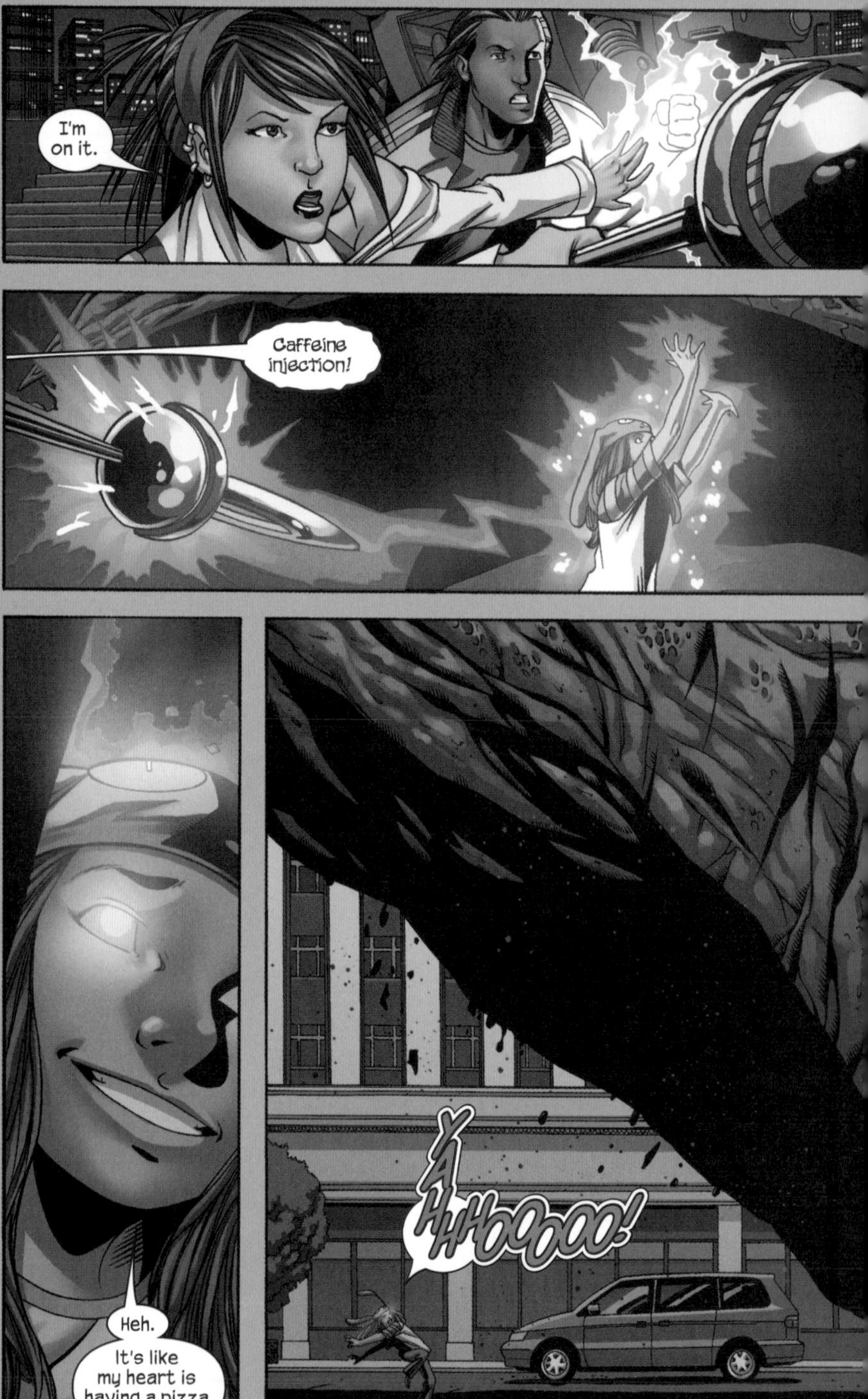
I'm on it.
Caffeine injection!
Heh.
It's like my heart is having a pizza party.
YAHHOOOOOO!

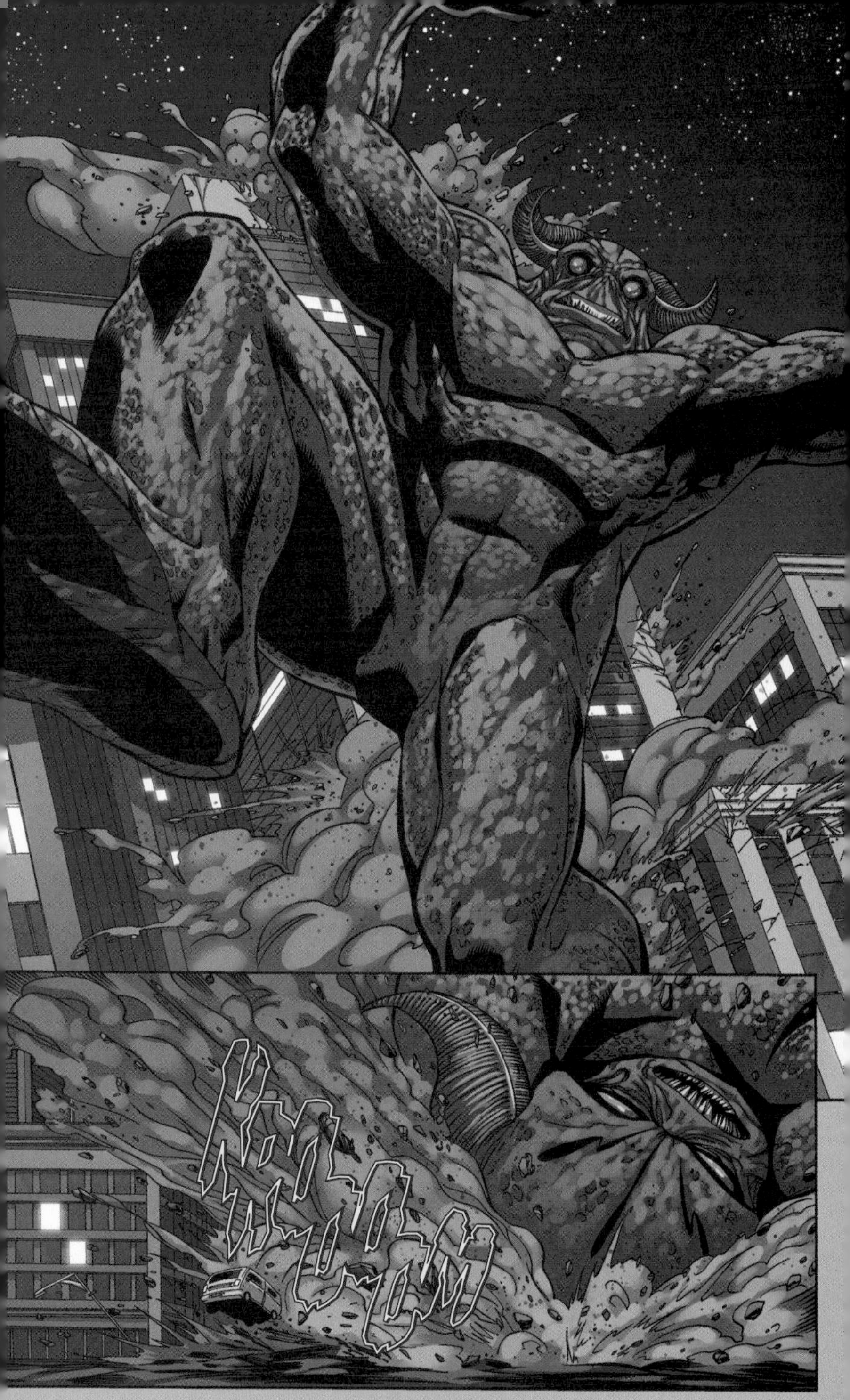

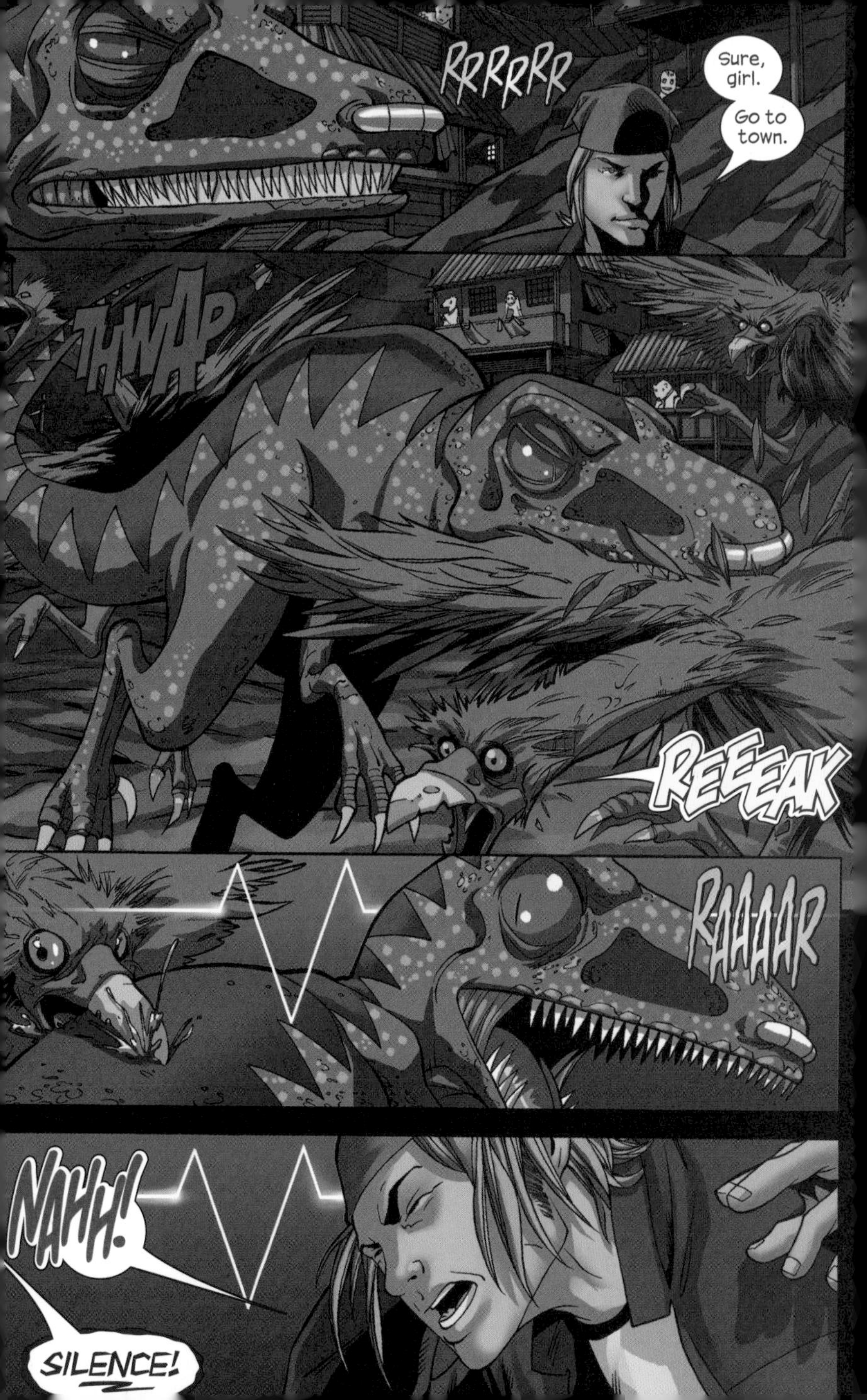
RRRRRR
Sure, girl.
Go to town.
THWAP
REEEAK
RAAAAR
NAHH!
SILENCE!

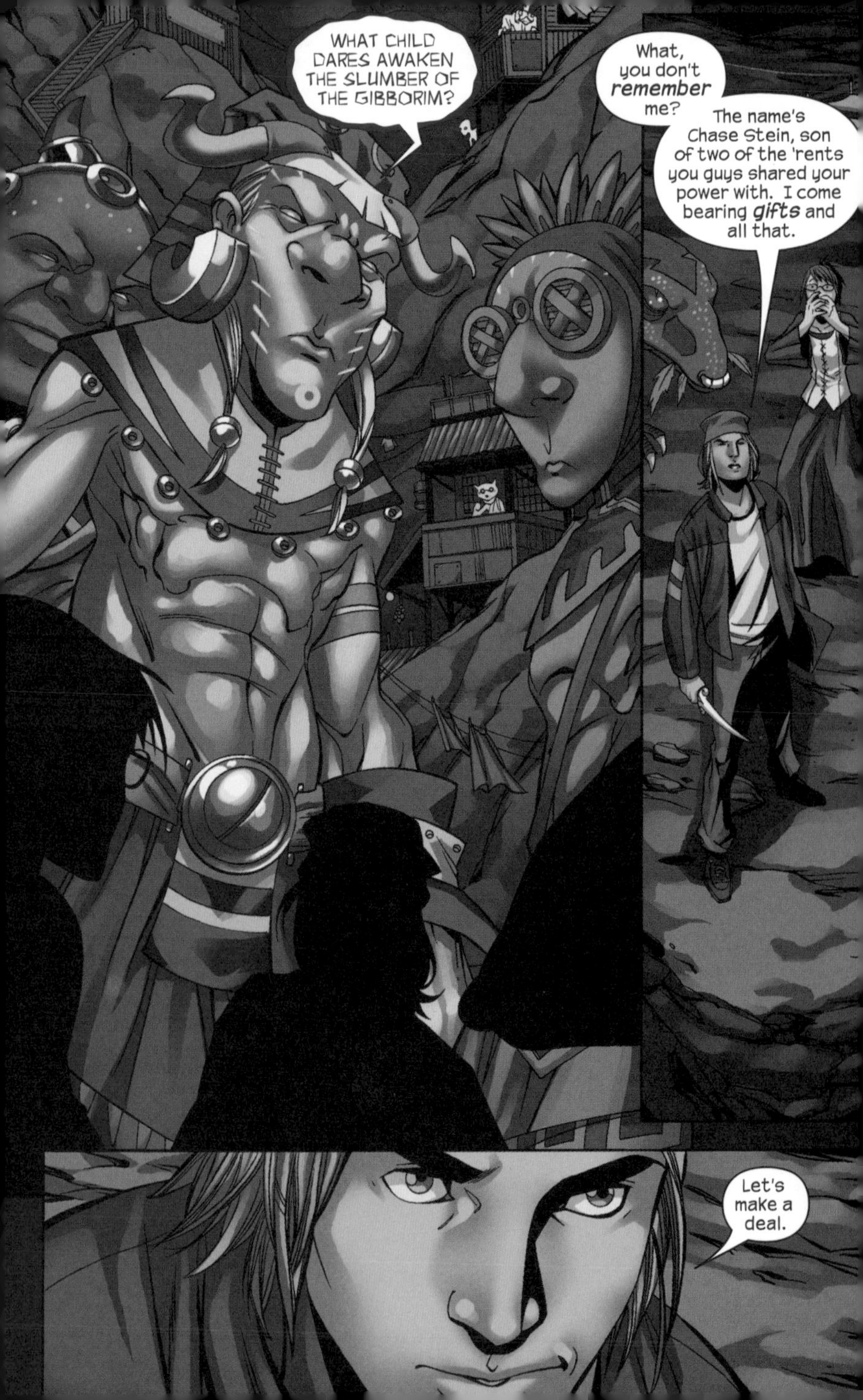
WHAT CHILD DARES AWAKEN THE SLUMBER OF THE GIBBORIM?
What, you don't **remember** me?
The name's Chase Stein, son of two of the 'rents you guys shared your power with. I come bearing **gifts** and all that.
Let's make a deal.

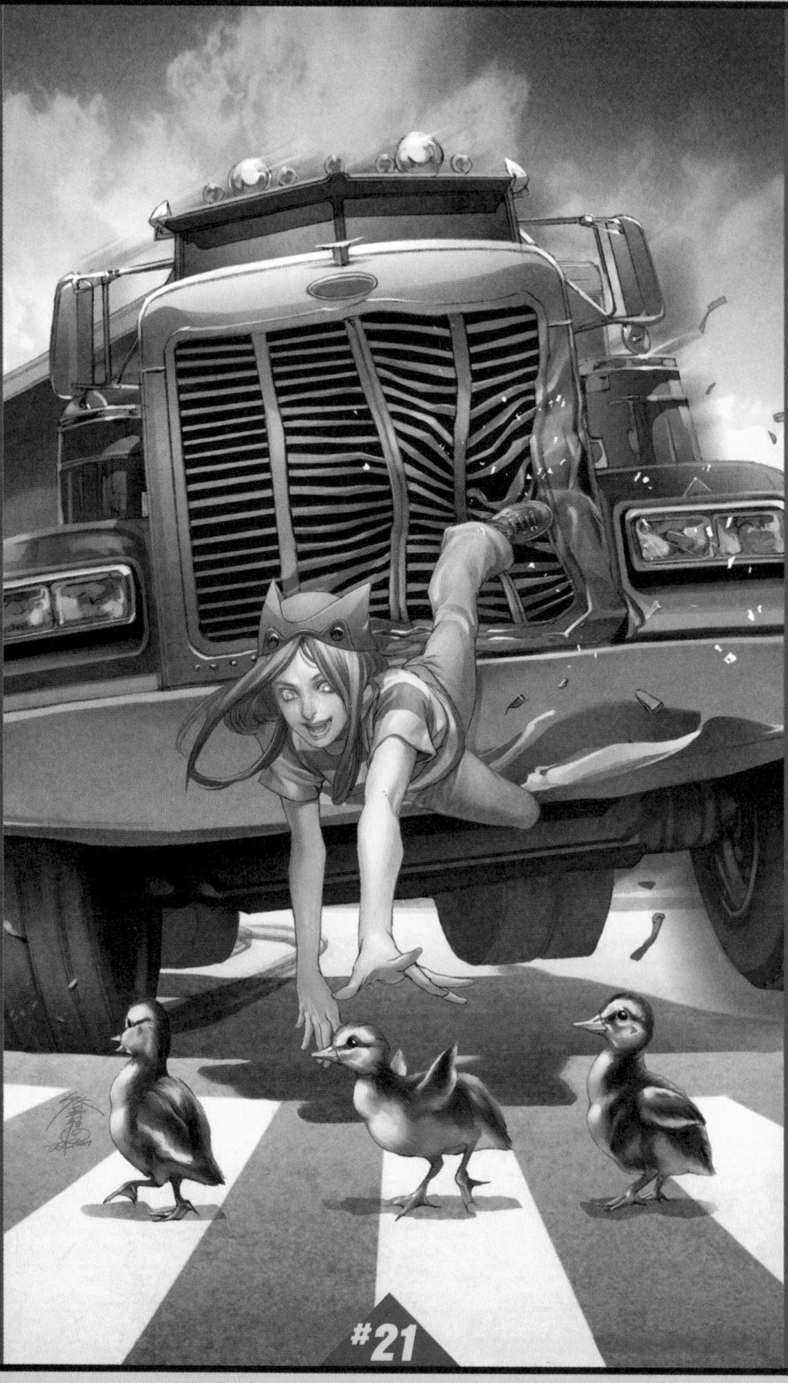
#21

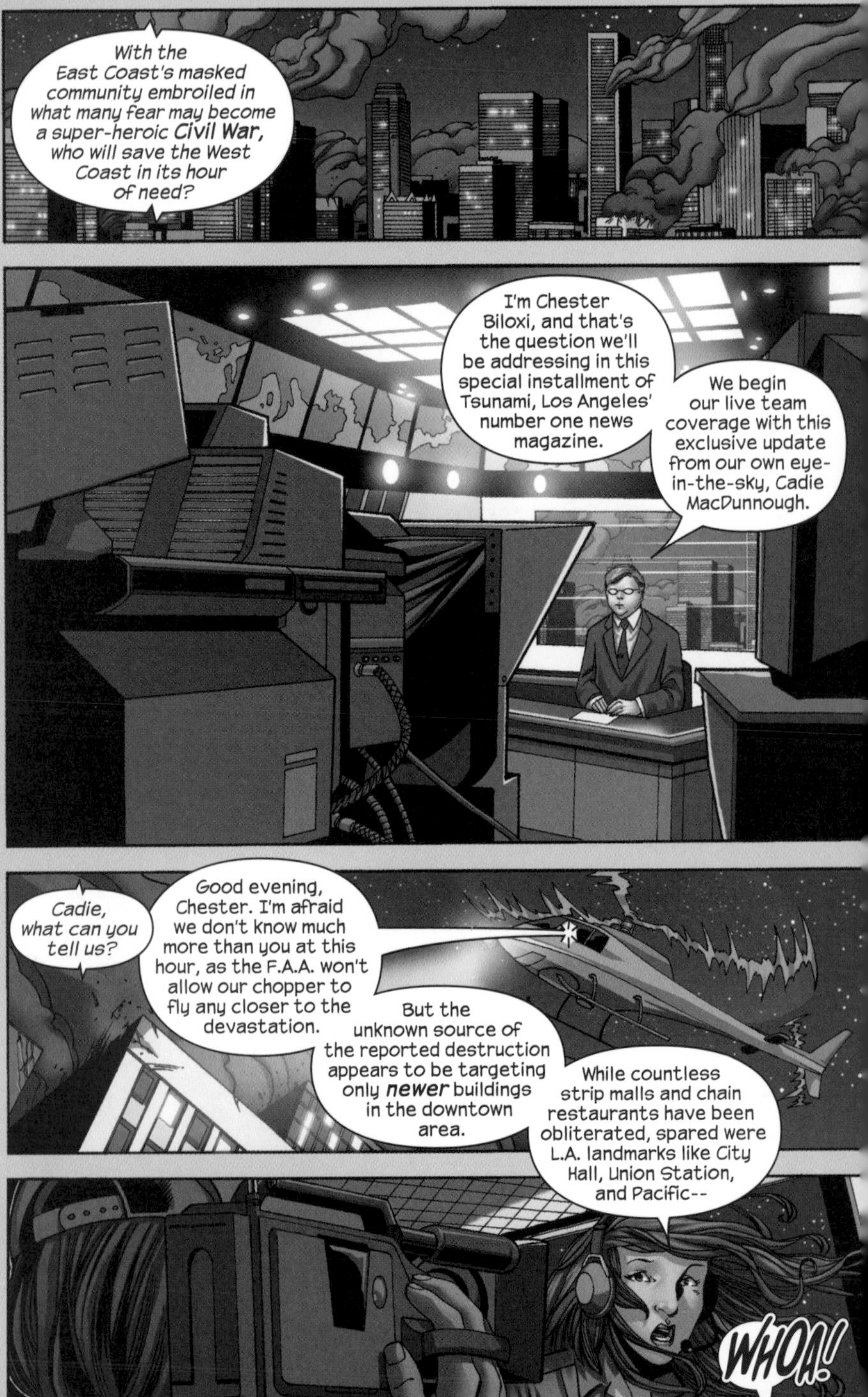
With the East Coast's masked community embroiled in what many fear may become a super-heroic Civil War, who will save the West Coast in its hour of need?
I'm Chester Biloxi, and that's the question we'll be addressing in this special installment of Tsunami, Los Angeles' number one news magazine.
We begin our live team coverage with this exclusive update from our own eye-in-the-sky, Cadie MacDunnough.
Cadie, what can you tell us?
Good evening, Chester. I'm afraid we don't know much more than you at this hour, as the F.A.A. won't allow our chopper to fly any closer to the devastation.
But the unknown source of the reported destruction appears to be targeting only newer buildings in the downtown area.
While countless strip malls and chain restaurants have been obliterated, spared were L.A. landmarks like City Hall, Union Station, and Pacific--
WHOA!

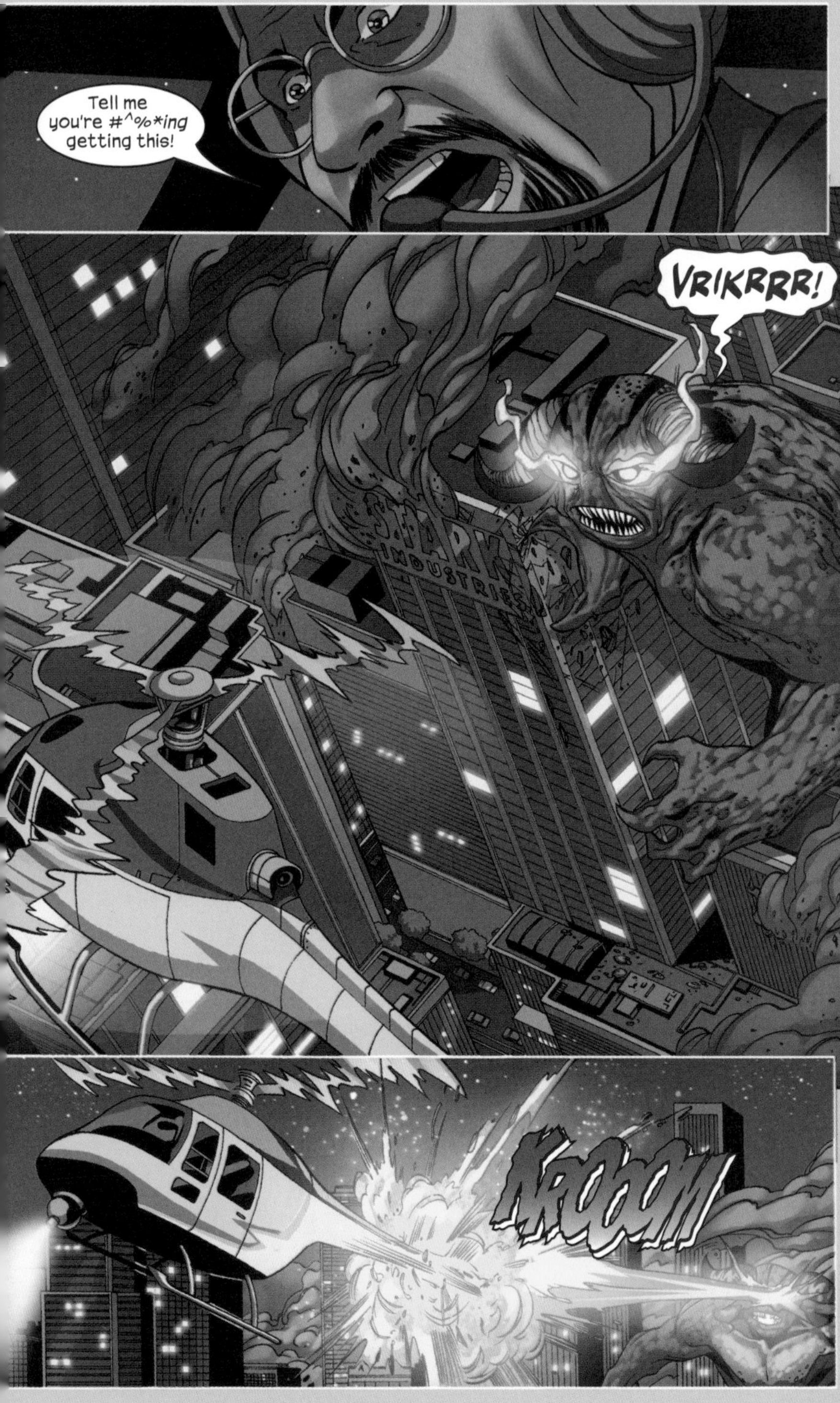

Tell me you're #^%*ing getting this!
VRIKRRR!
STARK INDUSTRIES
KROOOM

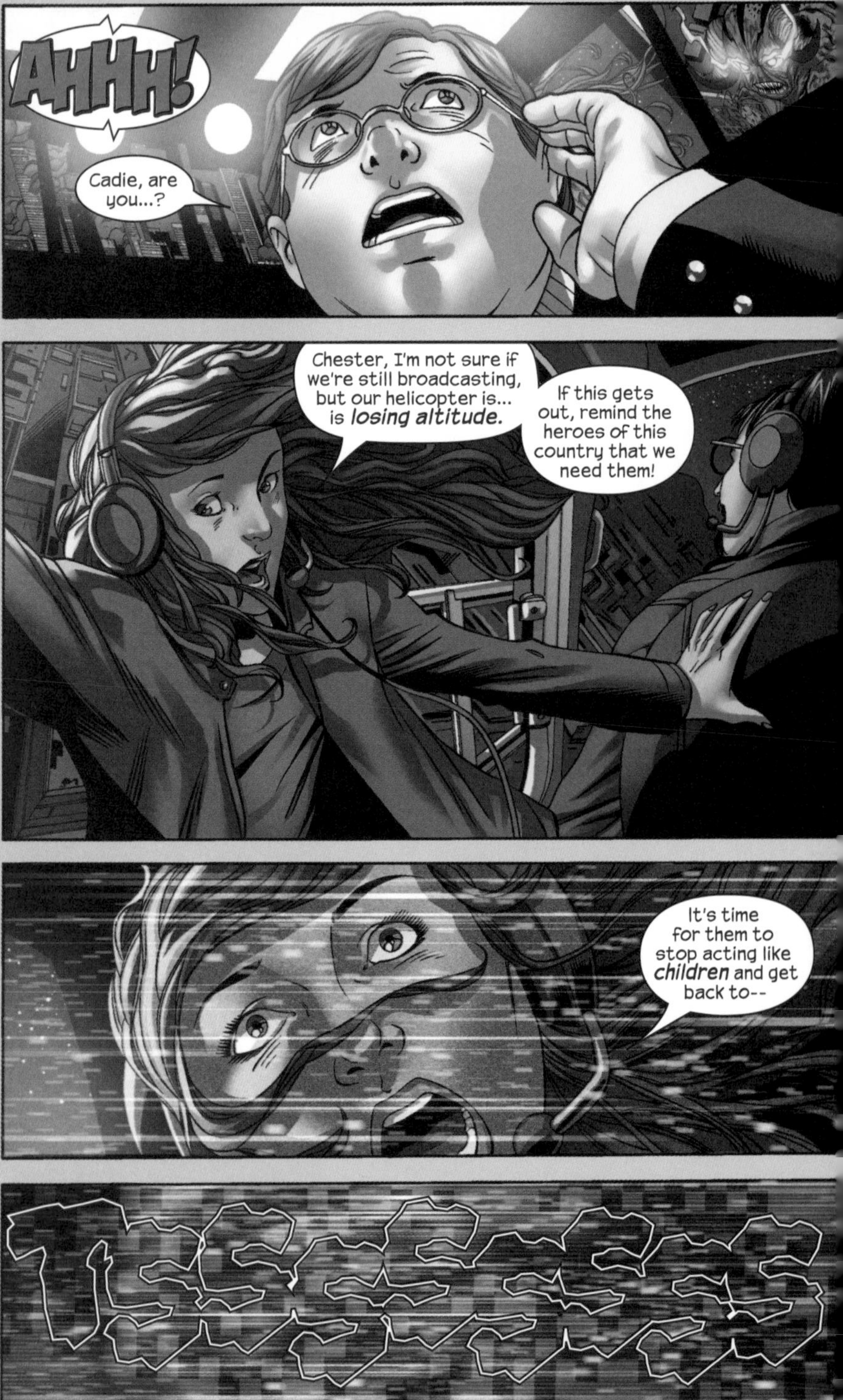
AHHH!
Cadie, are you...?
Chester, I'm not sure if we're still broadcasting, but our helicopter is... is *losing altitude.*
If this gets out, remind the heroes of this country that we need them!
It's time for them to stop acting like *children* and get back to--

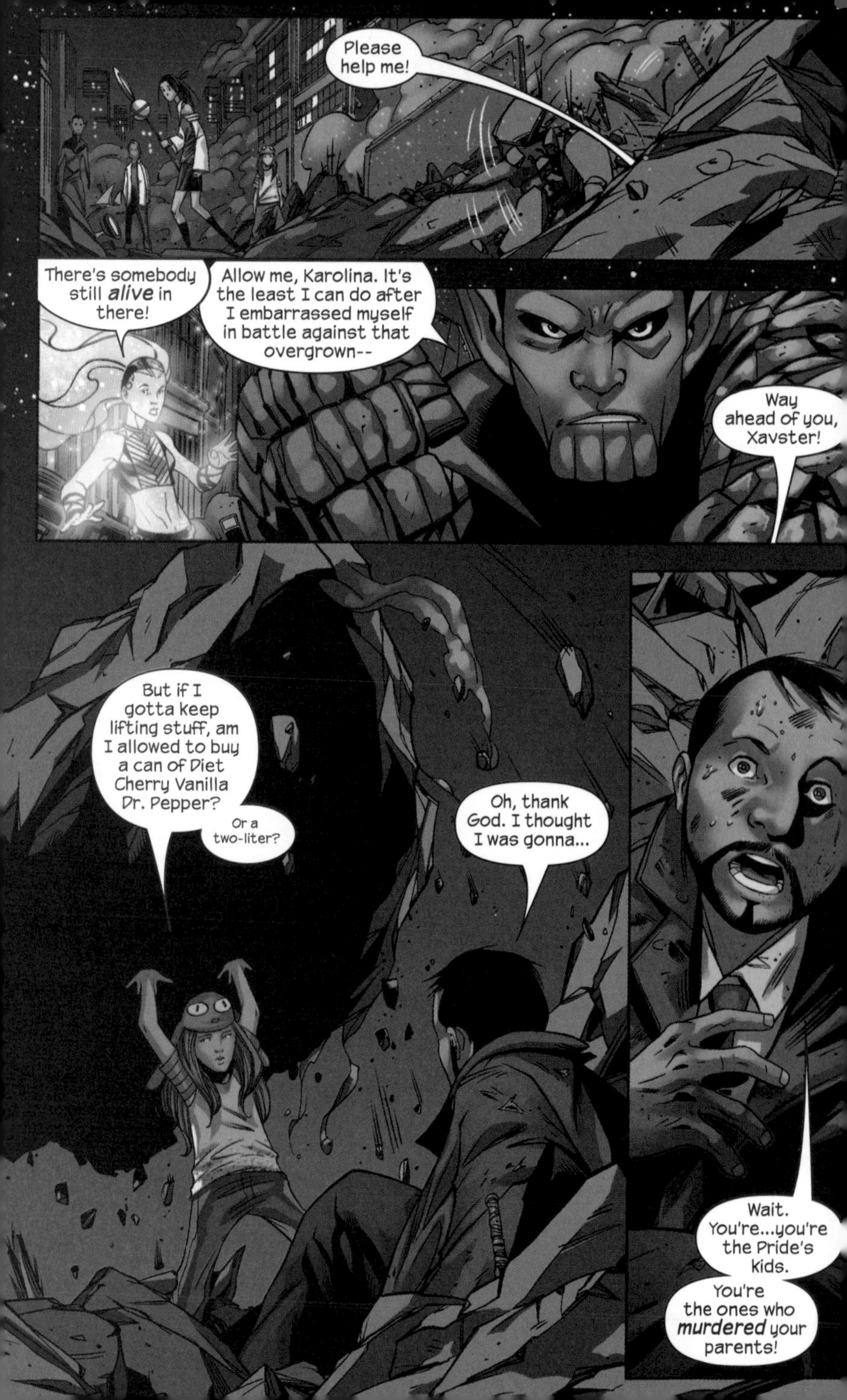

Please help me!
There's somebody still *alive* in there!
Allow me, Karolina. It's the least I can do after I embarrassed myself in battle against that overgrown--
Way ahead of you, Xavster!
But if I gotta keep lifting stuff, am I allowed to buy a can of Diet Cherry Vanilla Dr. Pepper?
Or a two-liter?
Oh, thank God. I thought I was gonna...
Wait. You're...you're the Pride's kids.
You're the ones who *murdered* your parents!

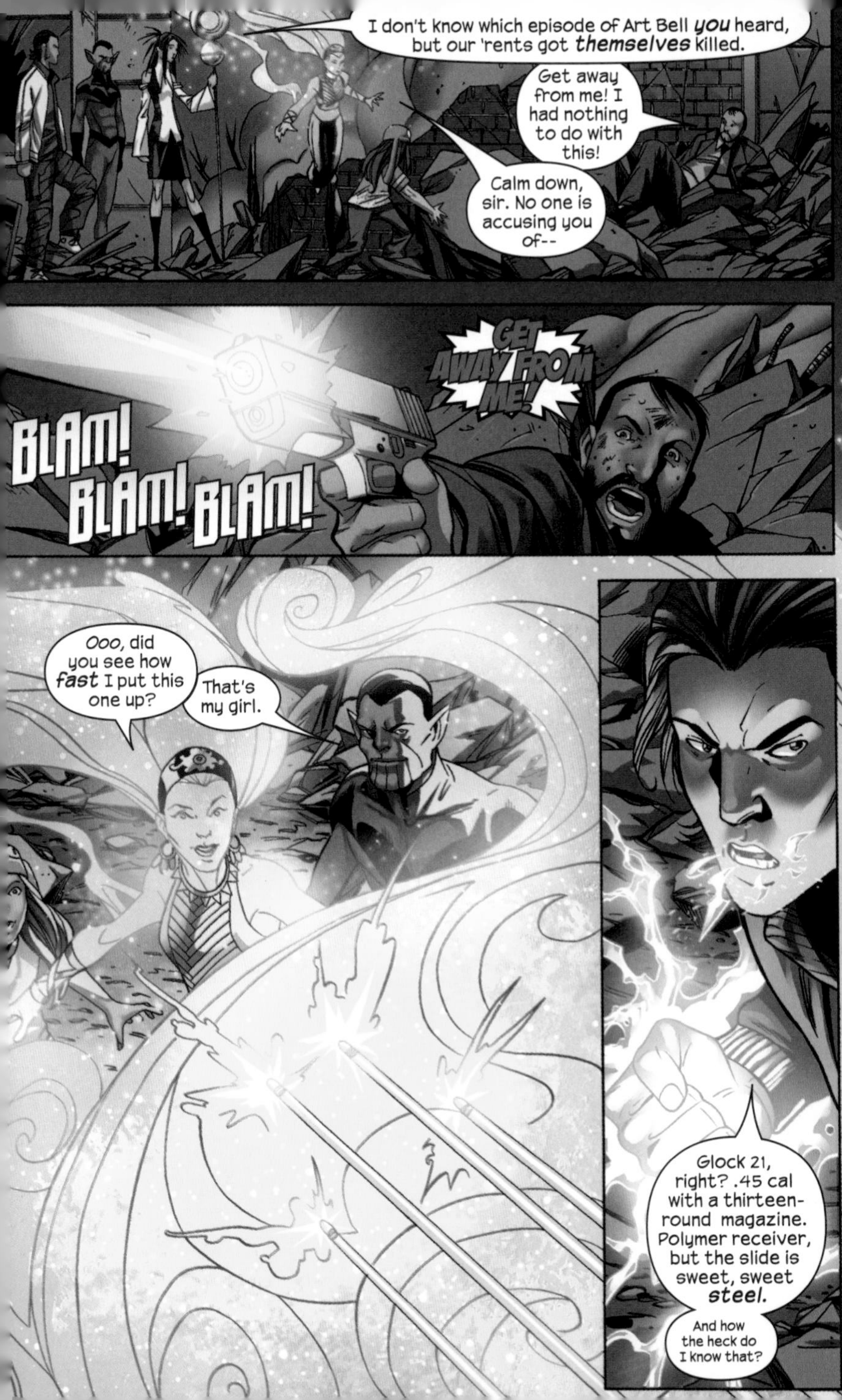
I don't know which episode of Art Bell *you* heard, but our 'rents got *themselves* killed.
Get away from me! I had nothing to do with this!
Calm down, sir. No one is accusing you of--
GET AWAY FROM ME!
BLAM! BLAM! BLAM!
Ooo, did you see how *fast* I put this one up?
That's my girl.
Glock 21, right? .45 cal with a thirteen-round magazine. Polymer receiver, but the slide is sweet, sweet *steel.*
And how the heck do I know that?

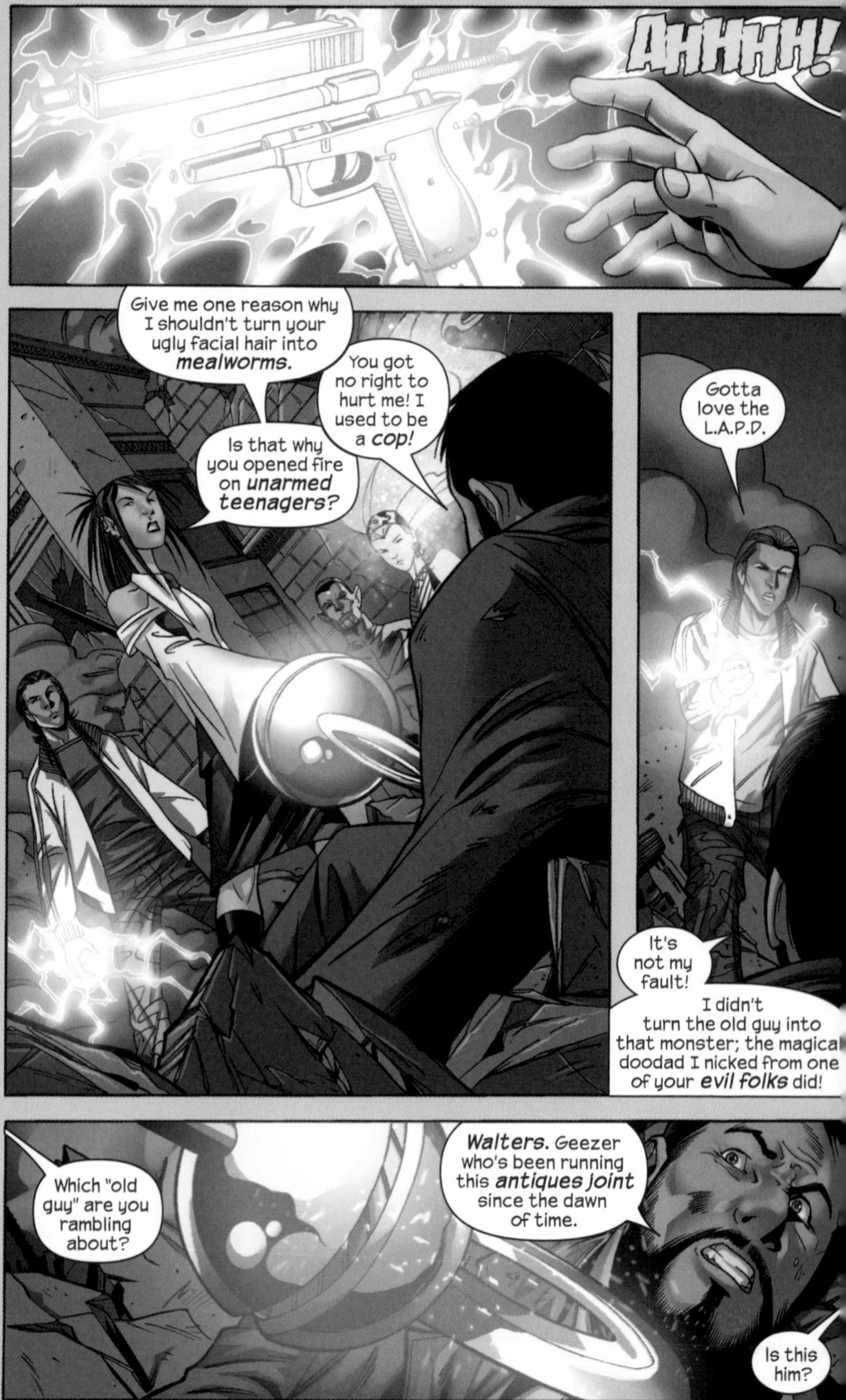
AHHHH!
Give me one reason why I shouldn't turn your ugly facial hair into mealworms.
You got no right to hurt me! I used to be a cop!
Is that why you opened fire on unarmed teenagers?
Gotta love the L.A.P.D.
It's not my fault!
I didn't turn the old guy into that monster; the magical doodad I nicked from one of your evil folks did!
Which "old guy" are you rambling about?
Walters. Geezer who's been running this antiques joint since the dawn of time.
Is this him?

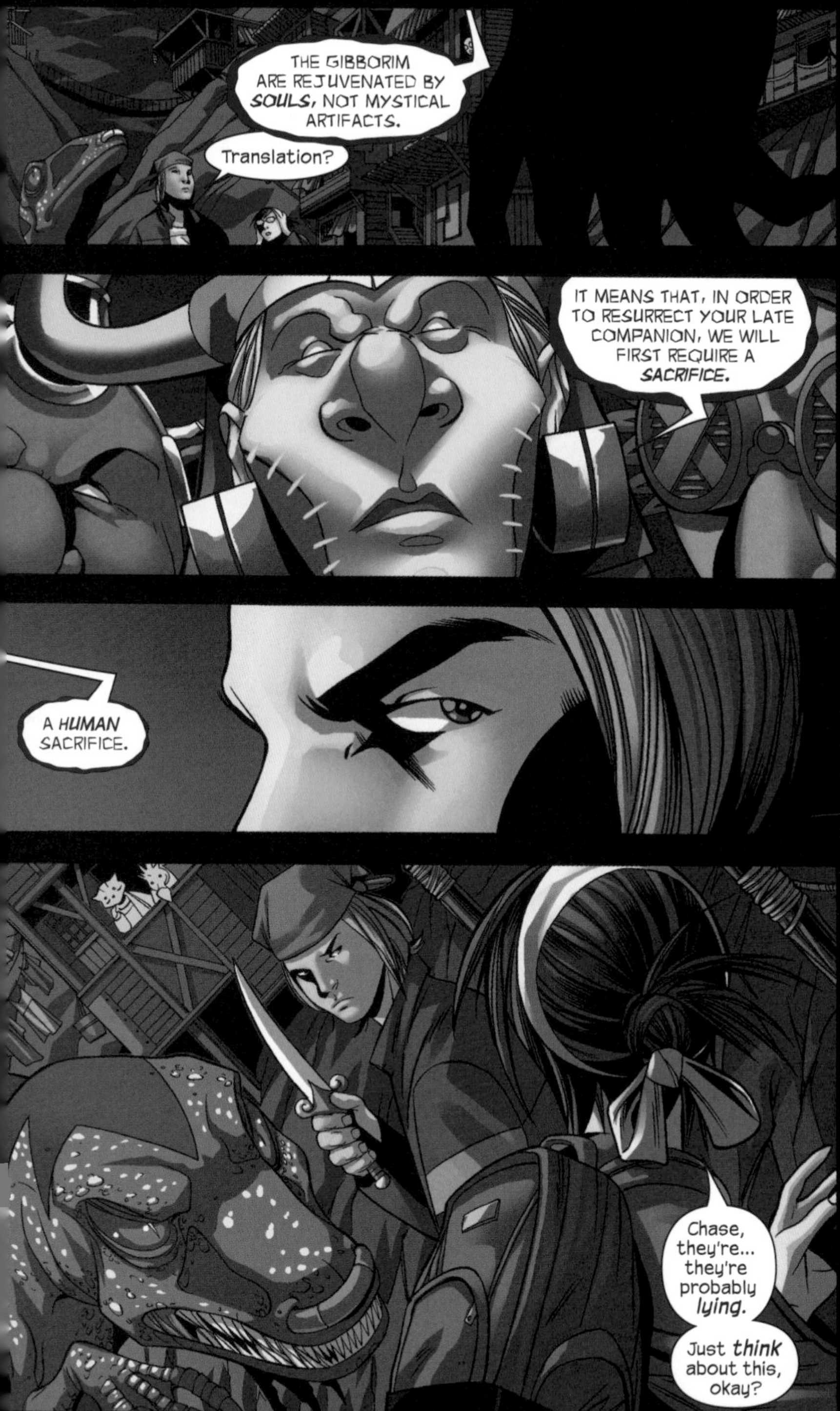
THE GIBBORIM ARE REJUVENATED BY SOULS, NOT MYSTICAL ARTIFACTS.
Translation?
IT MEANS THAT, IN ORDER TO RESURRECT YOUR LATE COMPANION, WE WILL FIRST REQUIRE A SACRIFICE.
A HUMAN SACRIFICE.
Chase, they're... they're probably lying.
Just think about this, okay?

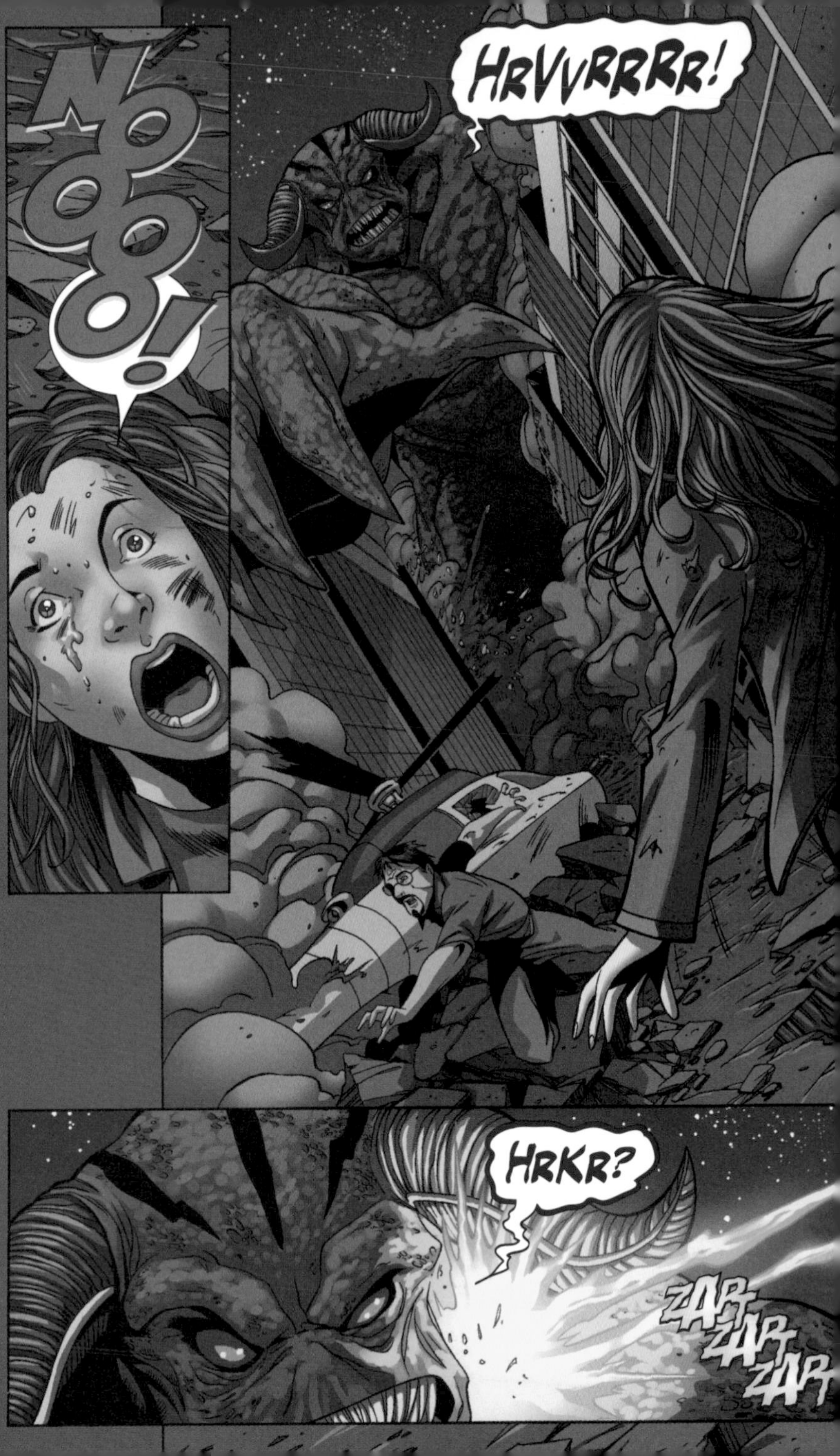
NOOOO!
HRVVRRRRR!
HRKR?
ZART ZART ZART

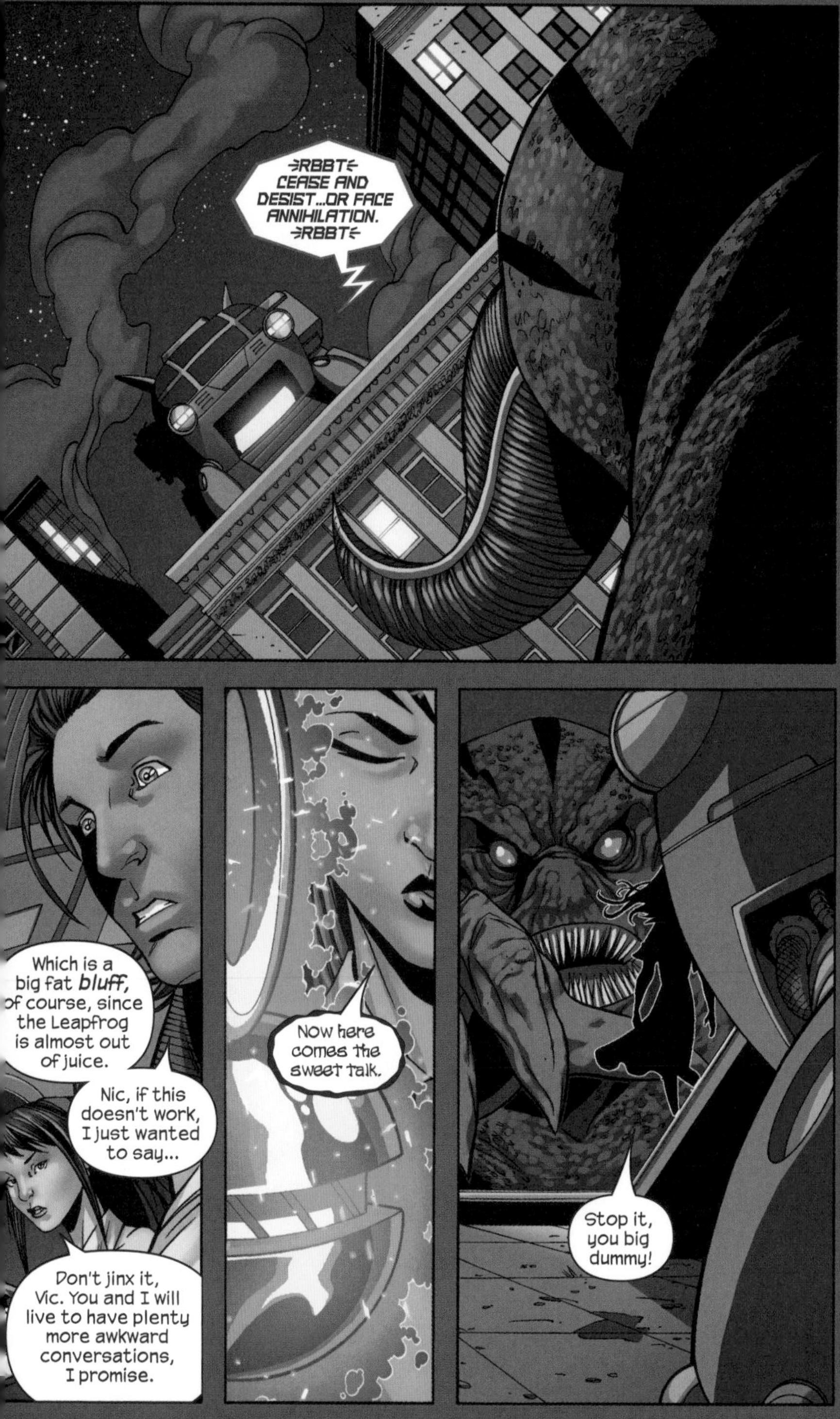

=RBBT= CEASE AND DESIST...OR FACE ANNIHILATION. =RBBT=
Which is a big fat *bluff,* of course, since the Leapfrog is almost out of juice.
Nic, if this doesn't work, I just wanted to say...
Don't jinx it, Vic. You and I will live to have plenty more awkward conversations, I promise.
Now here comes the sweet talk.
Stop it, you big dummy!

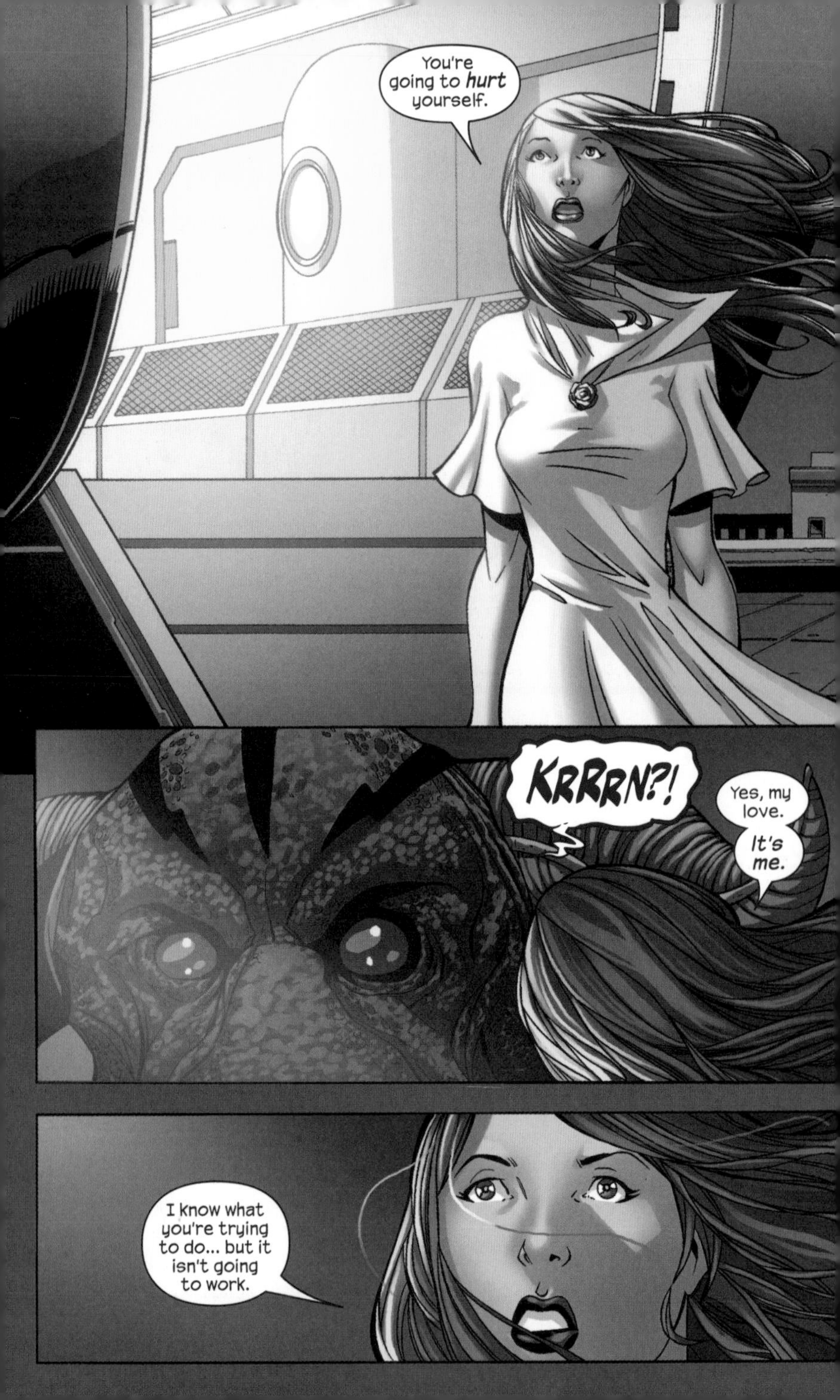
You're going to *hurt* yourself.
KRRRN?!
Yes, my love.
It's me.
I know what you're trying to do... but it isn't going to work.

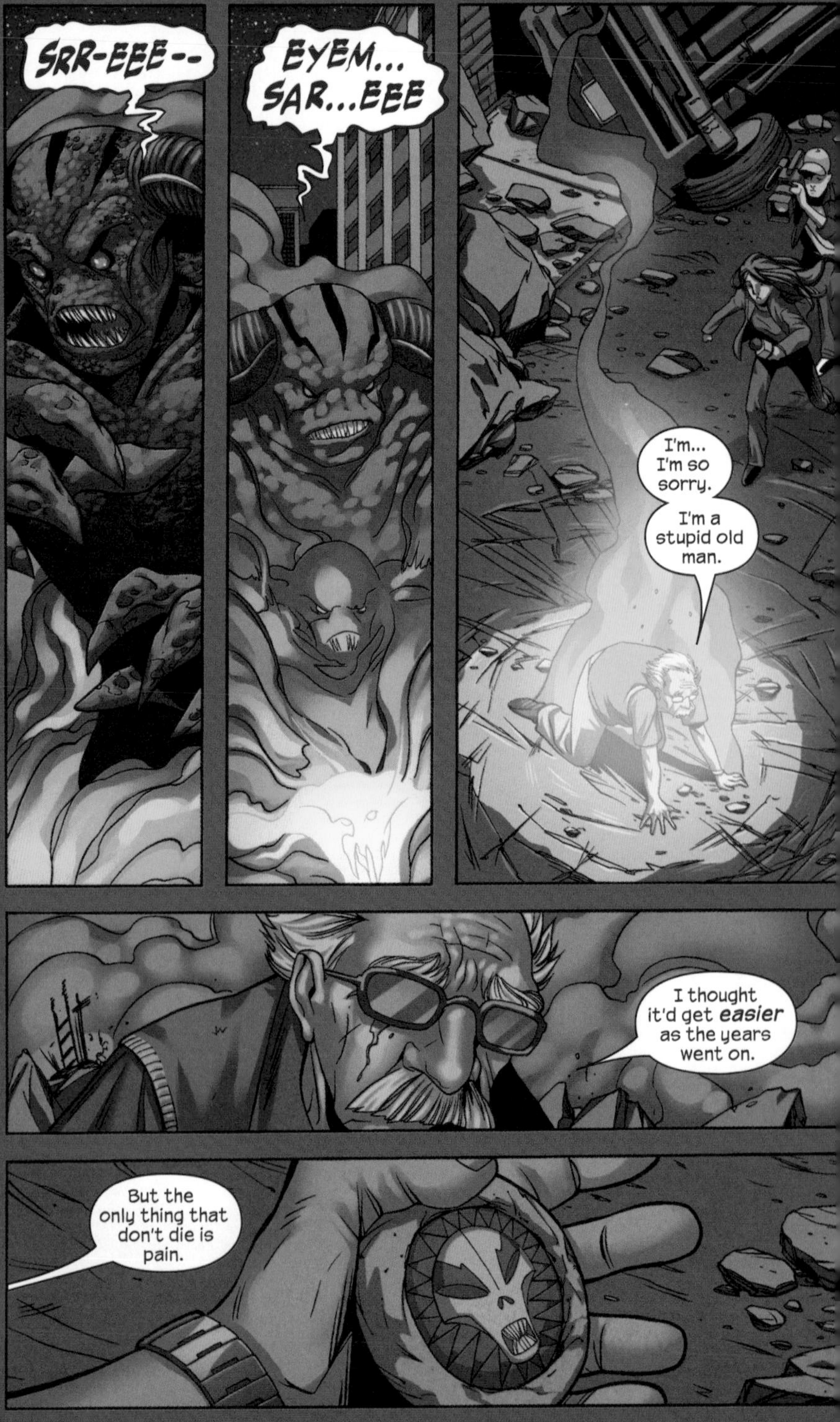
SRR-EEE--
EYEM... SAR...EEE
I'm... I'm so sorry.
I'm a stupid old man.
I thought it'd get *easier* as the years went on.
But the only thing that don't die is pain.

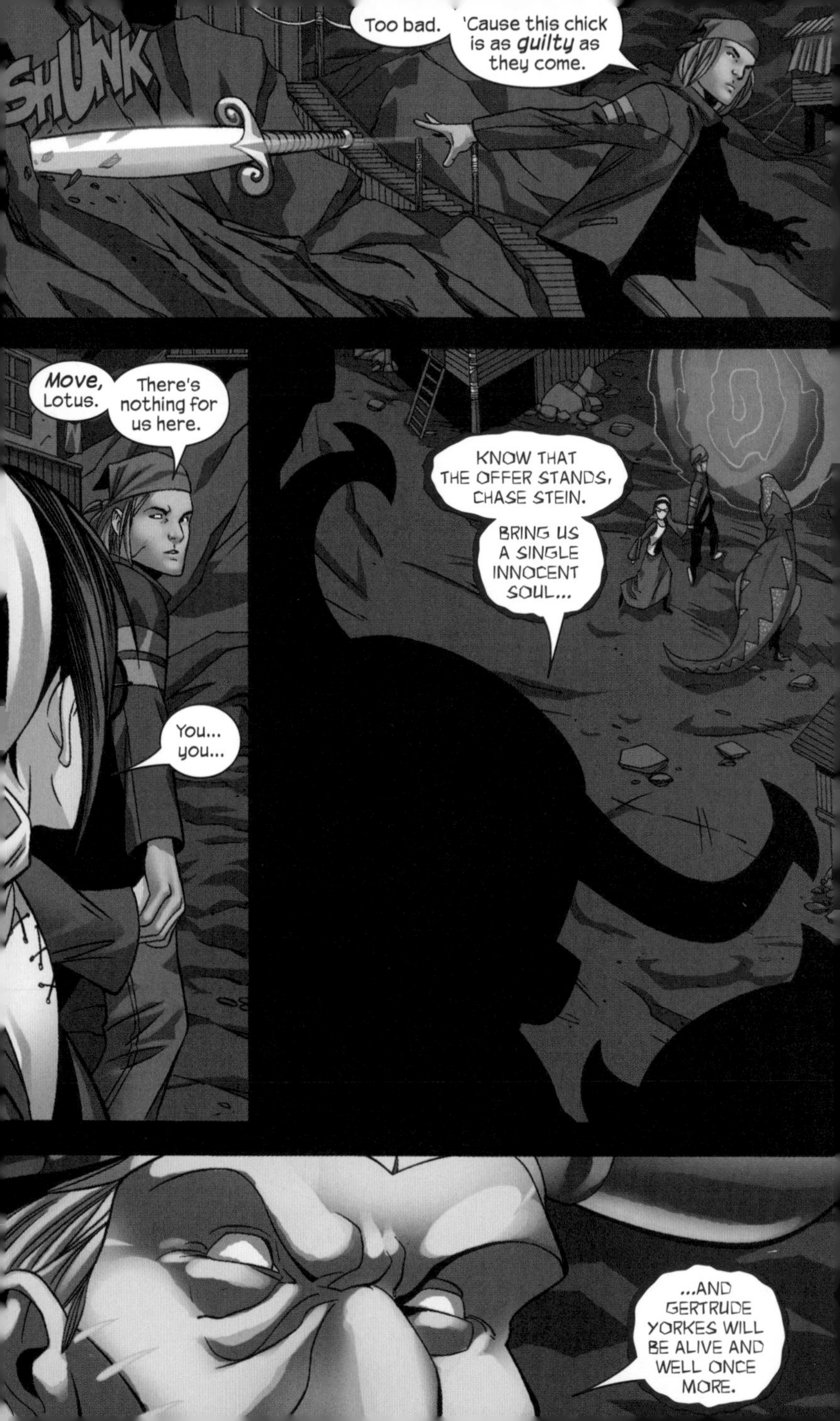
SHUNK
Too bad.
'Cause this chick is as *guilty* as they come.
Move, Lotus.
There's nothing for us here.
You... you...
KNOW THAT THE OFFER STANDS, CHASE STEIN.
BRING US A SINGLE INNOCENT SOUL...
...AND GERTRUDE YORKES WILL BE ALIVE AND WELL ONCE MORE.

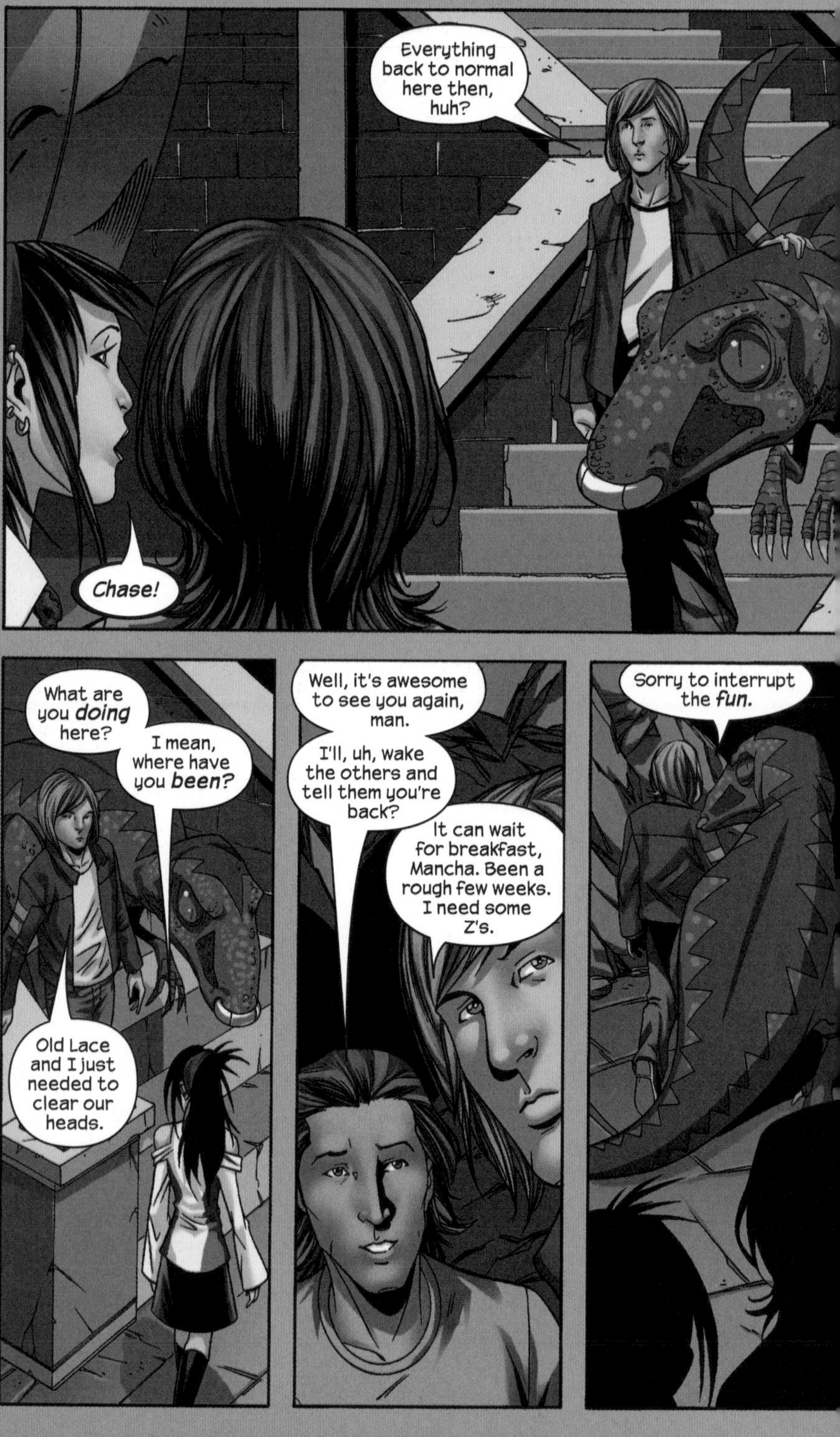
Everything back to normal here then, huh?
Chase!
What are you *doing* here?
I mean, where have you *been*?
Old Lace and I just needed to clear our heads.
Well, it's awesome to see you again, man.
I'll, uh, wake the others and tell them you're back?
It can wait for breakfast, Mancha. Been a rough few weeks. I need some Z's.
Sorry to interrupt the *fun.*

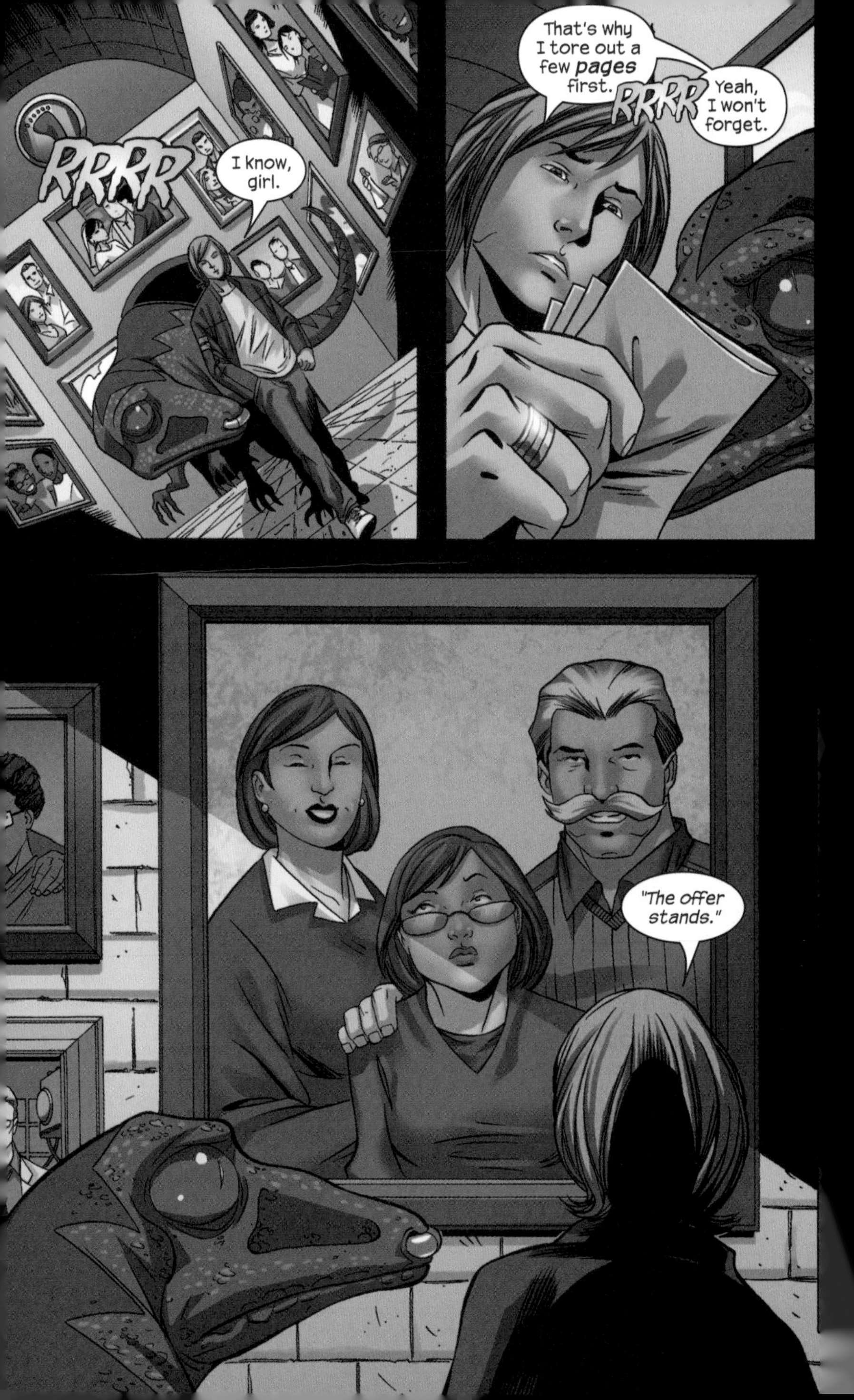
RRRR
I know, girl.
That's why I tore out a few *pages* first.
RRRR
Yeah, I won't forget.
"The offer stands."

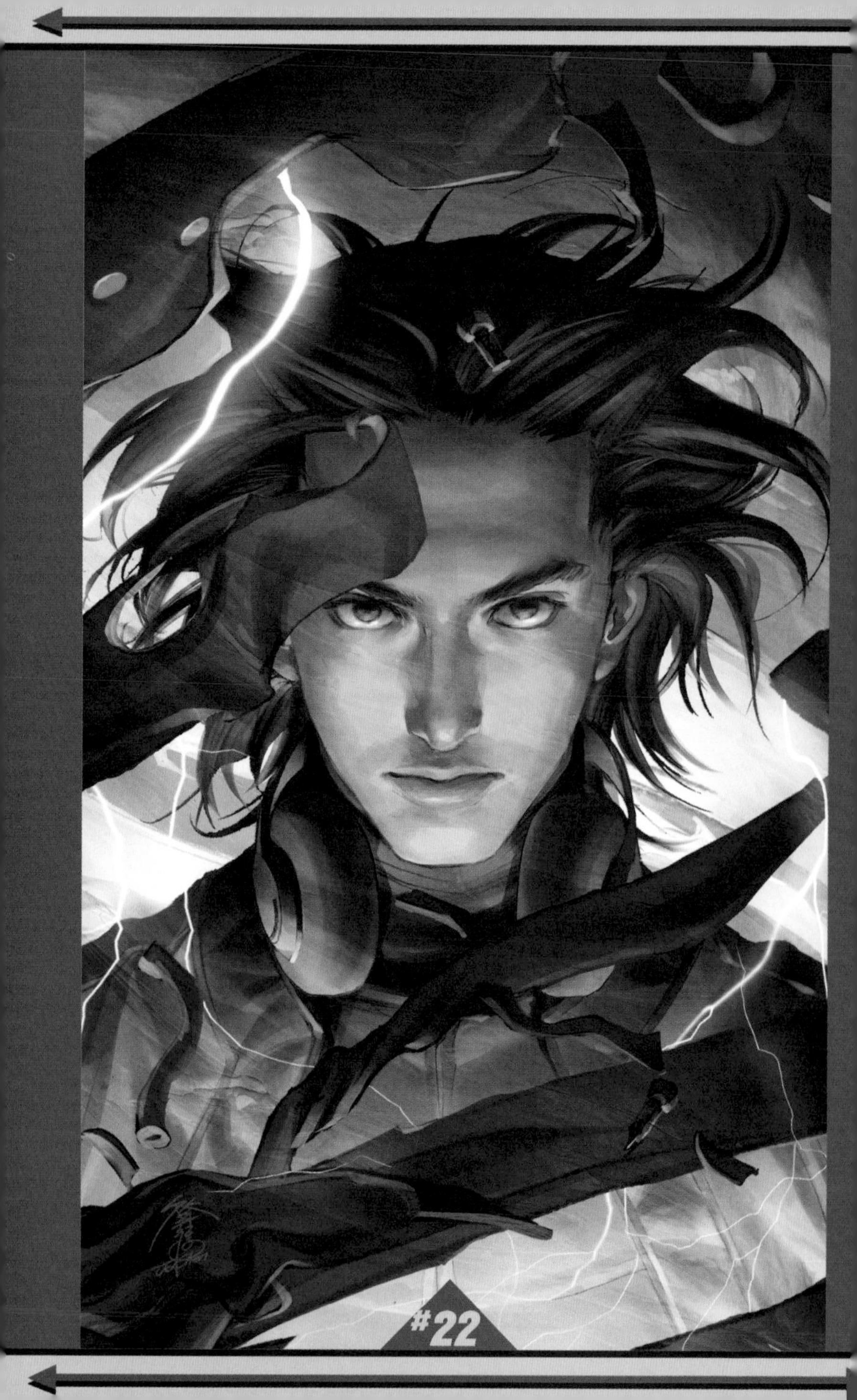
#22

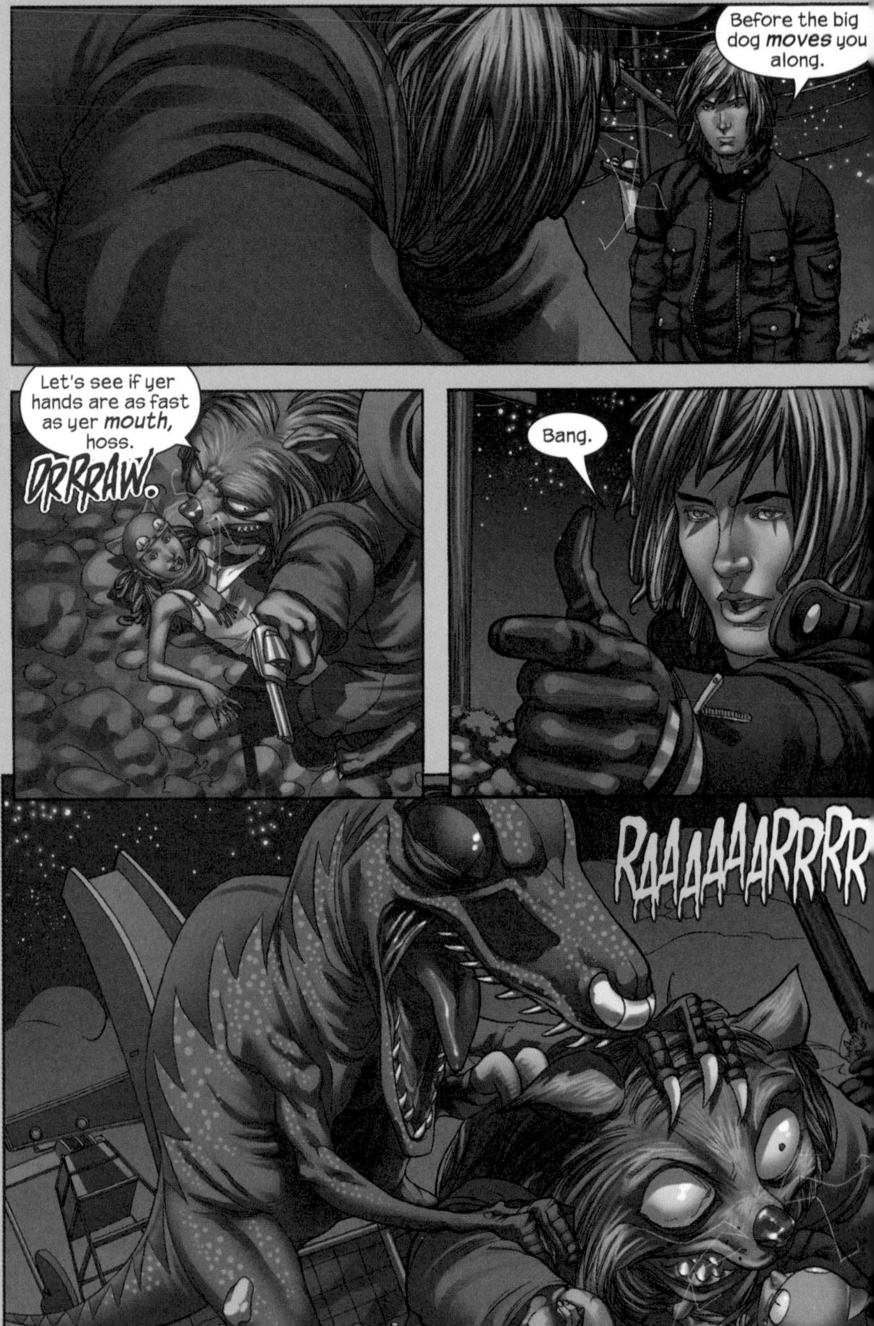

Before the big dog *moves* you along.
Let's see if yer hands are as fast as yer *mouth,* hoss.
DRRRAW.
Bang.
RAAAAARRRR

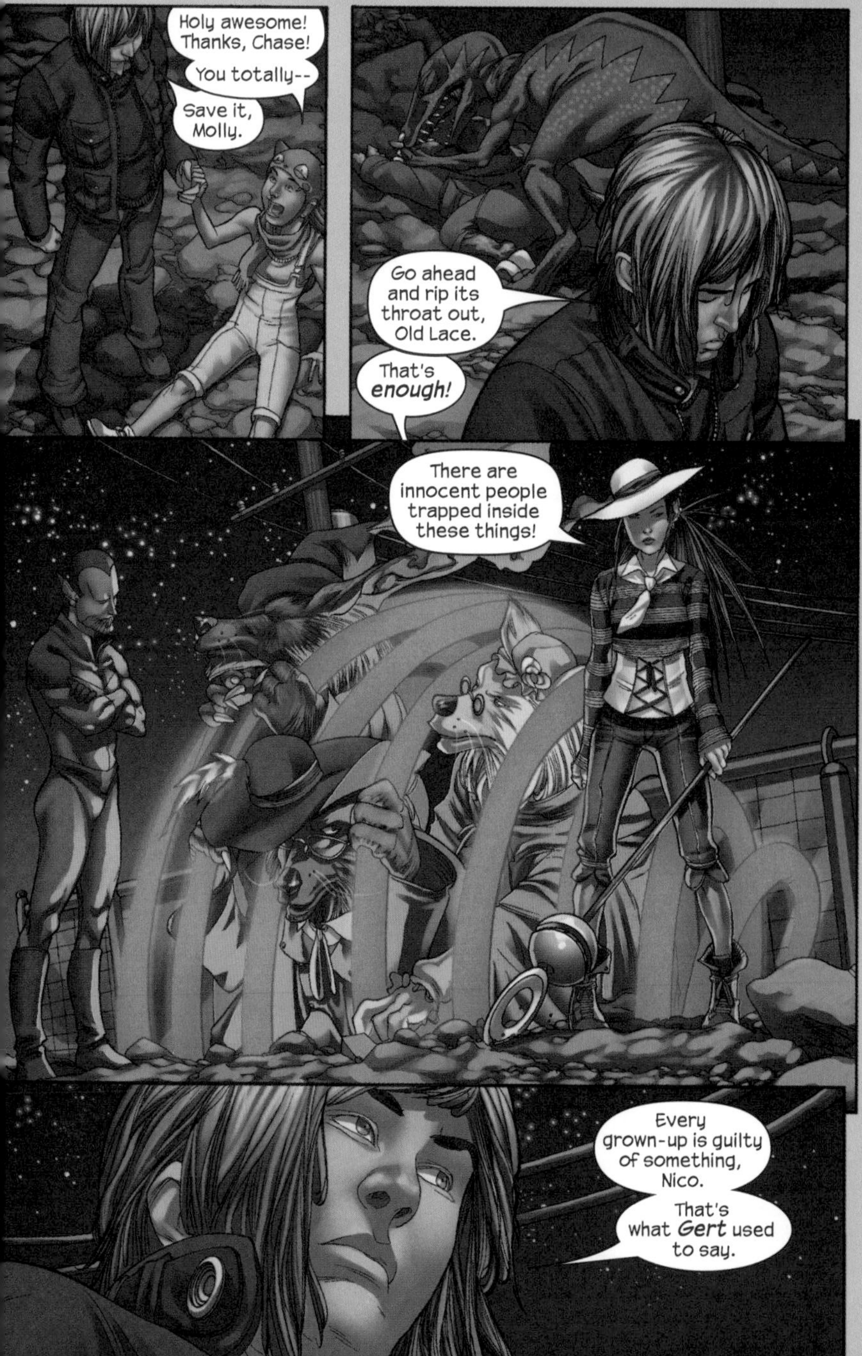
Holy awesome! Thanks, Chase!
You totally--
Save it, Molly.
Go ahead and rip its throat out, Old Lace.
That's *enough!*
There are innocent people trapped inside these things!
Every grown-up is guilty of something, Nico.
That's what *Gert* used to say.

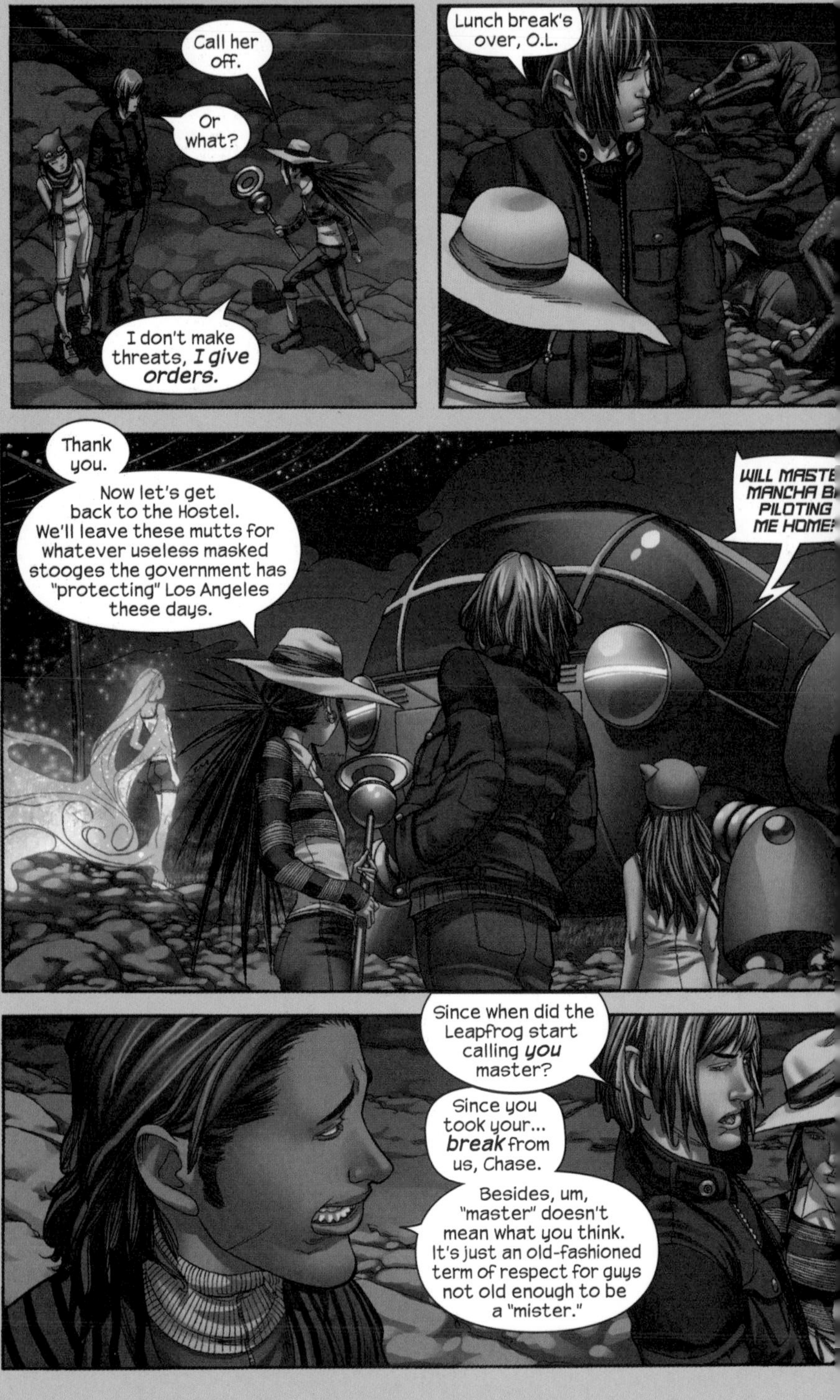

Call her off.
Or what?
I don't make threats, *I give orders.*
Lunch break's over, O.L.
Thank you.
Now let's get back to the Hostel. We'll leave these mutts for whatever useless masked stooges the government has "protecting" Los Angeles these days.
WILL MASTE MANCHA B PILOTING ME HOME
Since when did the Leapfrog start calling *you* master?
Since you took your... *break* from us, Chase.
Besides, um, "master" doesn't mean what you think. It's just an old-fashioned term of respect for guys not old enough to be a "mister."

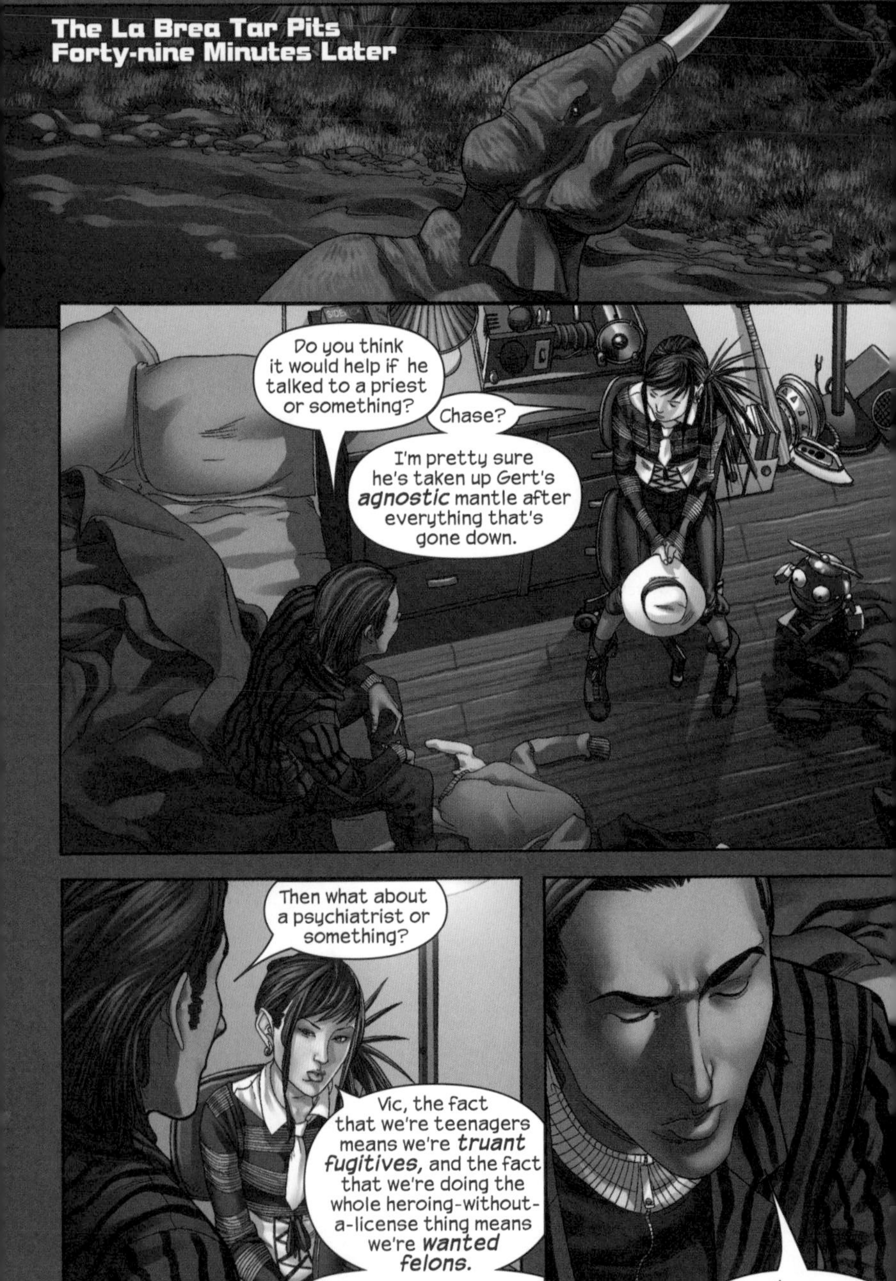

The La Brea Tar Pits
Forty-nine Minutes Later
Do you think it would help if he talked to a priest or something?
Chase?
I'm pretty sure he's taken up Gert's agnostic mantle after everything that's gone down.
Then what about a psychiatrist or something?
Vic, the fact that we're teenagers means we're truant fugitives, and the fact that we're doing the whole heroing-without-a-license thing means we're wanted felons.
Chase can't go to a shrink without getting the whole team in trouble.
Then maybe he doesn't belong on the team.

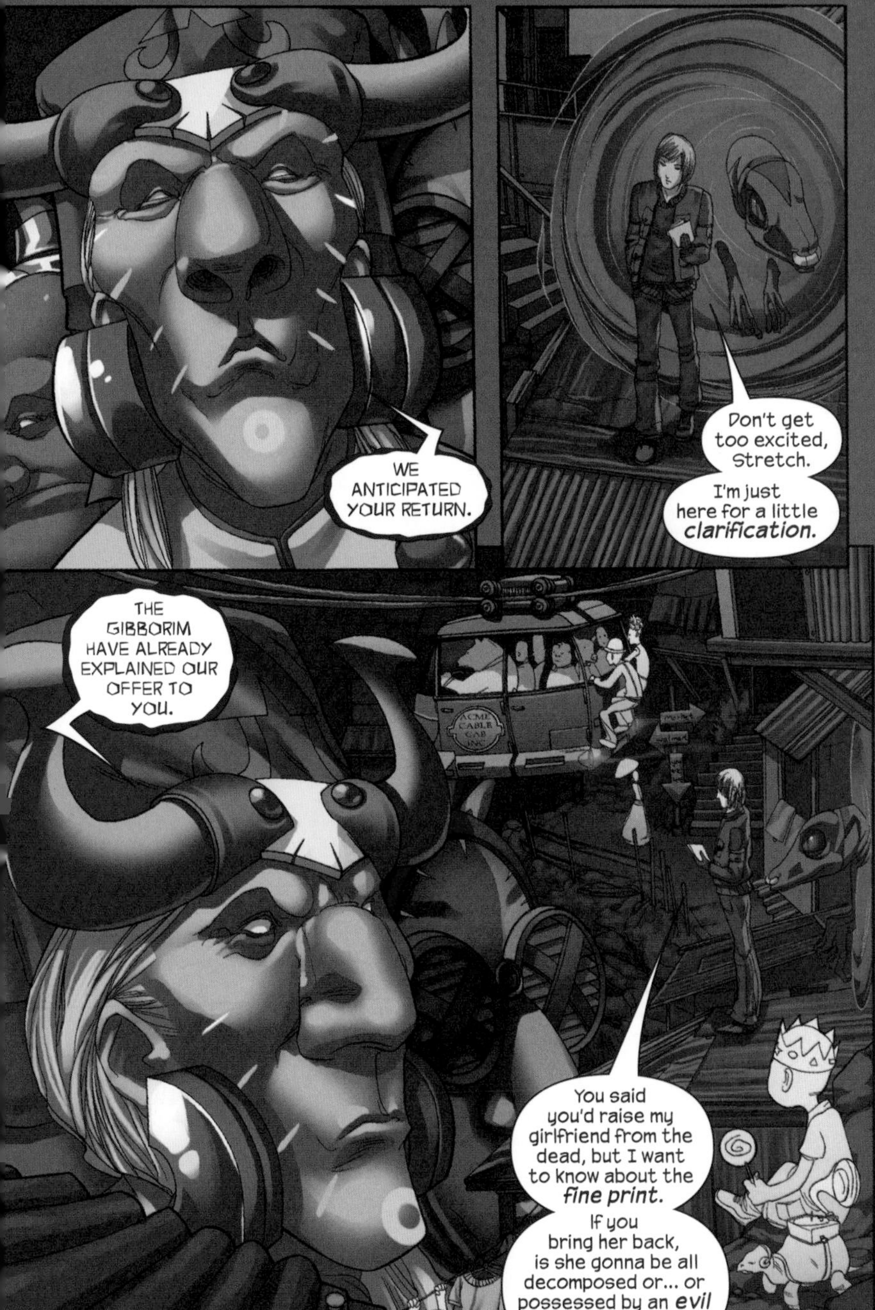
WE ANTICIPATED YOUR RETURN.
Don't get too excited, Stretch.
I'm just here for a little *clarification*.
THE GIBBORIM HAVE ALREADY EXPLAINED OUR OFFER TO YOU.
ACME CABLE CAB INC
You said you'd raise my girlfriend from the dead, but I want to know about the *fine print*.
If you bring her back, is she gonna be all decomposed or... or possessed by an *evil monkey demon* or something?

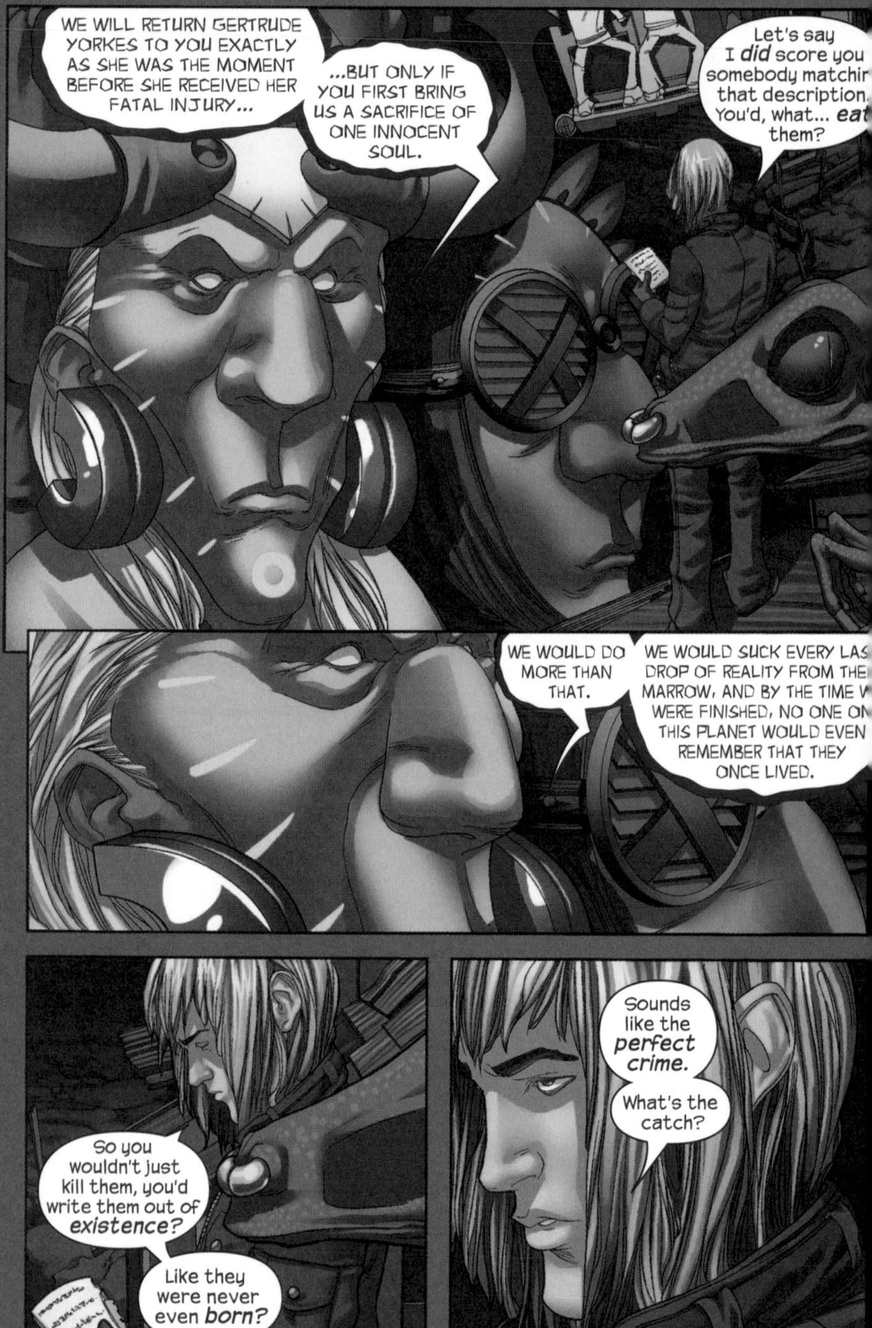
WE WILL RETURN GERTRUDE YORKES TO YOU EXACTLY AS SHE WAS THE MOMENT BEFORE SHE RECEIVED HER FATAL INJURY...
...BUT ONLY IF YOU FIRST BRING US A SACRIFICE OF ONE INNOCENT SOUL.
Let's say I *did* score you somebody matchir that description. You'd, what... *eat* them?
WE WOULD DO MORE THAN THAT.
WE WOULD SUCK EVERY LAS DROP OF REALITY FROM THE MARROW, AND BY THE TIME W WERE FINISHED, NO ONE ON THIS PLANET WOULD EVEN REMEMBER THAT THEY ONCE LIVED.
So you wouldn't just kill them, you'd write them out of *existence*?
Like they were never even *born*?
Sounds like the *perfect crime.*
What's the catch?

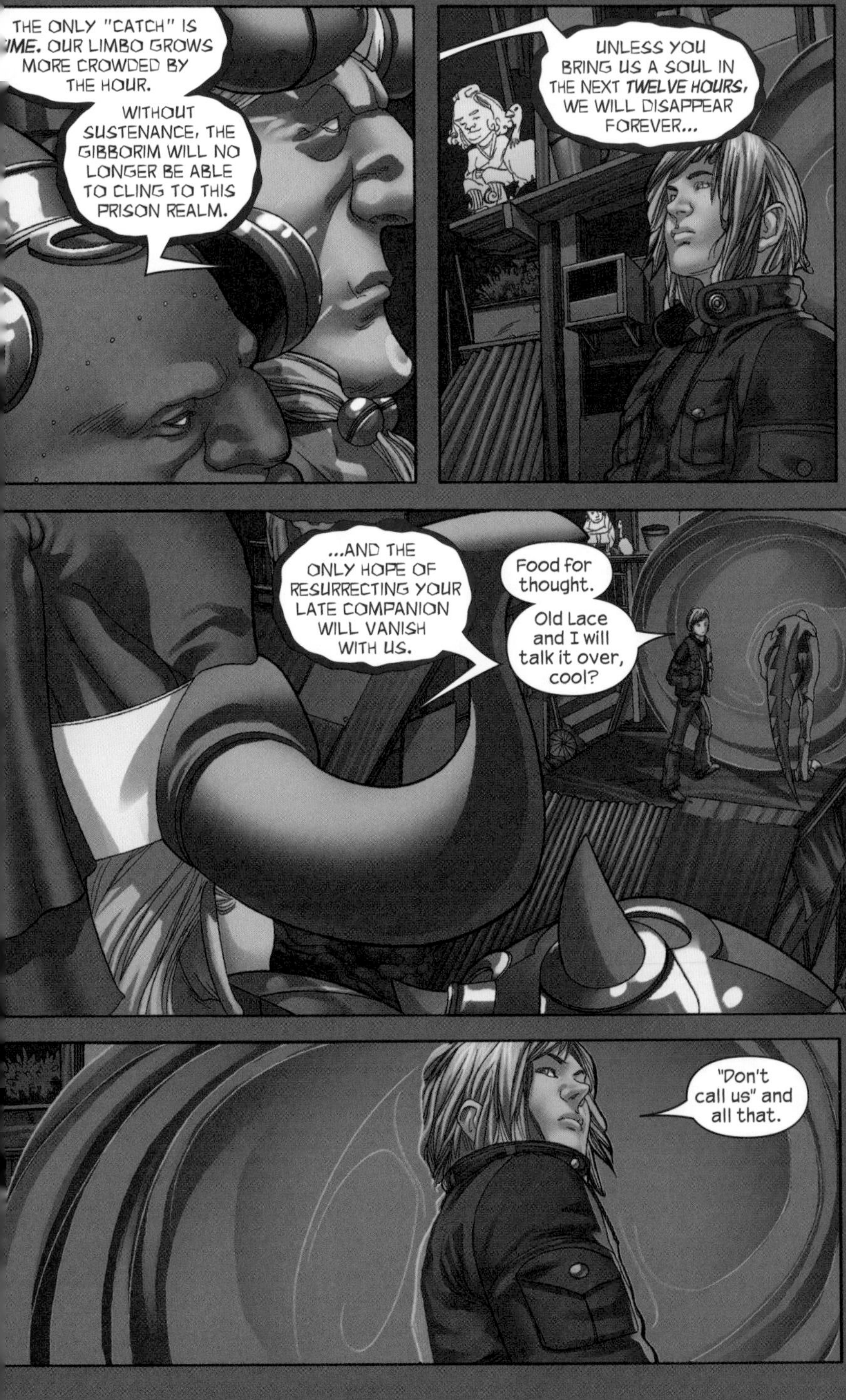
THE ONLY "CATCH" IS *IME.* OUR LIMBO GROWS MORE CROWDED BY THE HOUR.
WITHOUT SUSTENANCE, THE GIBBORIM WILL NO LONGER BE ABLE TO CLING TO THIS PRISON REALM.
UNLESS YOU BRING US A SOUL IN THE NEXT *TWELVE HOURS,* WE WILL DISAPPEAR FOREVER...
...AND THE ONLY HOPE OF RESURRECTING YOUR LATE COMPANION WILL VANISH WITH US.
Food for thought.
Old Lace and I will talk it over, cool?
"Don't call us" and all that.

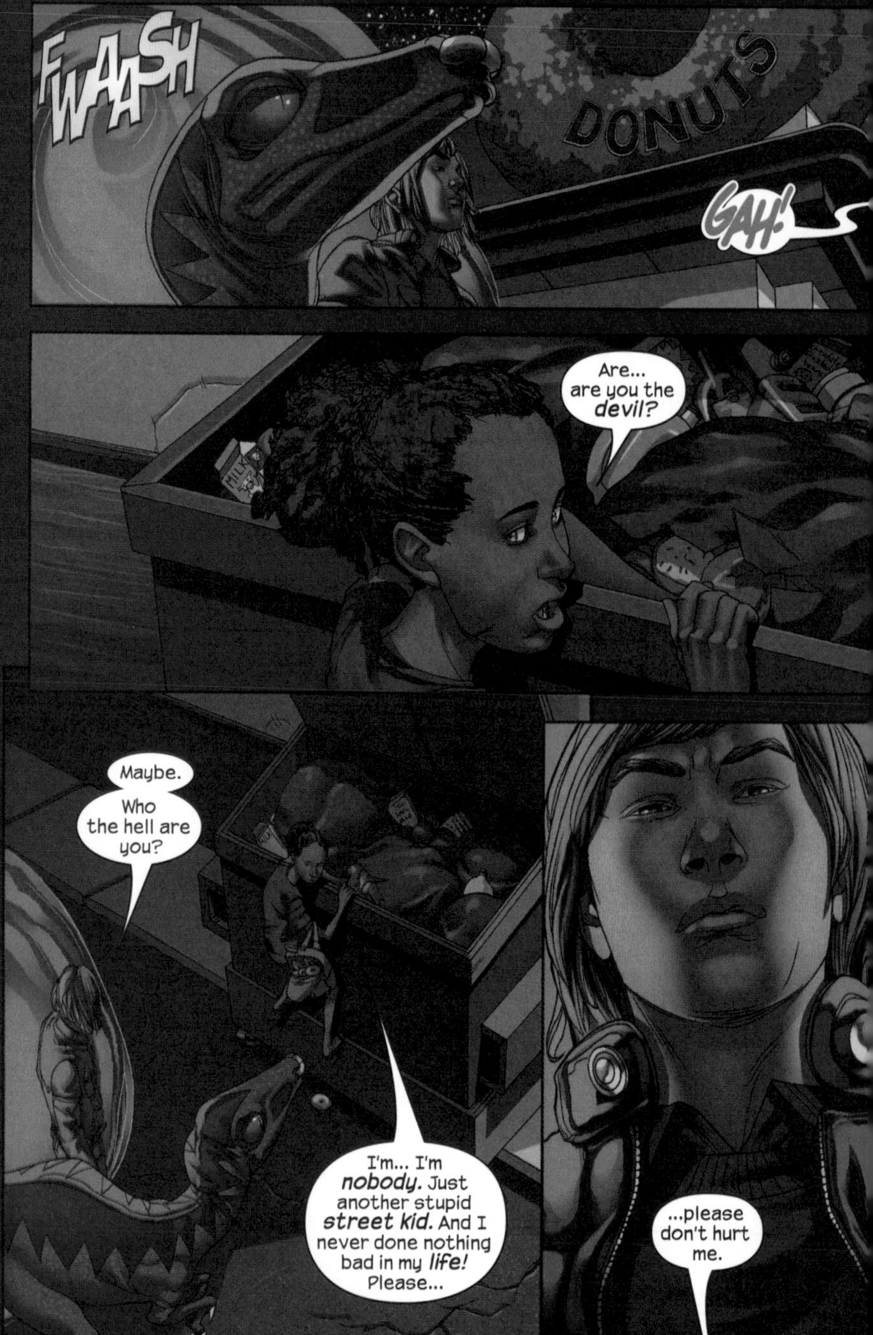
FWAASH
DONUTS
GAH!
Are... are you the devil?
MILK
Maybe.
Who the hell are you?
I'm... I'm nobody. Just another stupid street kid. And I never done nothing bad in my life! Please...
...please don't hurt me.

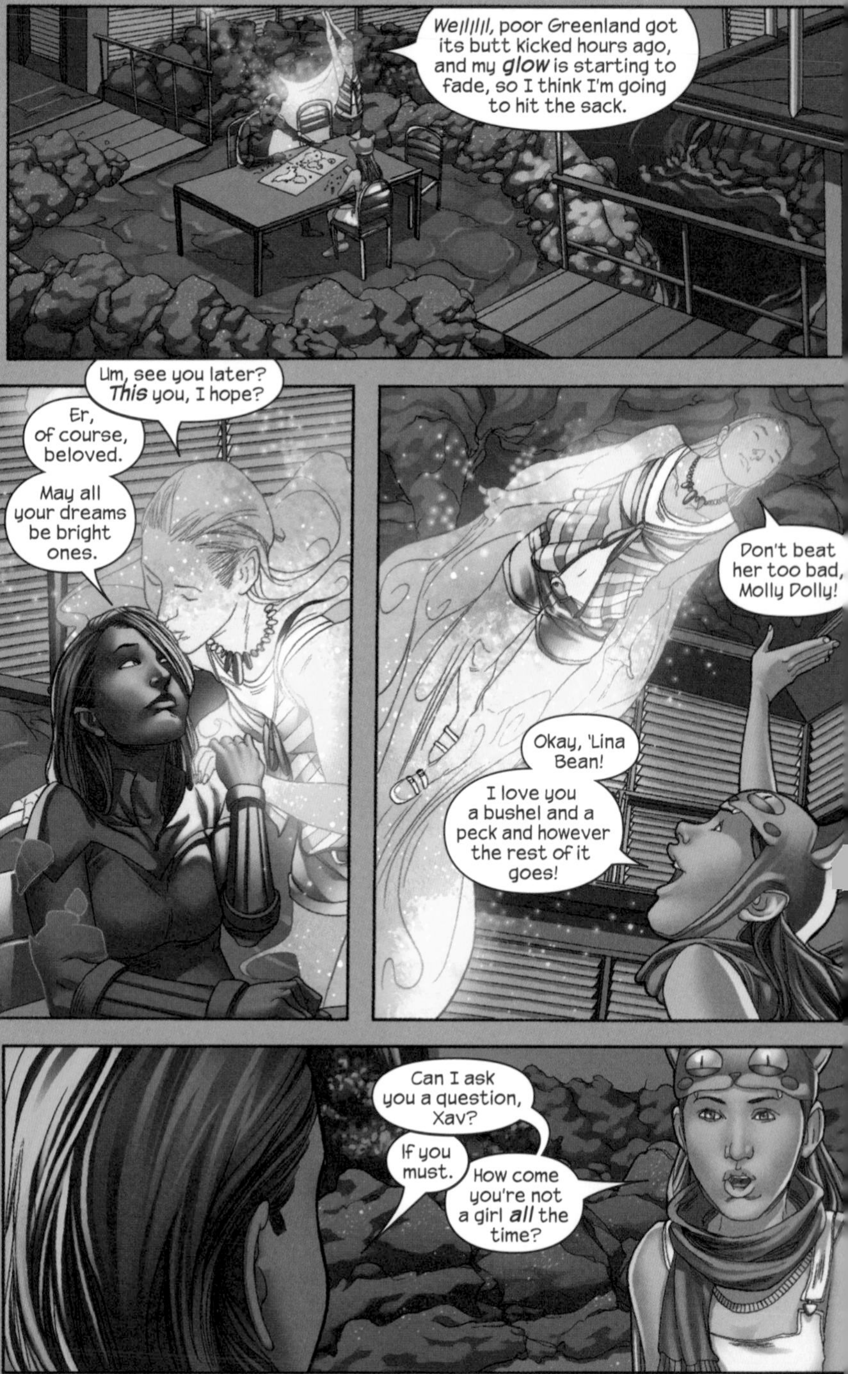
Wellllll, poor Greenland got its butt kicked hours ago, and my glow is starting to fade, so I think I'm going to hit the sack.
Um, see you later? This you, I hope?
Er, of course, beloved.
May all your dreams be bright ones.
Don't beat her too bad, Molly Dolly!
Okay, 'Lina Bean!
I love you a bushel and a peck and however the rest of it goes!
Can I ask you a question, Xav?
If you must.
How come you're not a girl all the time?

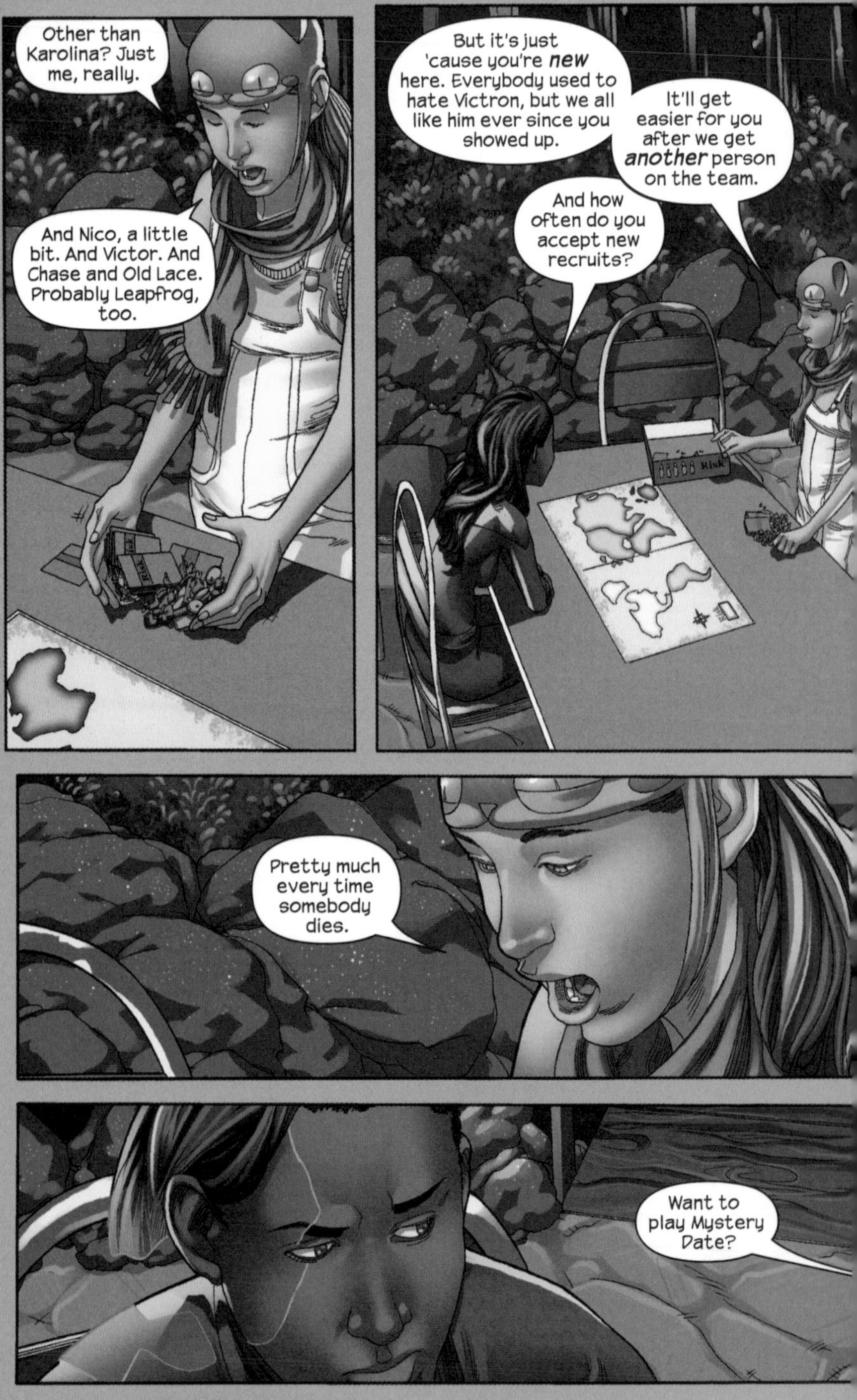
Other than Karolina? Just me, really.
And Nico, a little bit. And Victor. And Chase and Old Lace. Probably Leapfrog, too.
But it's just 'cause you're *new* here. Everybody used to hate Victron, but we all like him ever since you showed up.
It'll get easier for you after we get ***another*** person on the team.
And how often do you accept new recruits?
Risk
Pretty much every time somebody dies.
Want to play Mystery Date?

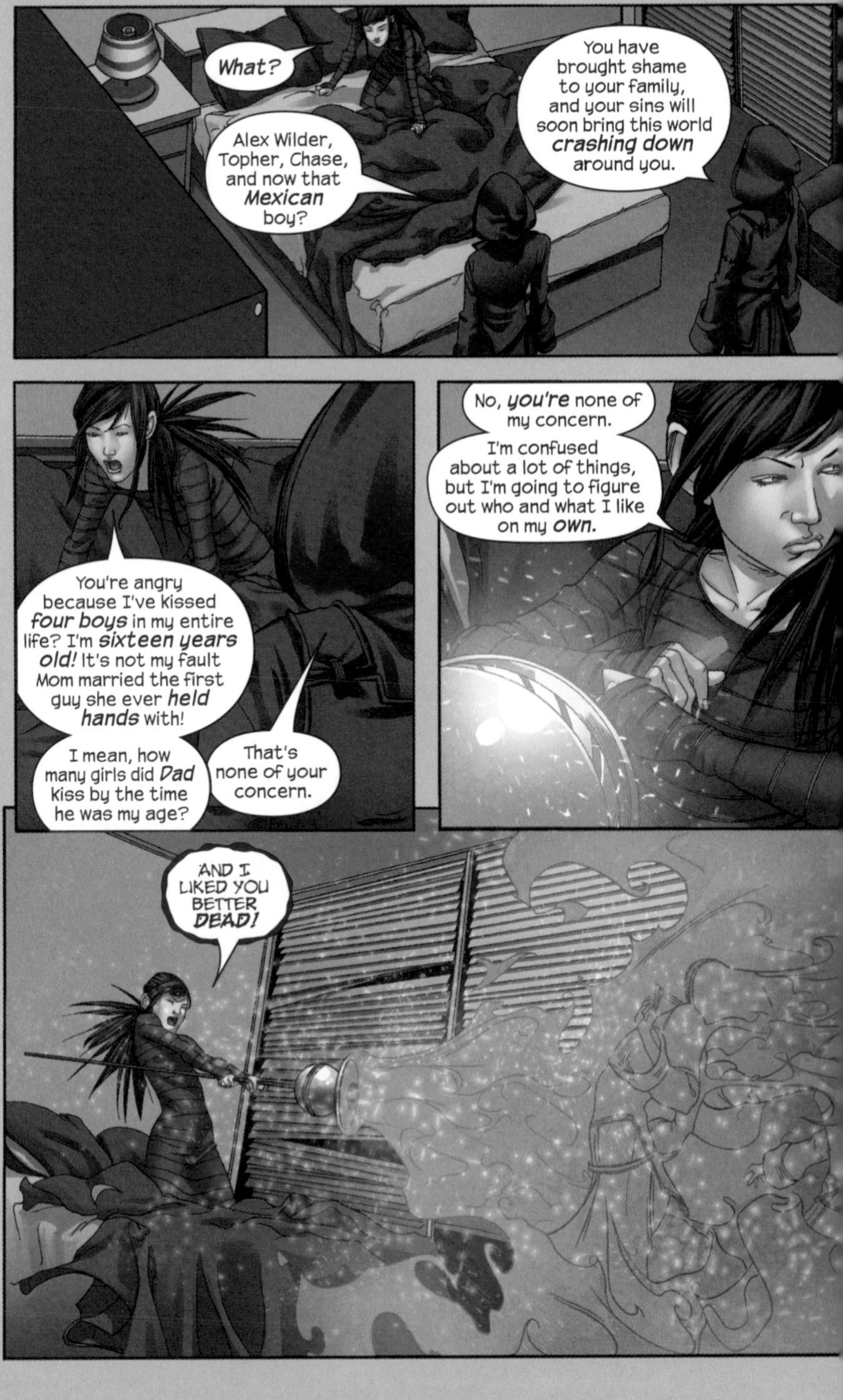
What?
You have brought shame to your family, and your sins will soon bring this world crashing down around you.
Alex Wilder, Topher, Chase, and now that Mexican boy?
You're angry because I've kissed four boys in my entire life? I'm sixteen years old! It's not my fault Mom married the first guy she ever held hands with!
I mean, how many girls did Dad kiss by the time he was my age?
That's none of your concern.
No, you're none of my concern.
I'm confused about a lot of things, but I'm going to figure out who and what I like on my own.
AND I LIKED YOU BETTER DEAD!

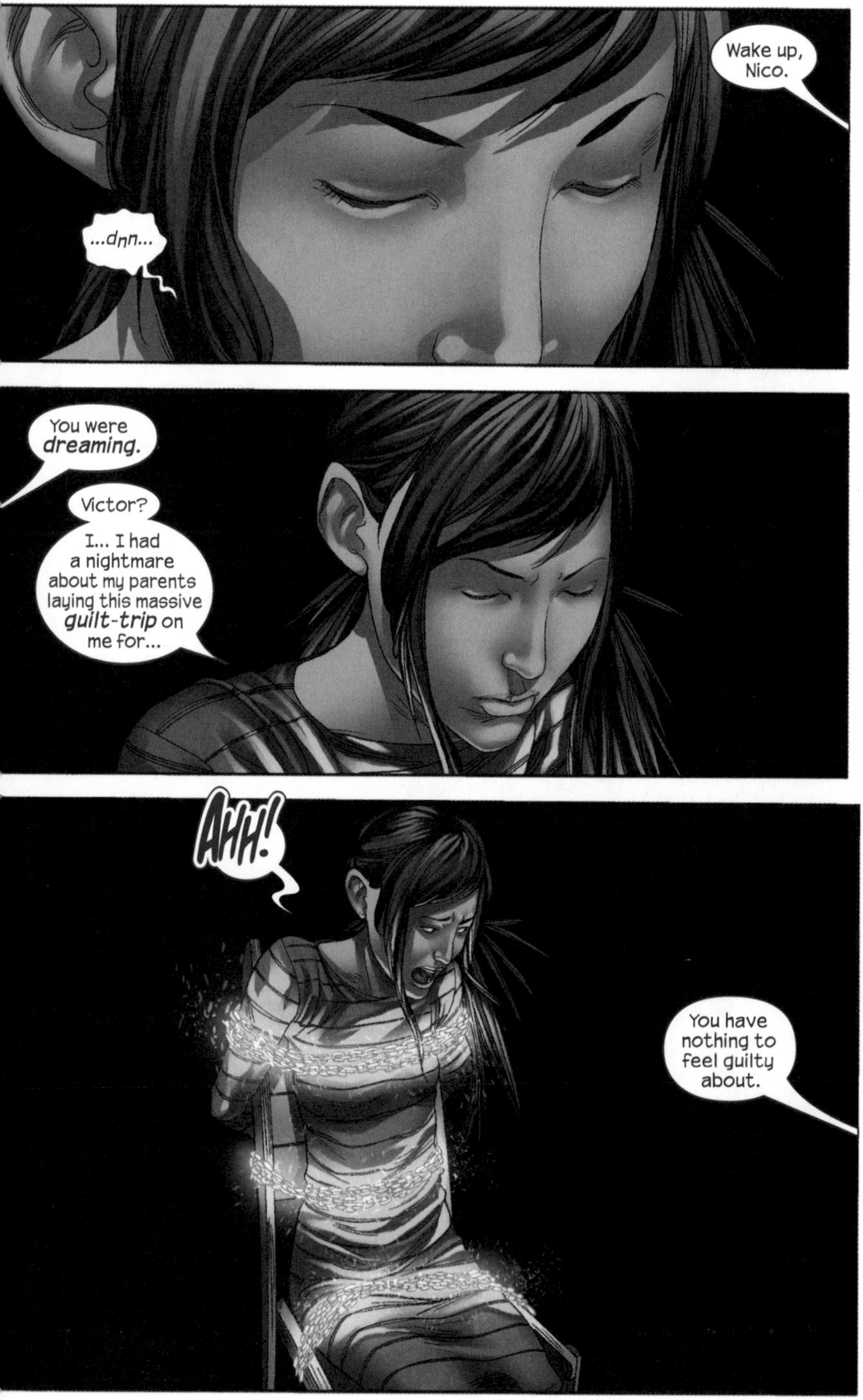
Wake up, Nico.
...dnn...
You were *dreaming.*
Victor?
I... I had a nightmare about my parents laying this massive *guilt-trip* on me for...
AHH!
You have nothing to feel guilty about.

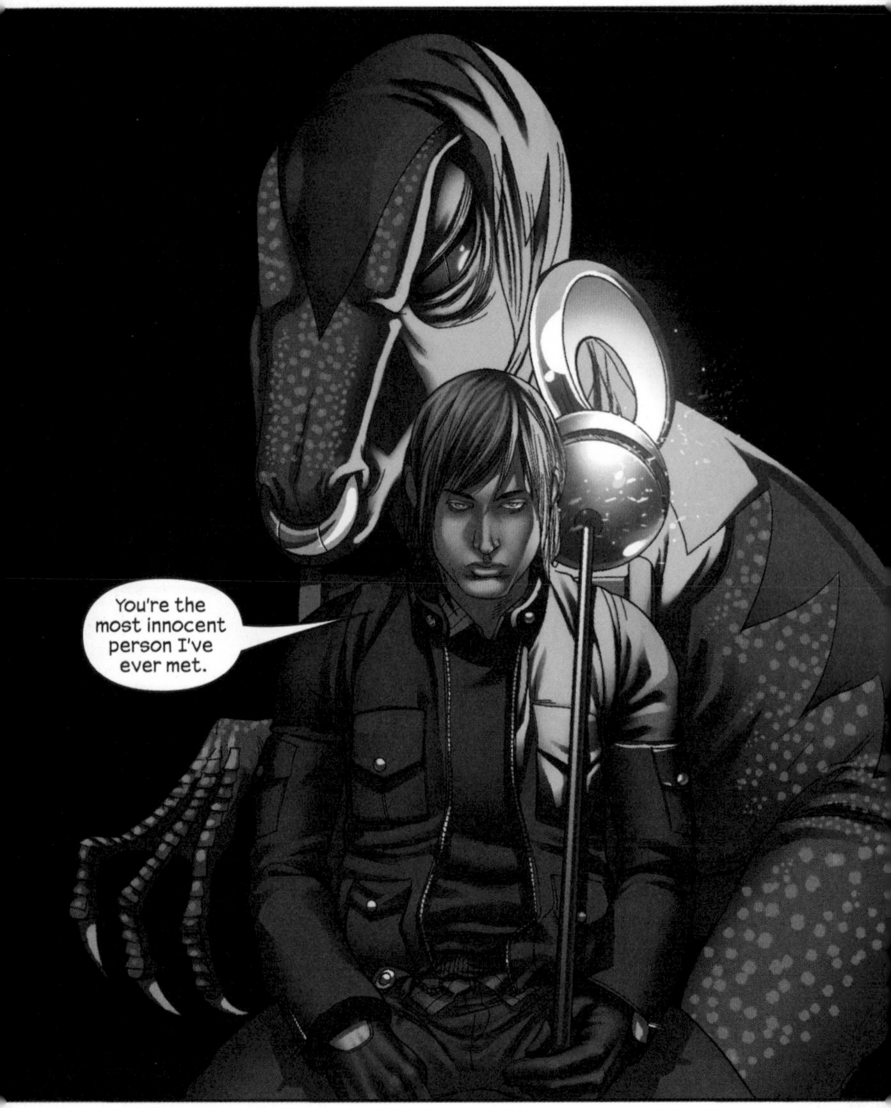
You're the most innocent person I've ever met.

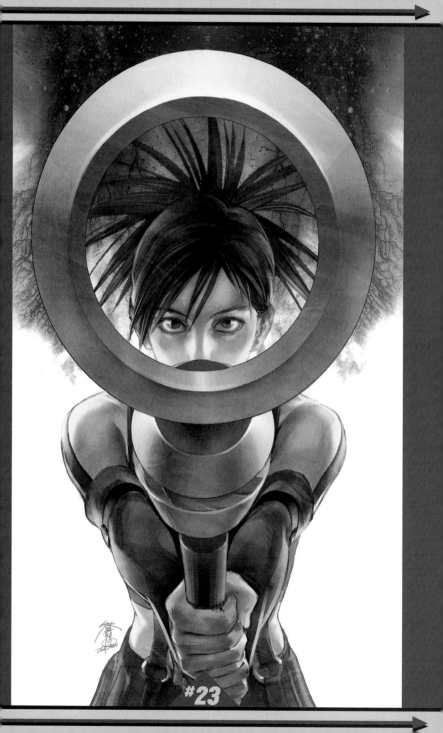

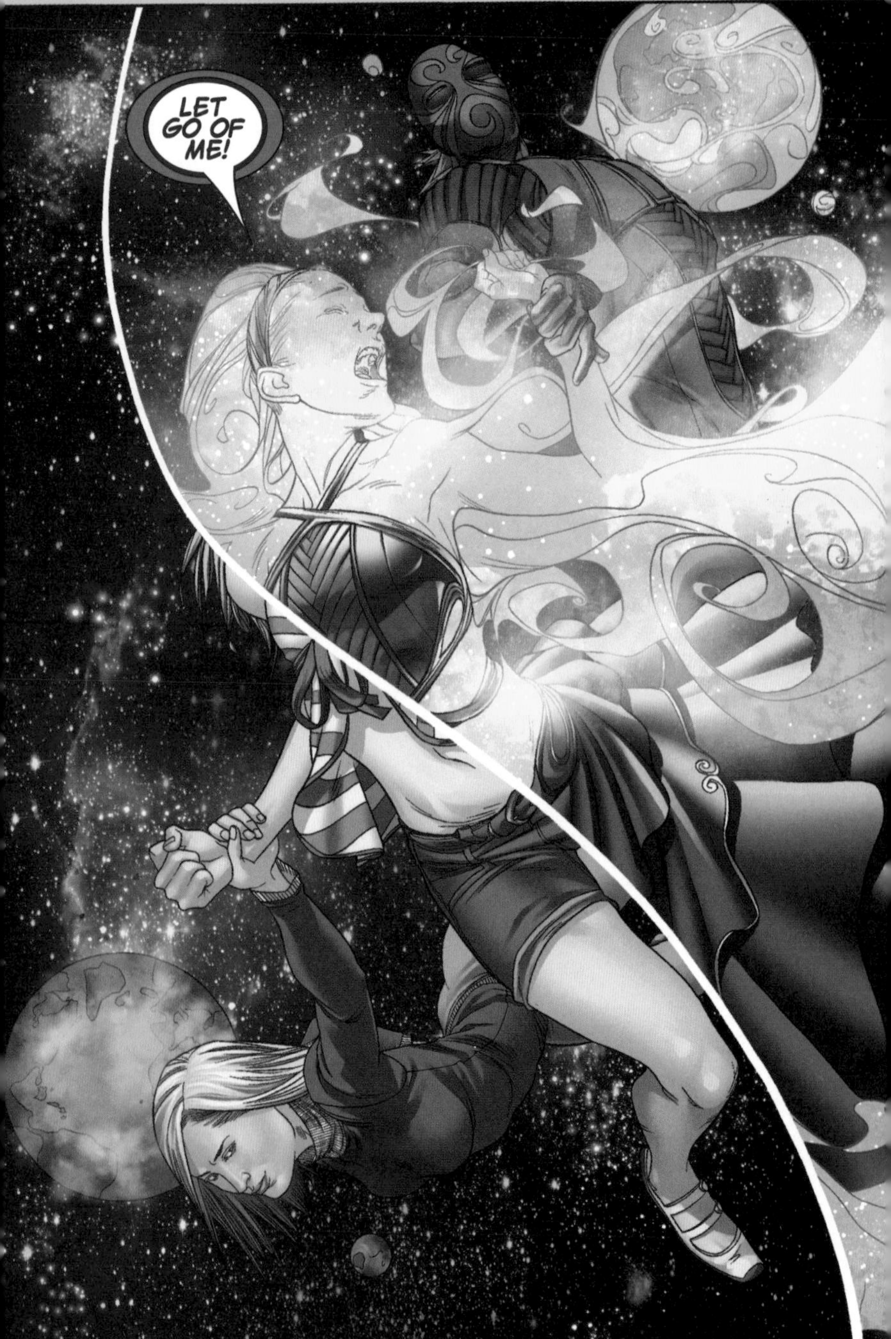
LET GO OF ME!

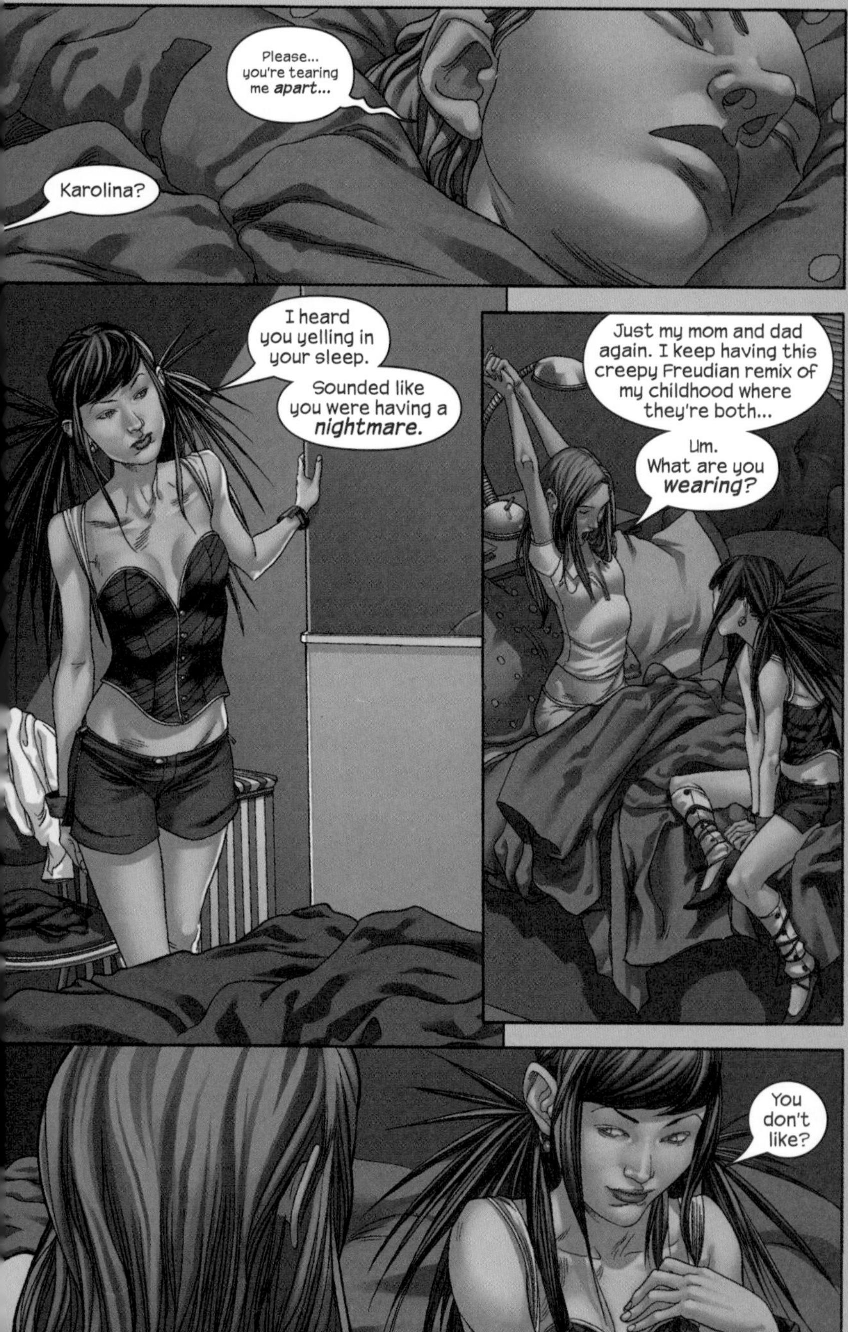
Please... you're tearing me *apart*...
Karolina?
I heard you yelling in your sleep.
Sounded like you were having a *nightmare.*
Just my mom and dad again. I keep having this creepy Freudian remix of my childhood where they're both...
Um. What are you *wearing?*
You don't like?

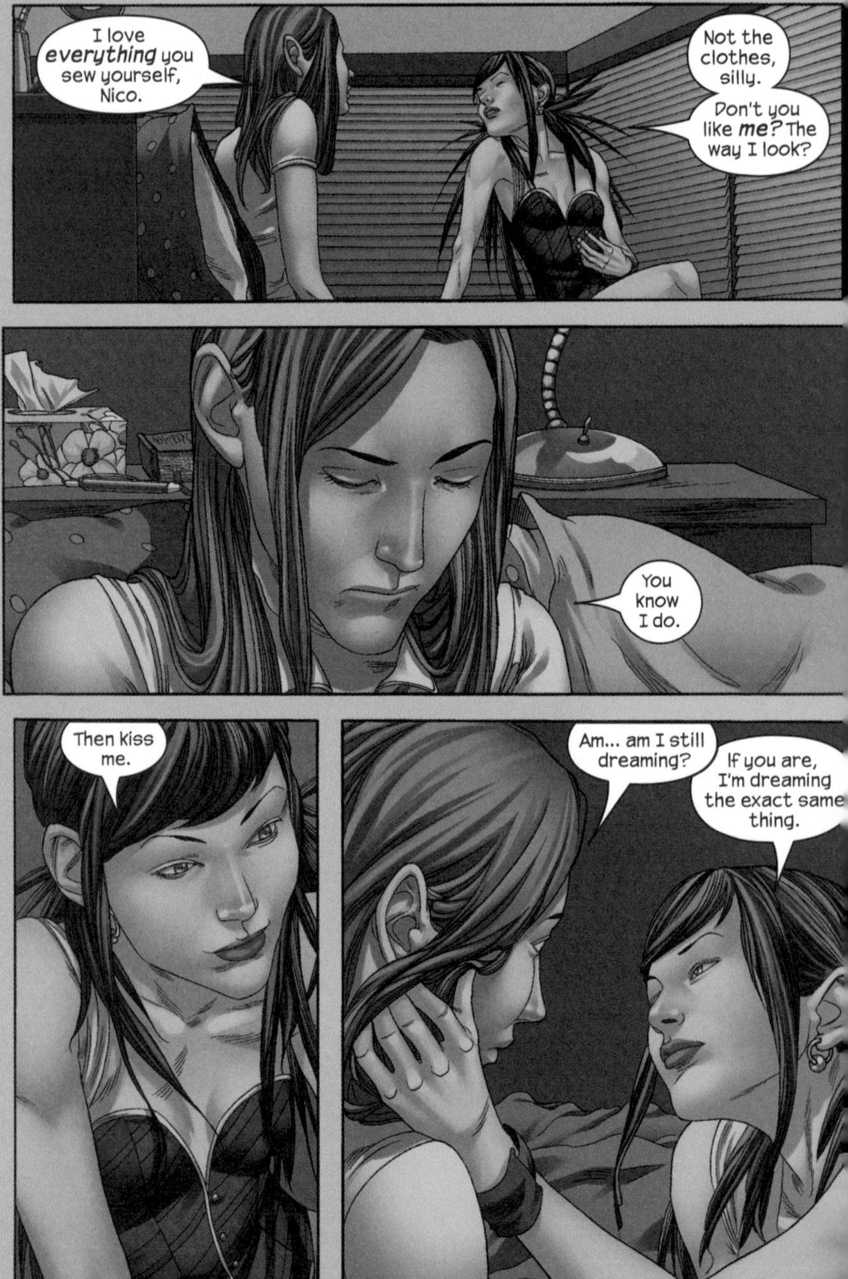
I love *everything* you sew yourself, Nico.
Not the clothes, silly.
Don't you like *me?* The way I look?
You know I do.
Then kiss me.
Am... am I still dreaming?
If you are, I'm dreaming the exact same thing.

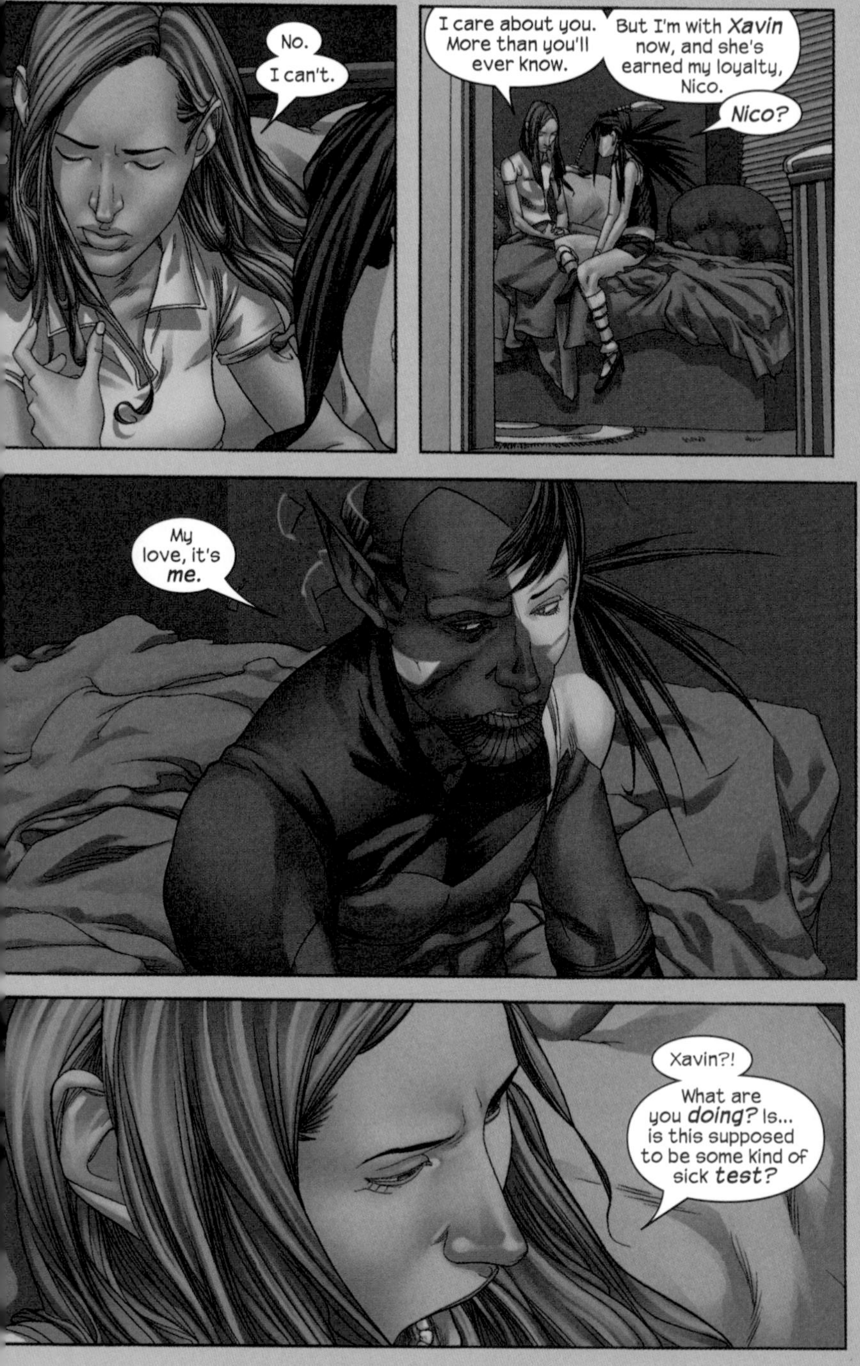
No.
I can't.
I care about you. More than you'll ever know.
But I'm with Xavin now, and she's earned my loyalty, Nico.
Nico?
My love, it's me.
Xavin?!
What are you doing? Is... is this supposed to be some kind of sick test?

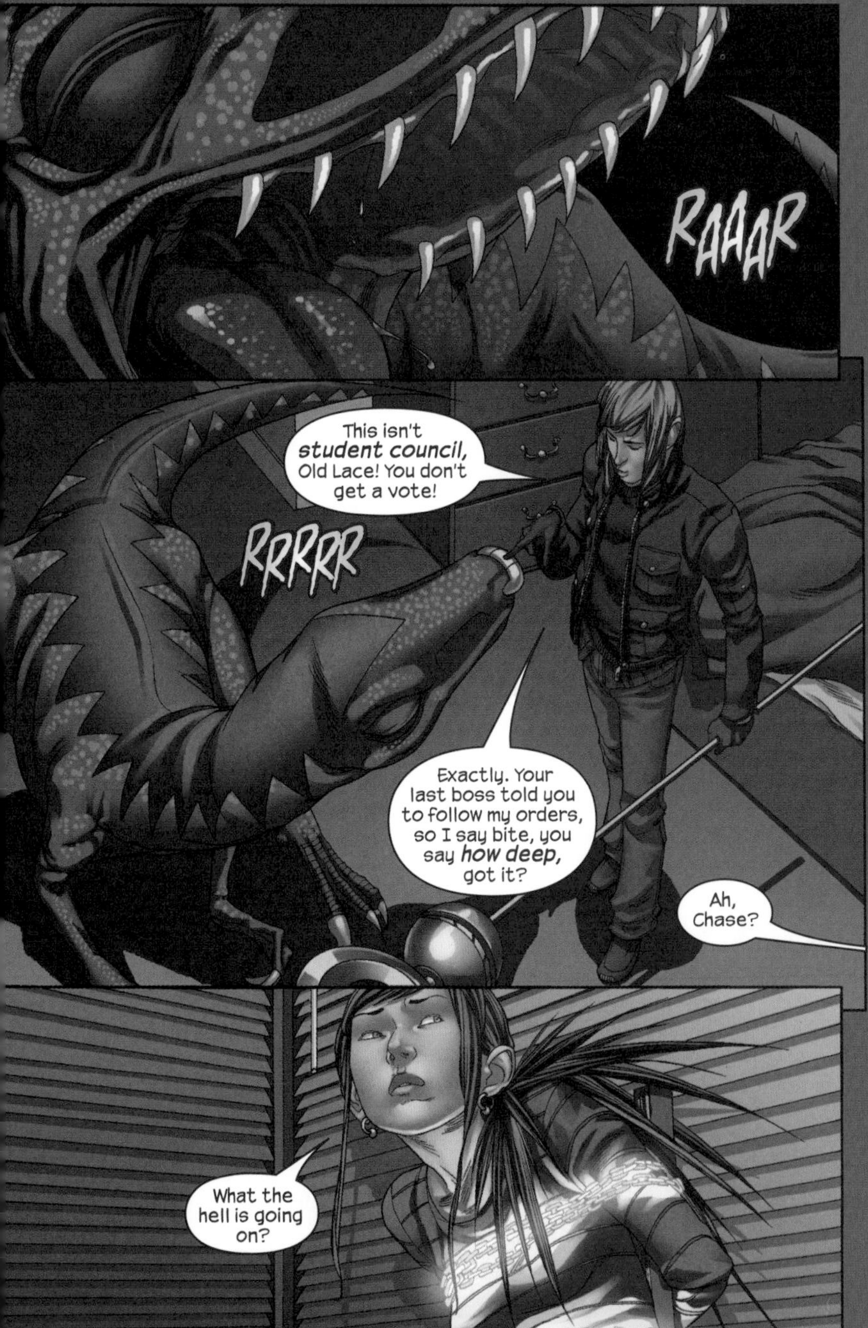
RAAAR
This isn't **student council,** Old Lace! You don't get a vote!
RRRRR
Exactly. Your last boss told you to follow my orders, so I say bite, you say **how deep,** got it?
Ah, Chase?
What the hell is going on?

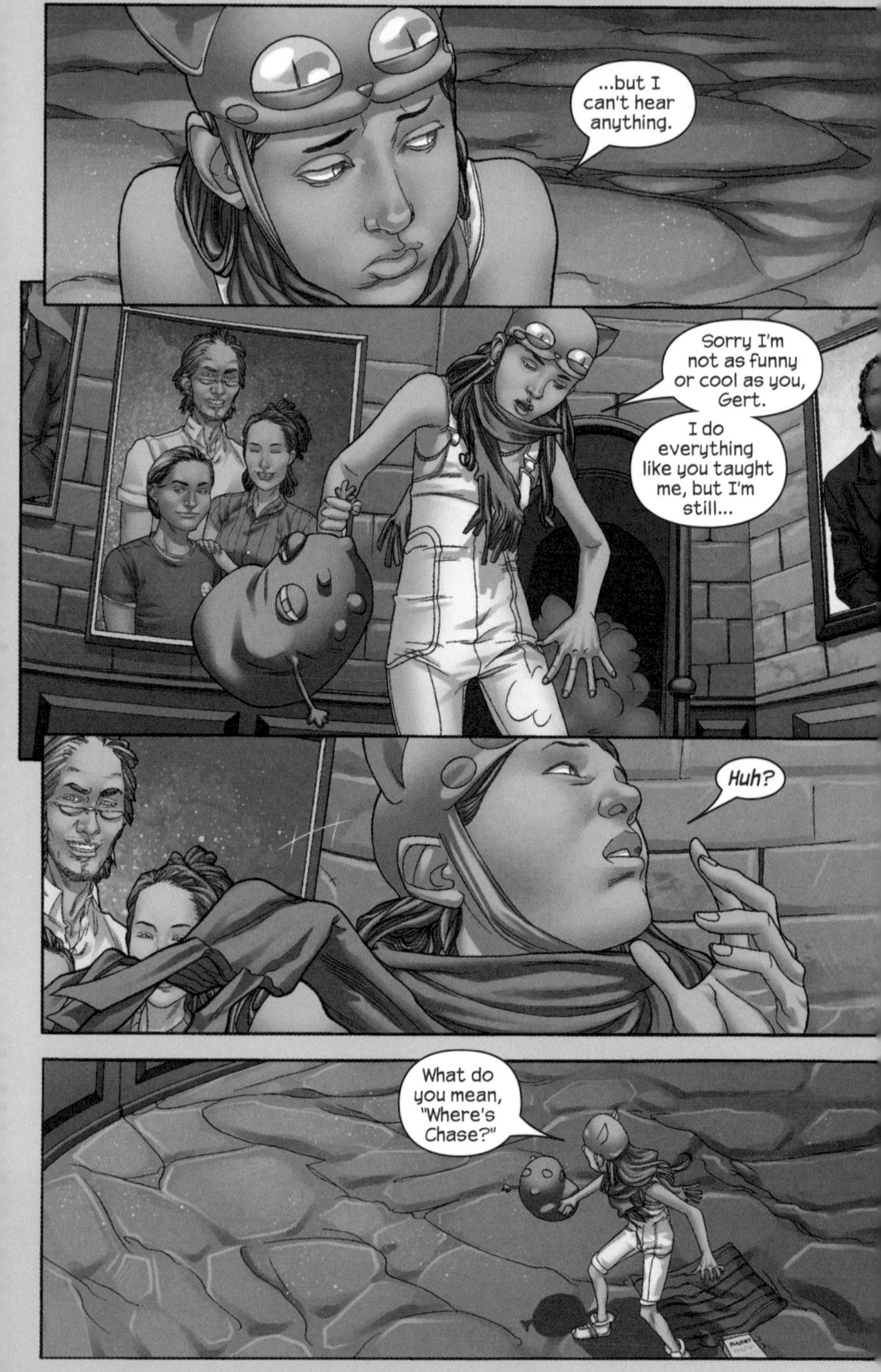
...but I can't hear anything.
Sorry I'm not as funny or cool as you, Gert.
I do everything like you taught me, but I'm still...
Huh?
What do you mean, "Where's Chase?"

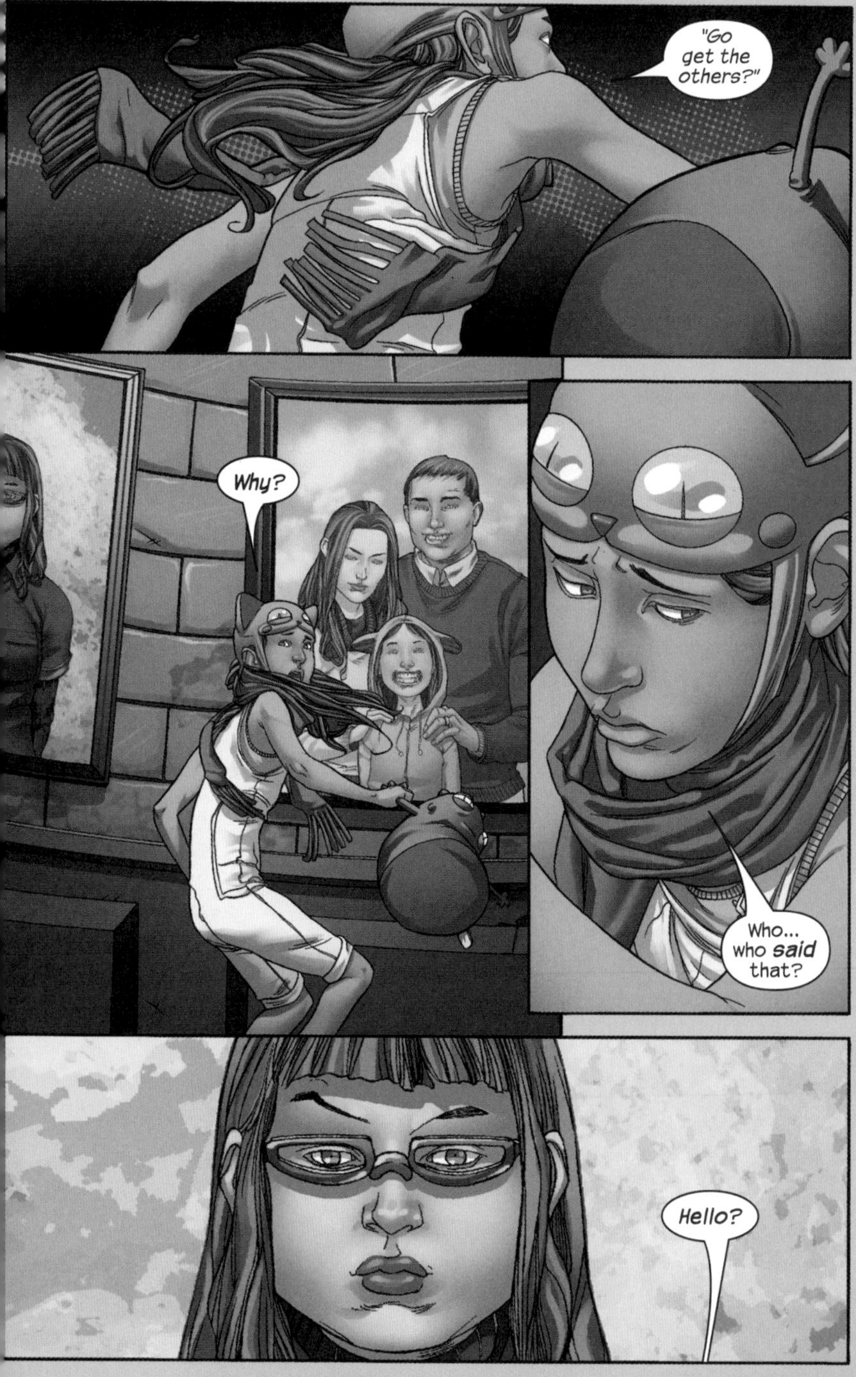
"Go get the others?"
Why?
Who... who said that?
Hello?

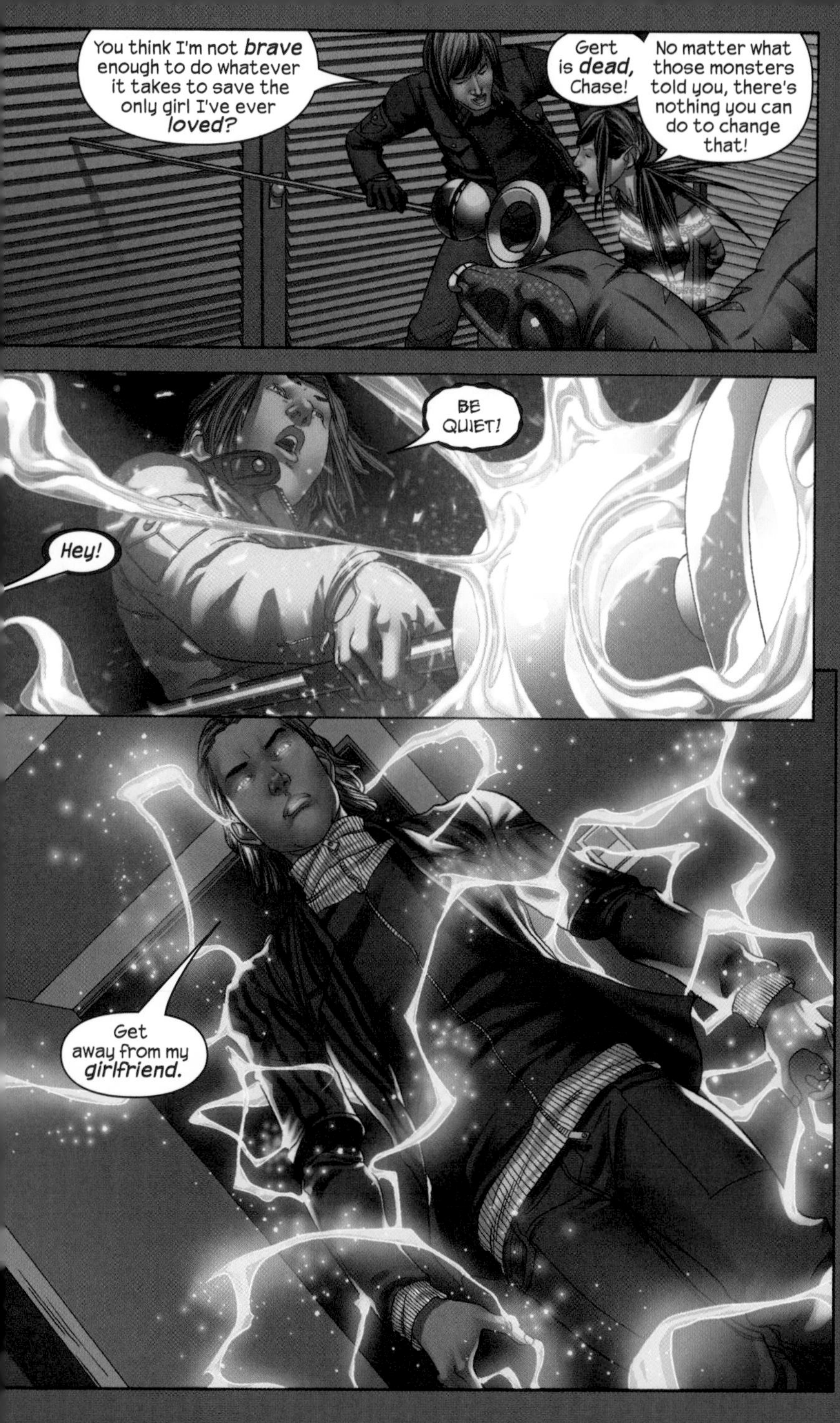
You think I'm not brave enough to do whatever it takes to save the only girl I've ever loved?
Gert is dead, Chase!
No matter what those monsters told you, there's nothing you can do to change that!
BE QUIET!
Hey!
Get away from my girlfriend.

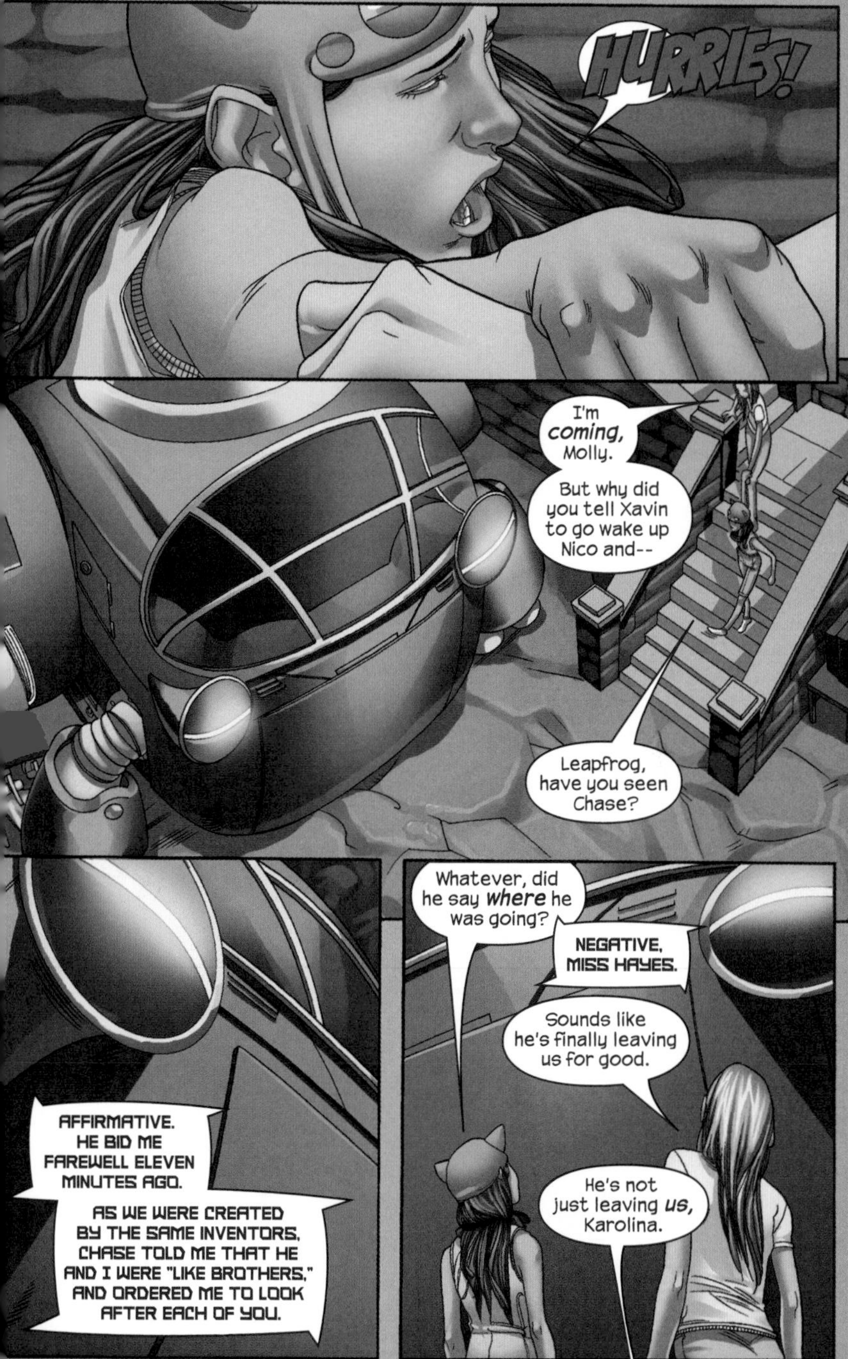
HURRIES!
I'm *coming,* Molly.
But why did you tell Xavin to go wake up Nico and--
Leapfrog, have you seen Chase?
AFFIRMATIVE. HE BID ME FAREWELL ELEVEN MINUTES AGO.
AS WE WERE CREATED BY THE SAME INVENTORS, CHASE TOLD ME THAT HE AND I WERE "LIKE BROTHERS," AND ORDERED ME TO LOOK AFTER EACH OF YOU.
Whatever, did he say *where* he was going?
NEGATIVE, MISS HAYES.
Sounds like he's finally leaving us for good.
He's not just leaving *us,* Karolina.

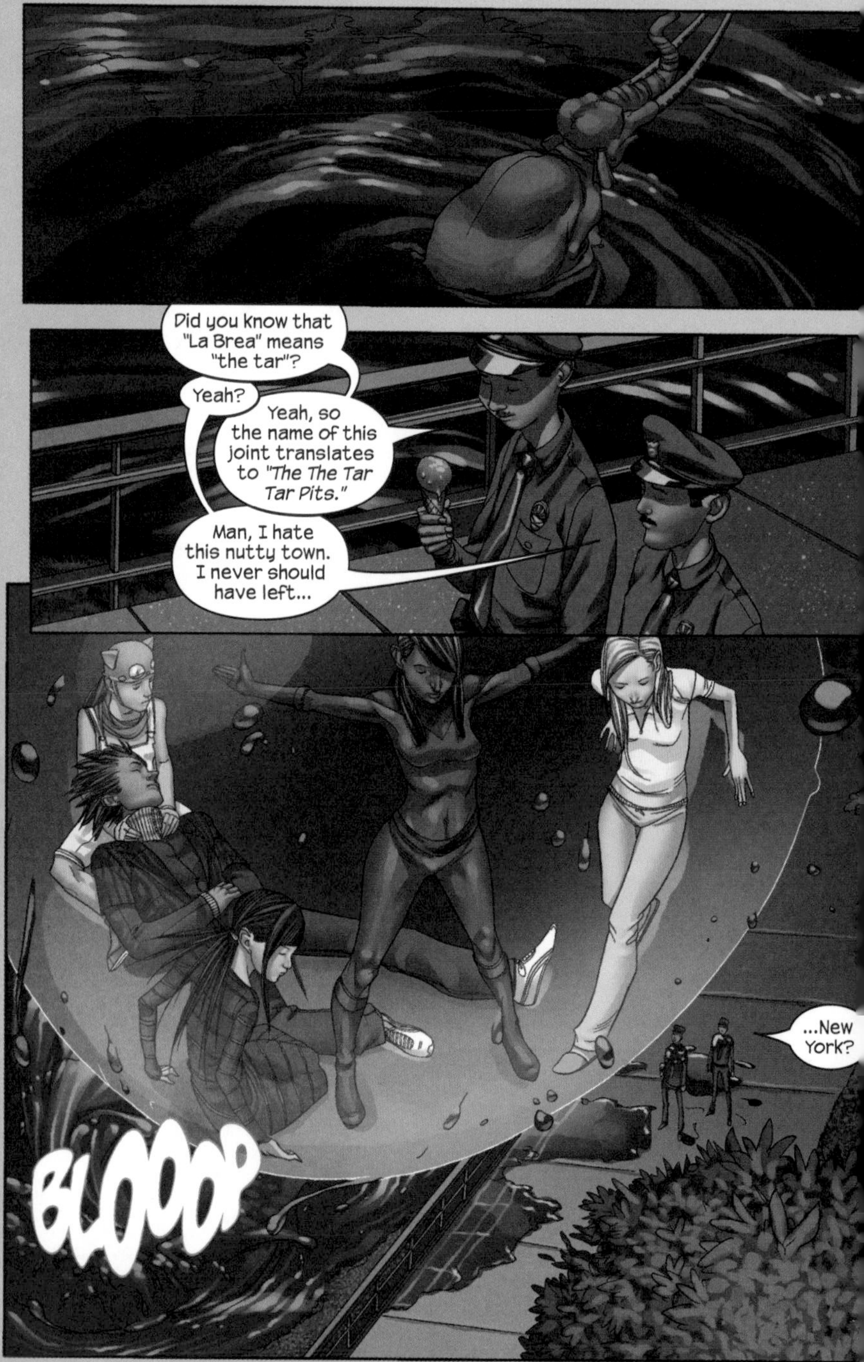

Did you know that "La Brea" means "the tar"?
Yeah?
Yeah, so the name of this joint translates to "The The Tar Tar Pits."
Man, I hate this nutty town. I never should have left...
BLOOOP
...New York?

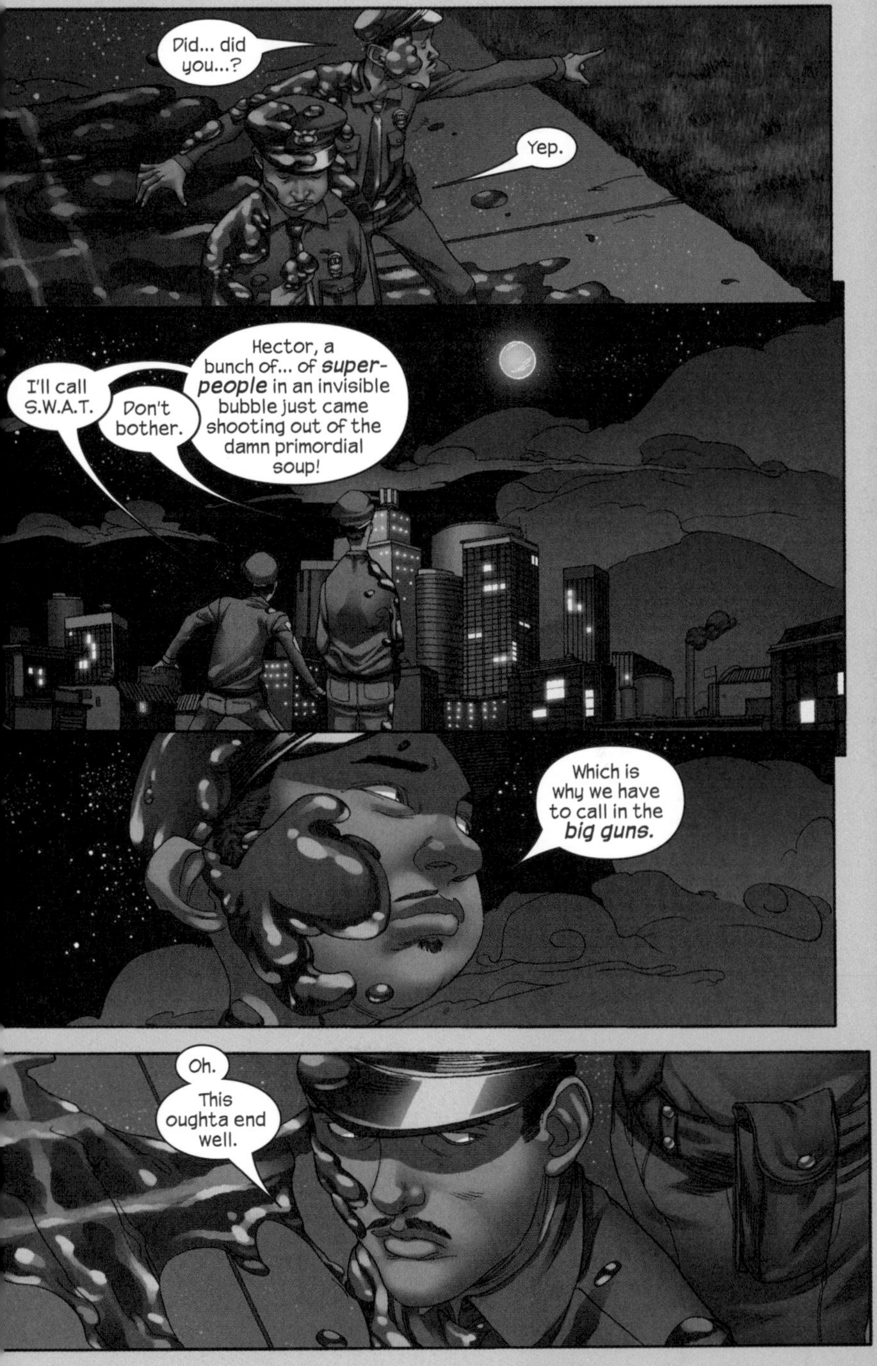

Did... did you...?
Yep.
I'll call S.W.A.T.
Hector, a bunch of... of super-people in an invisible bubble just came shooting out of the damn primordial soup!
Don't bother.
Which is why we have to call in the big guns.
Oh.
This oughta end well.

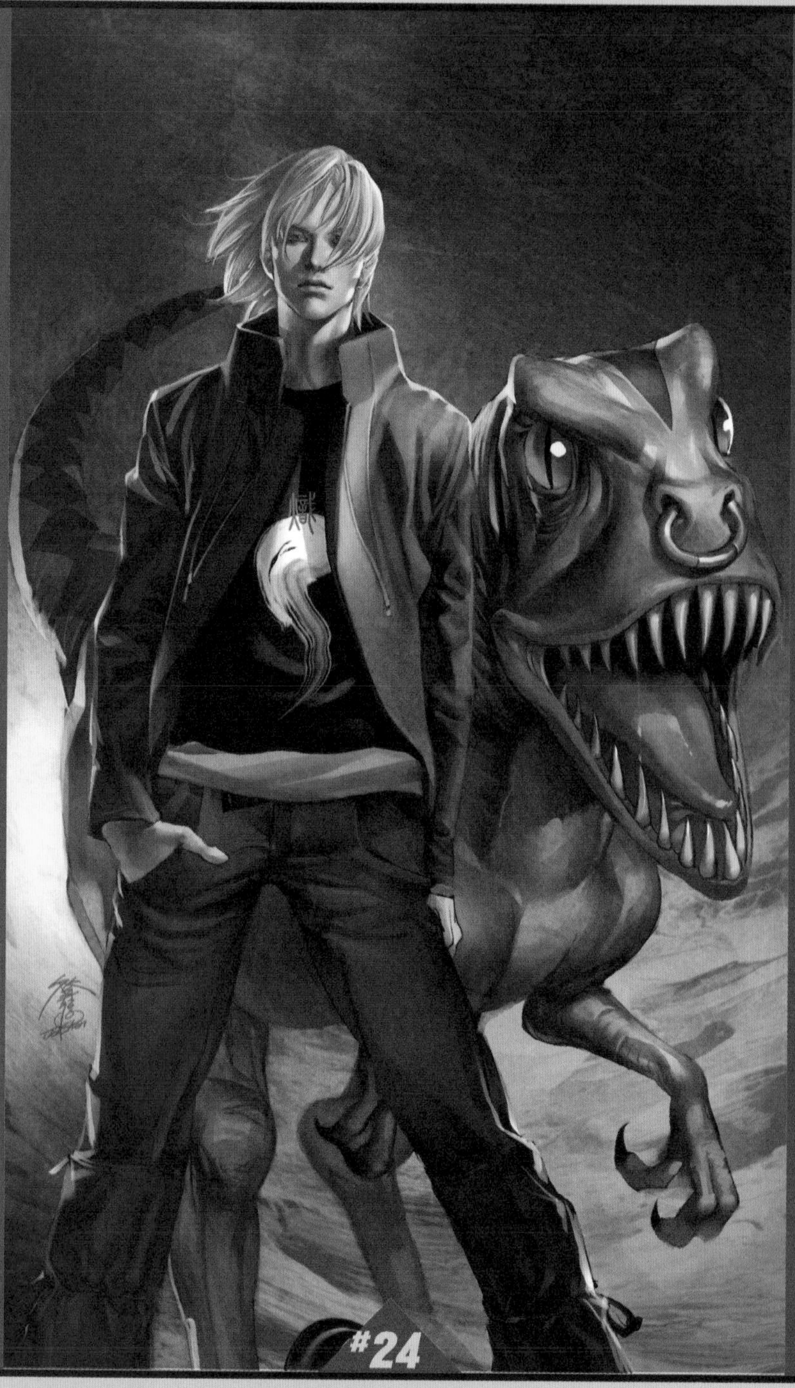
#24

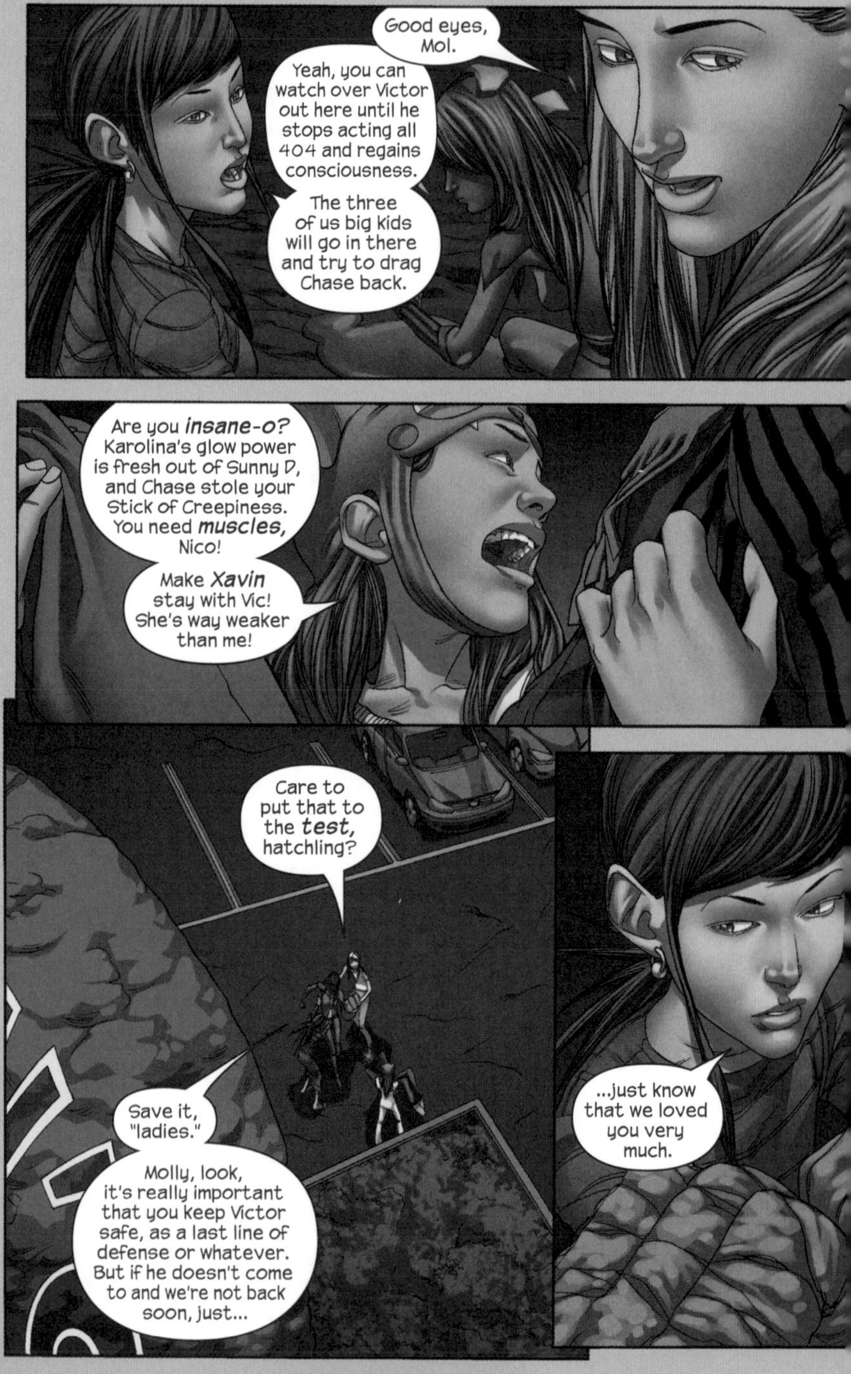
Good eyes, Mol.
Yeah, you can watch over Victor out here until he stops acting all 404 and regains consciousness.
The three of us big kids will go in there and try to drag Chase back.
Are you *insane-o?* Karolina's glow power is fresh out of Sunny D, and Chase stole your Stick of Creepiness. You need *muscles,* Nico!
Make *Xavin* stay with Vic! She's way weaker than me!
Care to put that to the *test,* hatchling?
Save it, "ladies."
Molly, look, it's really important that you keep Victor safe, as a last line of defense or whatever. But if he doesn't come to and we're not back soon, just...
...just know that we loved you very much.

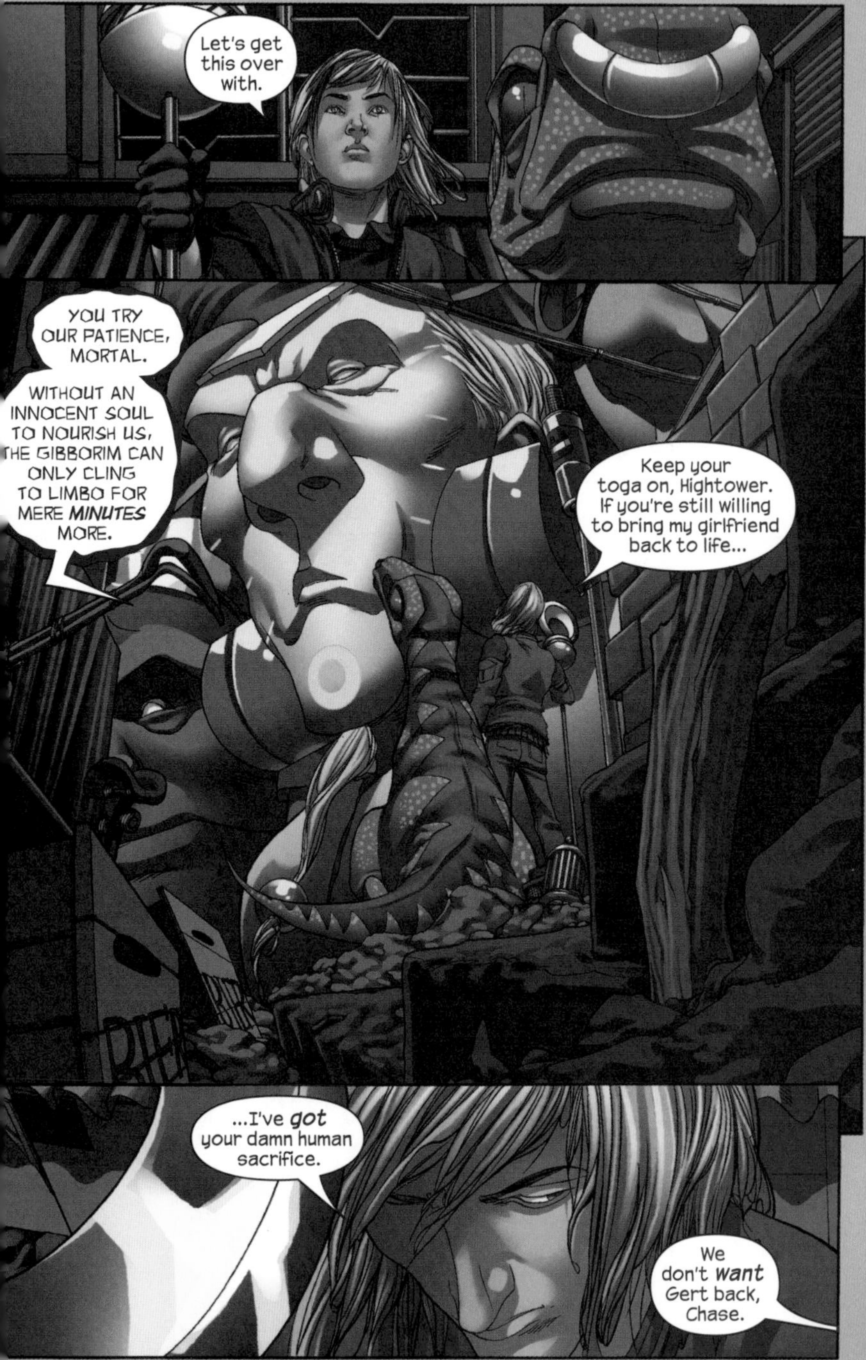

Let's get this over with.
YOU TRY OUR PATIENCE, MORTAL.
WITHOUT AN INNOCENT SOUL TO NOURISH US, THE GIBBORIM CAN ONLY CLING TO LIMBO FOR MERE *MINUTES* MORE.
Keep your toga on, Hightower. If you're still willing to bring my girlfriend back to life...
...I've *got* your damn human sacrifice.
We don't *want* Gert back, Chase.

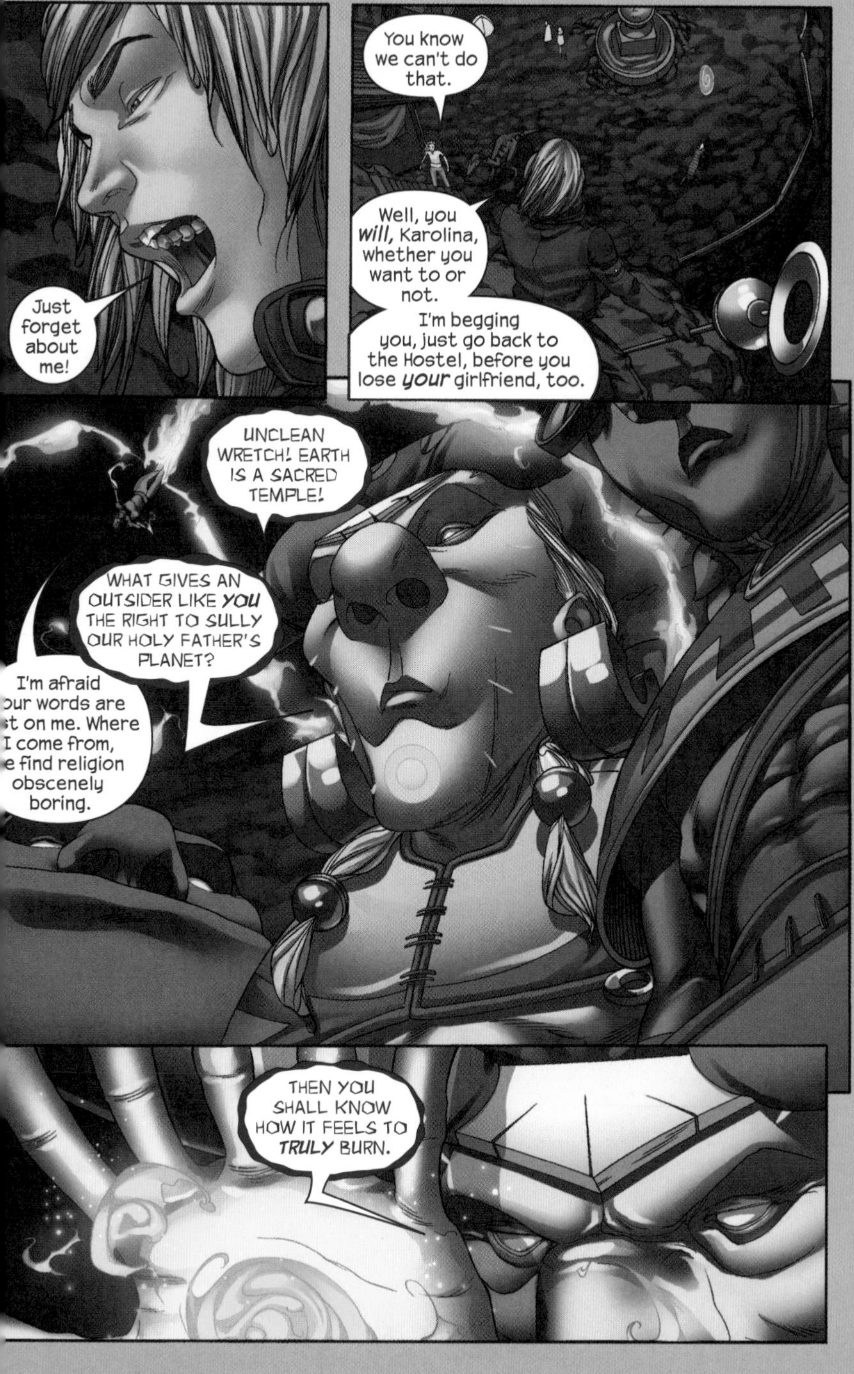
Just forget about me!
You know we can't do that.
Well, you *will,* Karolina, whether you want to or not.
I'm begging you, just go back to the Hostel, before you lose ***your*** girlfriend, too.
UNCLEAN WRETCH! EARTH IS A SACRED TEMPLE!
WHAT GIVES AN OUTSIDER LIKE ***YOU*** THE RIGHT TO SULLY OUR HOLY FATHER'S PLANET?
I'm afraid our words are st on me. Where I come from, e find religion obscenely boring.
THEN YOU SHALL KNOW HOW IT FEELS TO ***TRULY*** BURN.

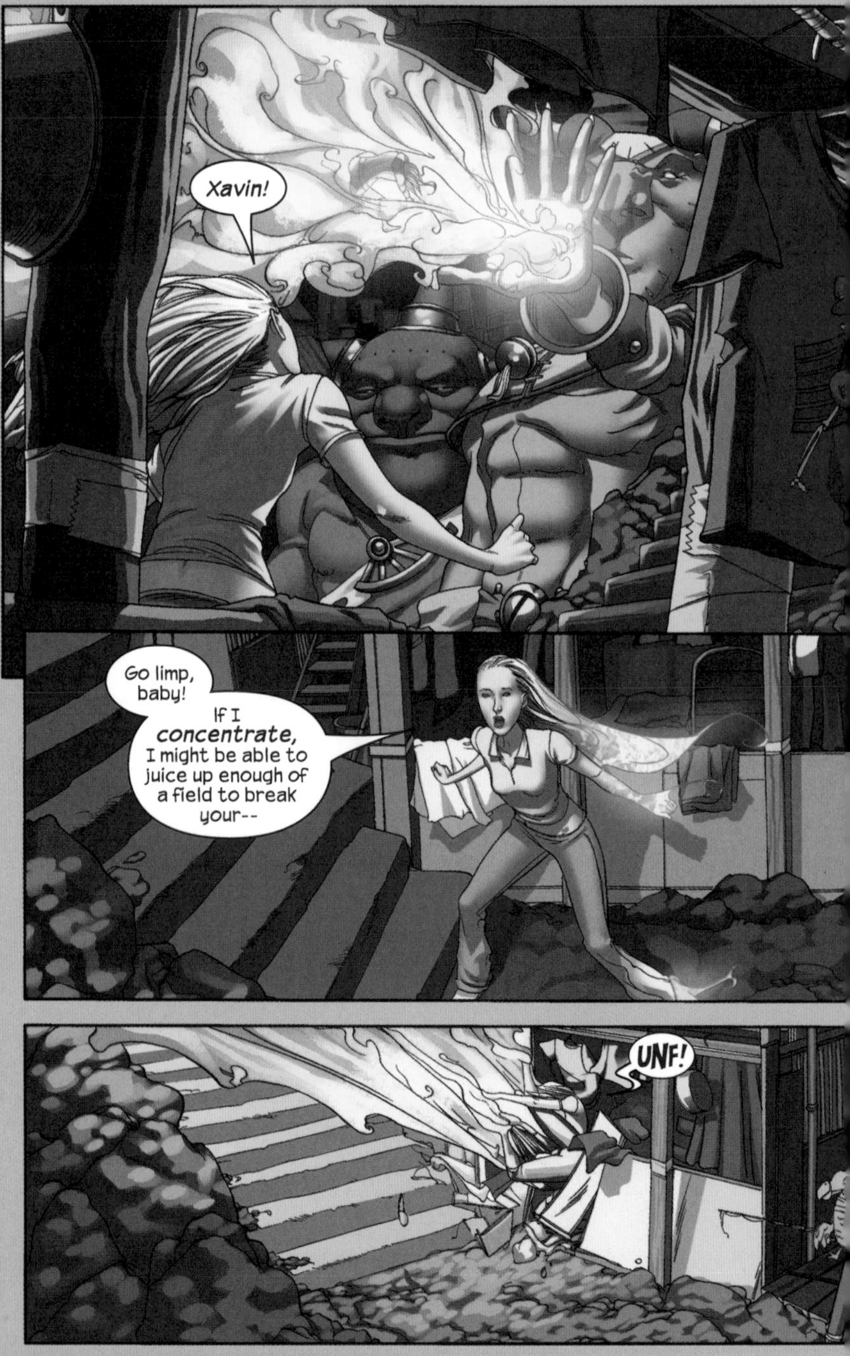
Xavin!
Go limp, baby!
If I concentrate, I might be able to juice up enough of a field to break your--
UNF!

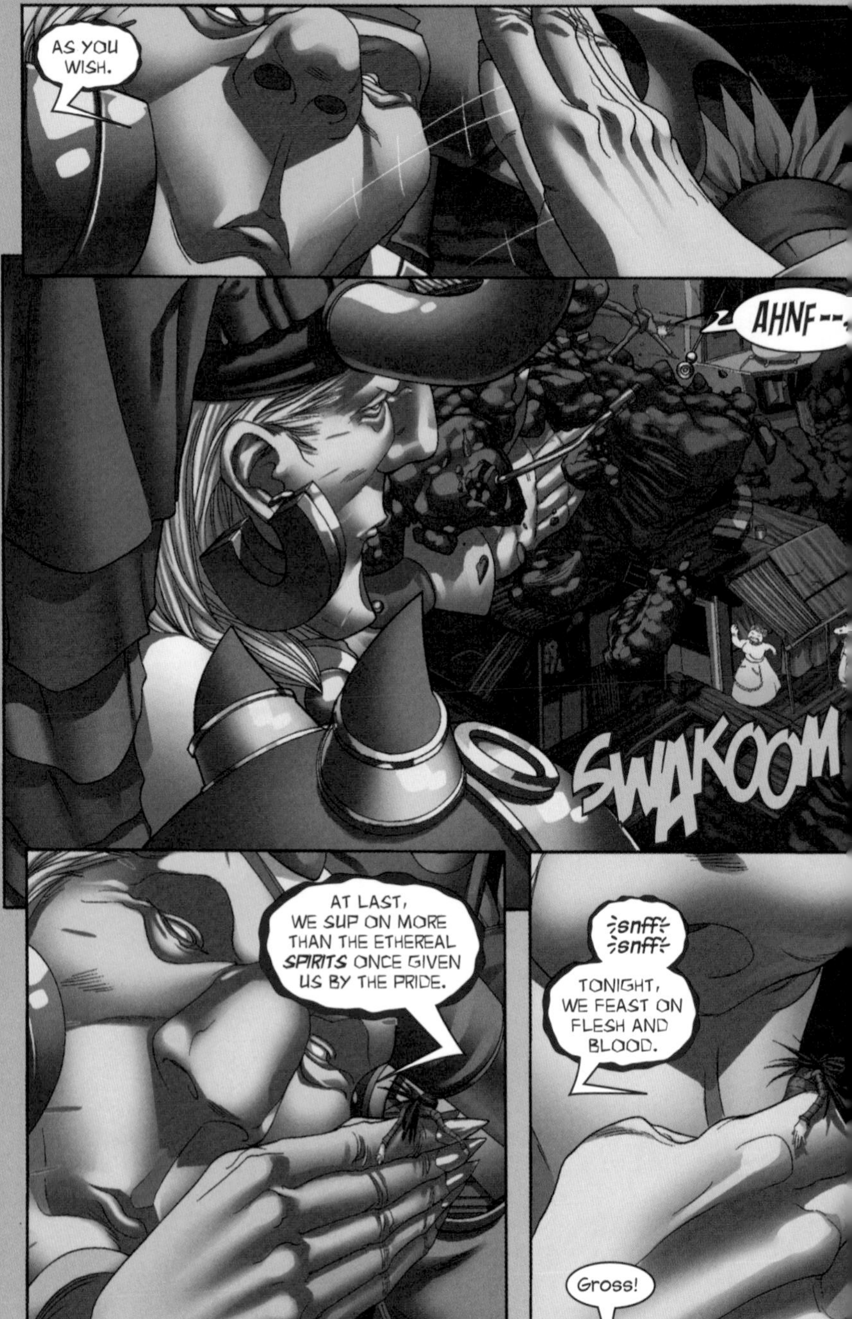
AS YOU WISH.
AHNF--
SWAKOOM
AT LAST, WE SUP ON MORE THAN THE ETHEREAL SPIRITS ONCE GIVEN US BY THE PRIDE.
snff snff
TONIGHT, WE FEAST ON FLESH AND BLOOD.
Gross!

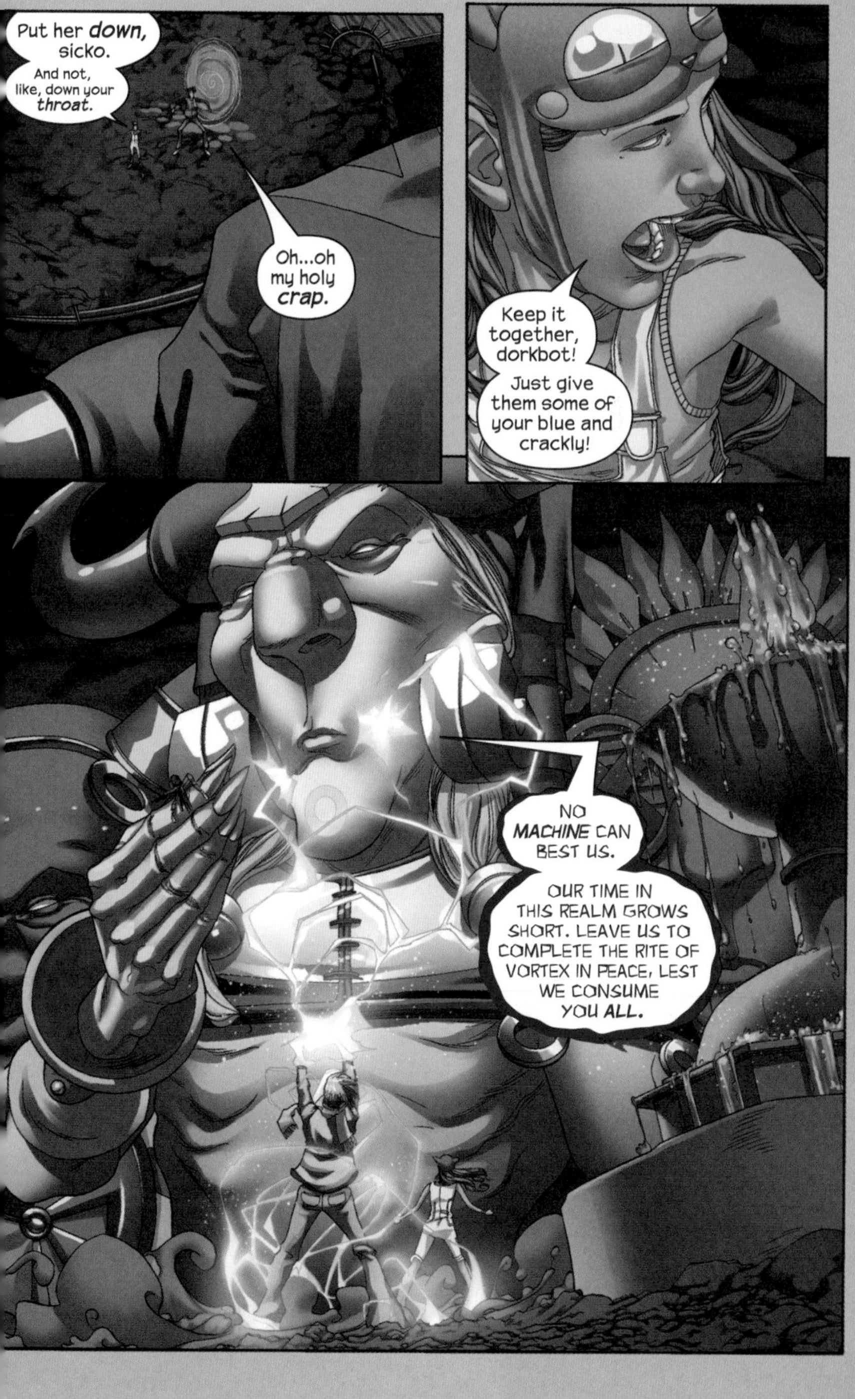
Put her *down,* sicko.
And not, like, down your *throat*.
Oh...oh my holy *crap*.
Keep it together, dorkbot!
Just give them some of your blue and crackly!
NO *MACHINE* CAN BEST US.
OUR TIME IN THIS REALM GROWS SHORT. LEAVE US TO COMPLETE THE RITE OF VORTEX IN PEACE, LEST WE CONSUME YOU *ALL*.

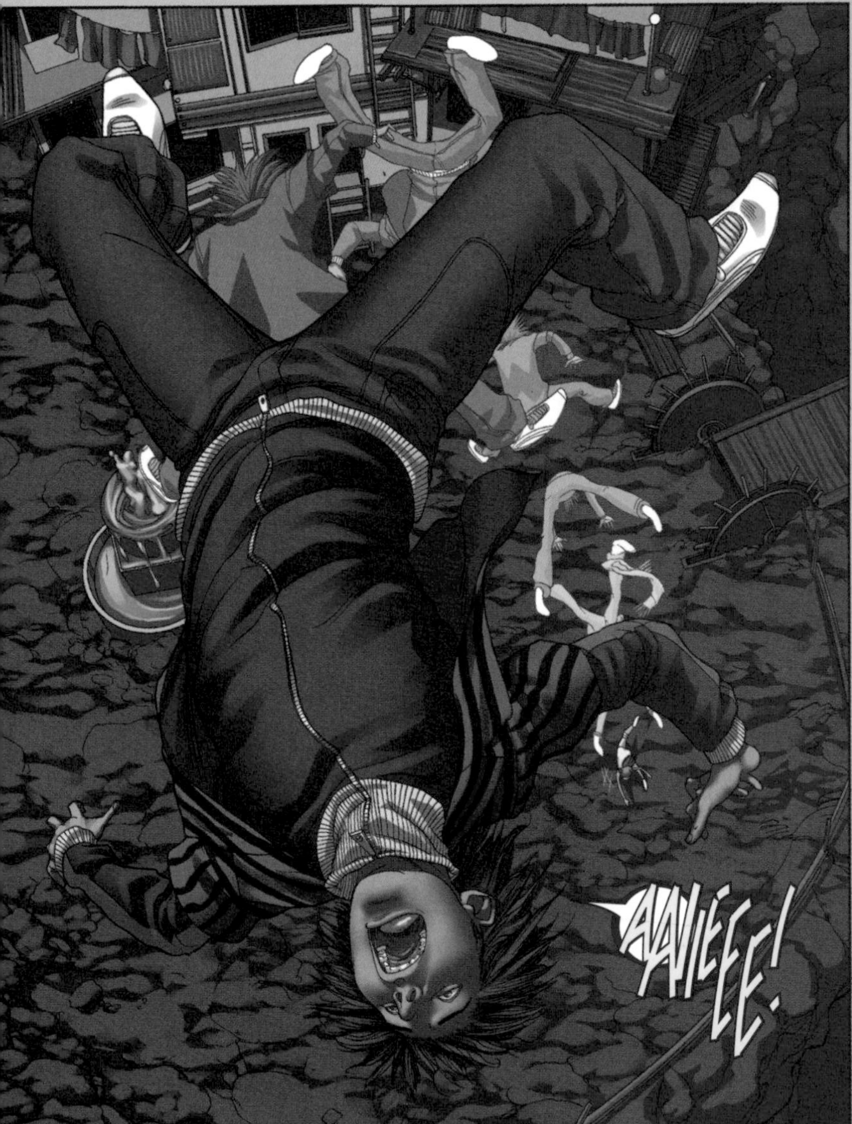
AAAIIEEE!

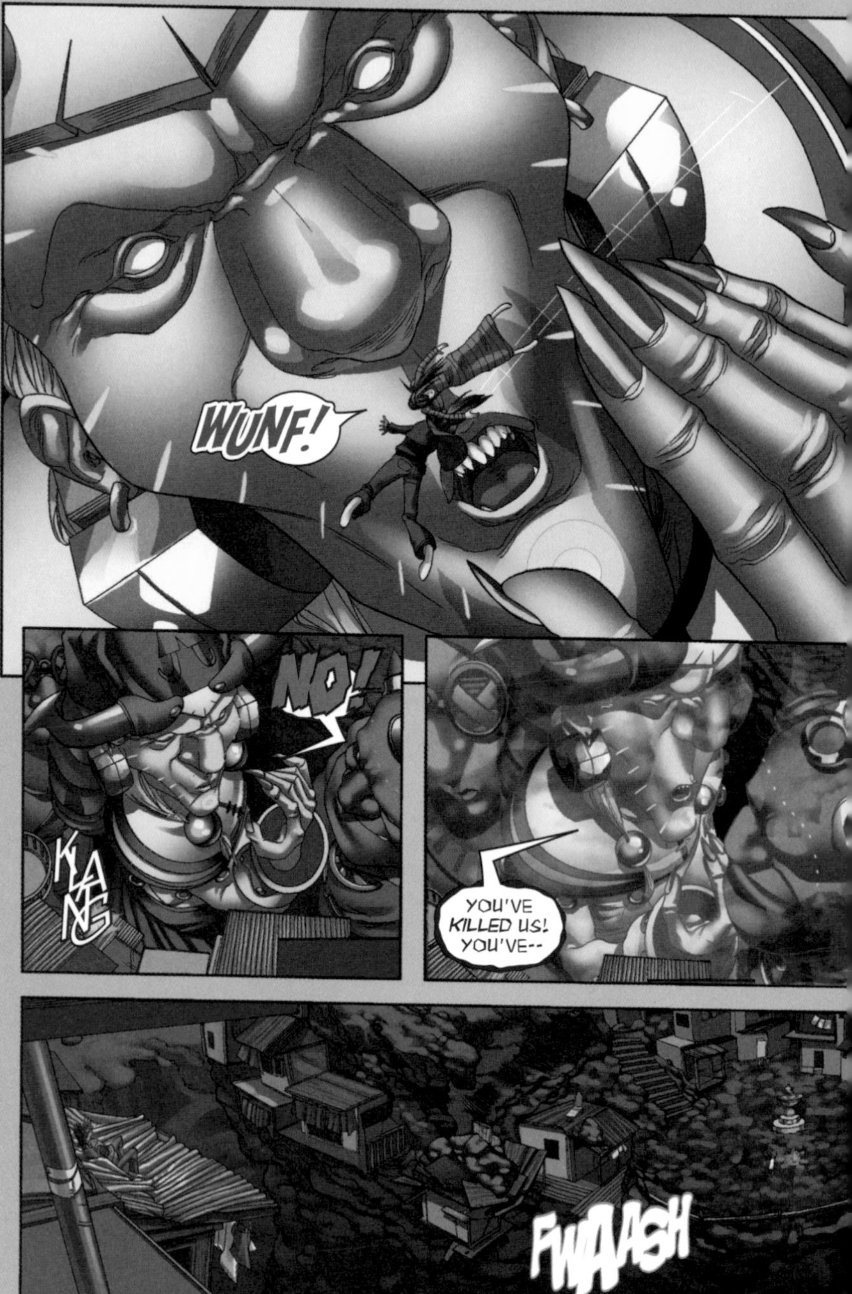
WUNF!
NO!
KLANG
YOU'VE KILLED US! YOU'VE--
FWAASH

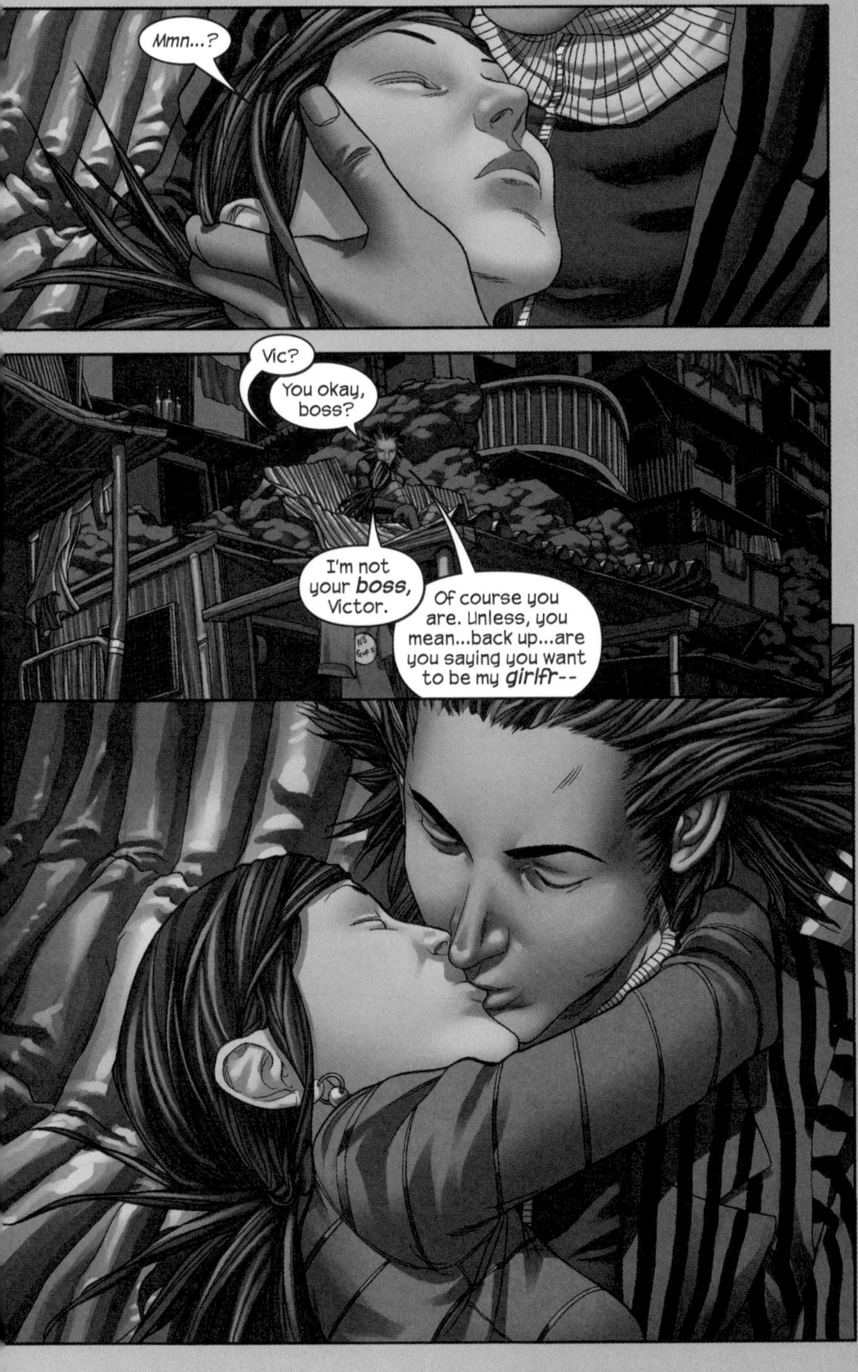
Mmn...?
Vic?
You okay, boss?
I'm not your **boss,** Victor.
Of course you are. Unless, you mean...back up...are you saying you want to be my *girlfr--*

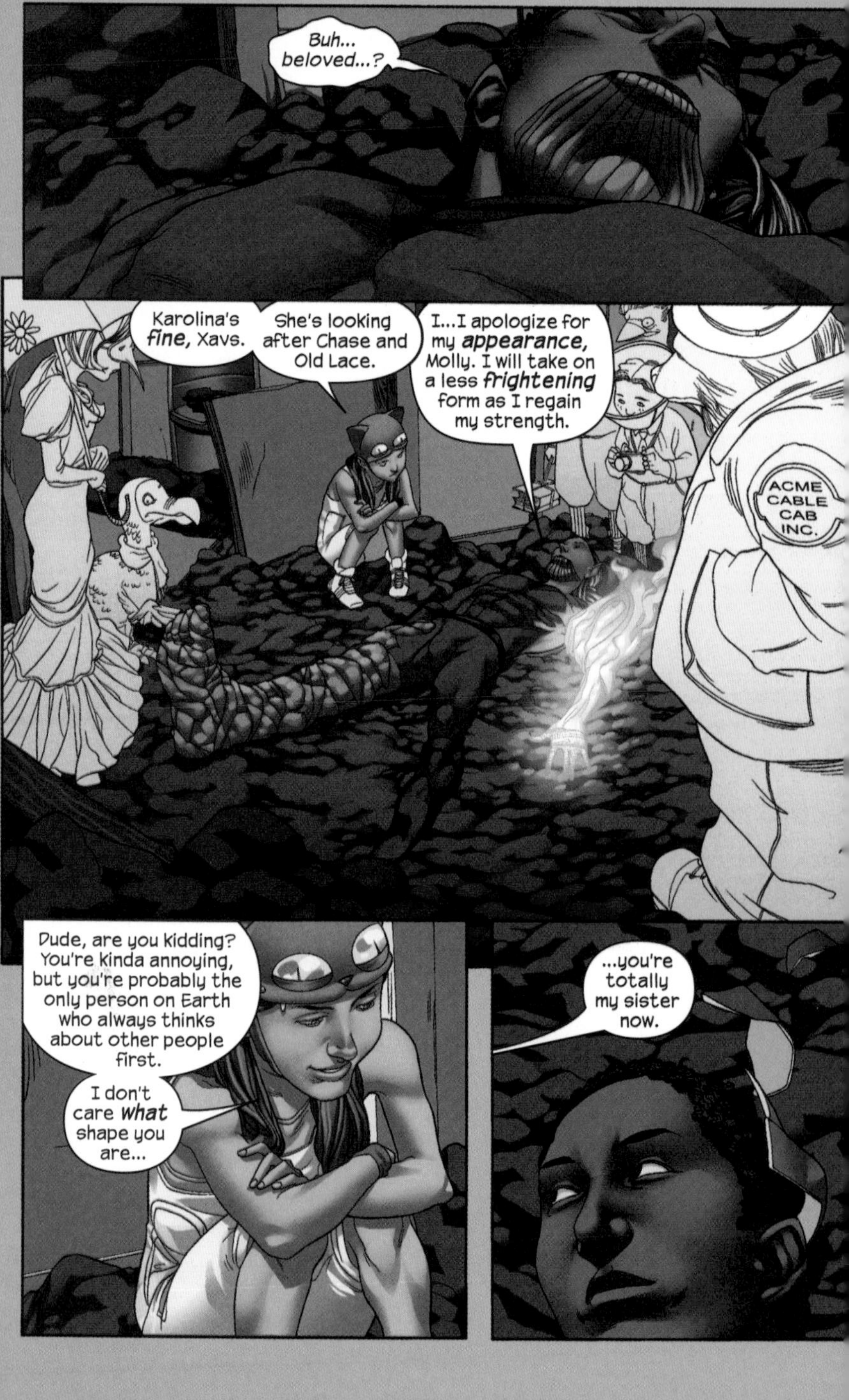

Buh... beloved...?
Karolina's *fine,* Xavs.
She's looking after Chase and Old Lace.
I...I apologize for my *appearance,* Molly. I will take on a less *frightening* form as I regain my strength.
ACME CABLE CAB INC.
Dude, are you kidding? You're kinda annoying, but you're probably the only person on Earth who always thinks about other people first.
I don't care *what* shape you are...
...you're totally my sister now.

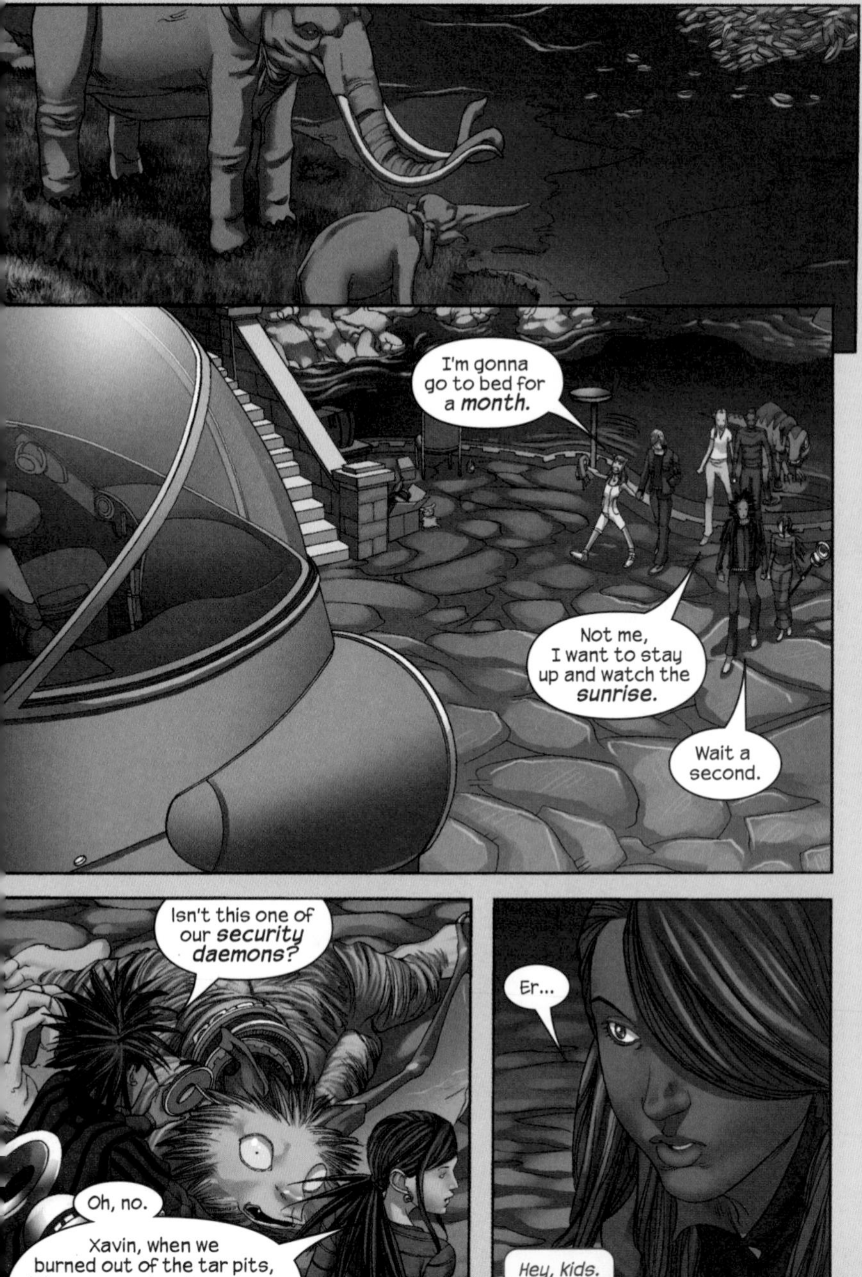
I'm gonna go to bed for a *month.*
Not me, I want to stay up and watch the *sunrise.*
Wait a second.
Isn't this one of our *security daemons?*
Oh, no.
Xavin, when we burned out of the tar pits, did you remember to make *us* invisible, or just the bubble we were zooming around in?
Er...
Hey, kids.

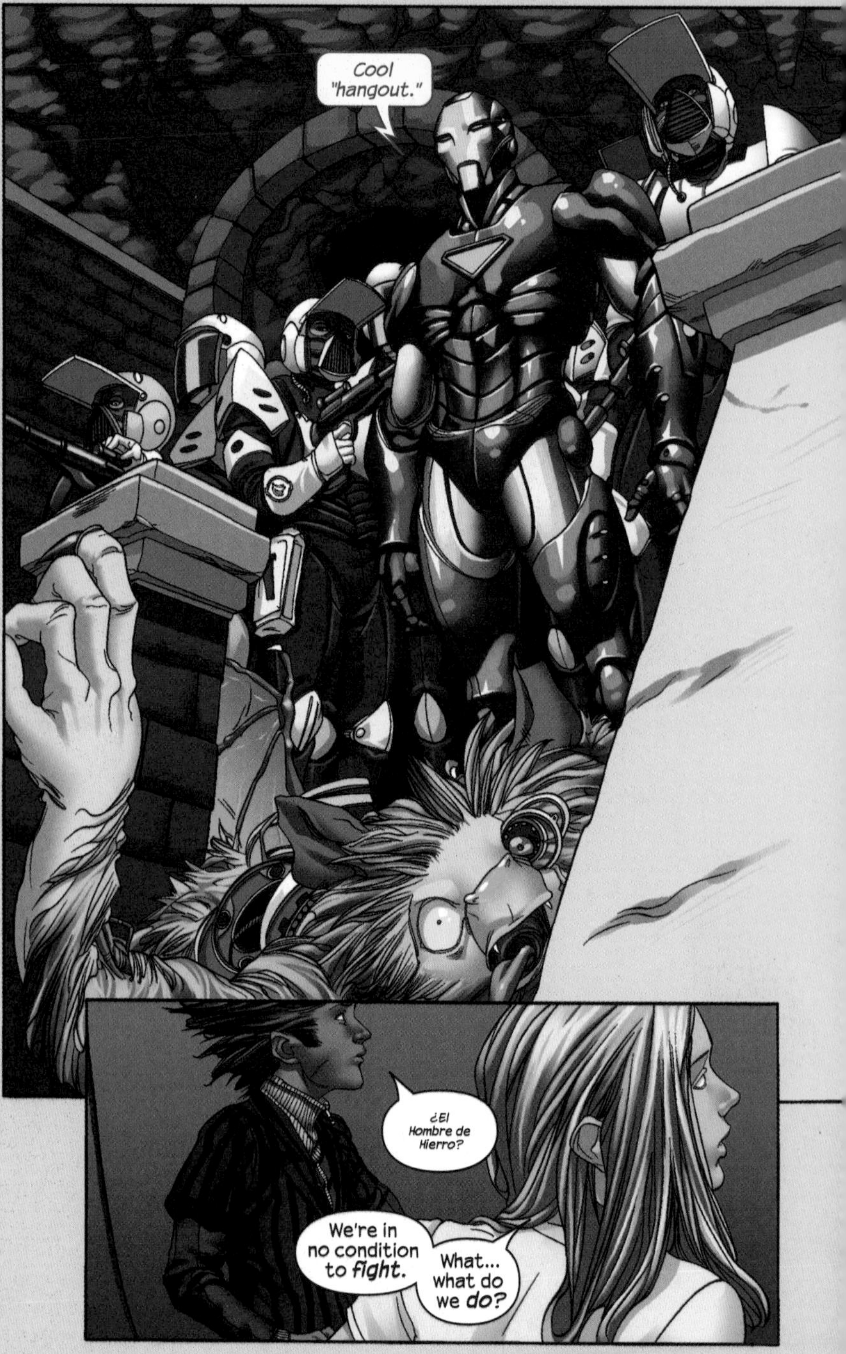
Cool "hangout."
¿El Hombre de Hierro?
We're in no condition to fight.
What... what do we do?

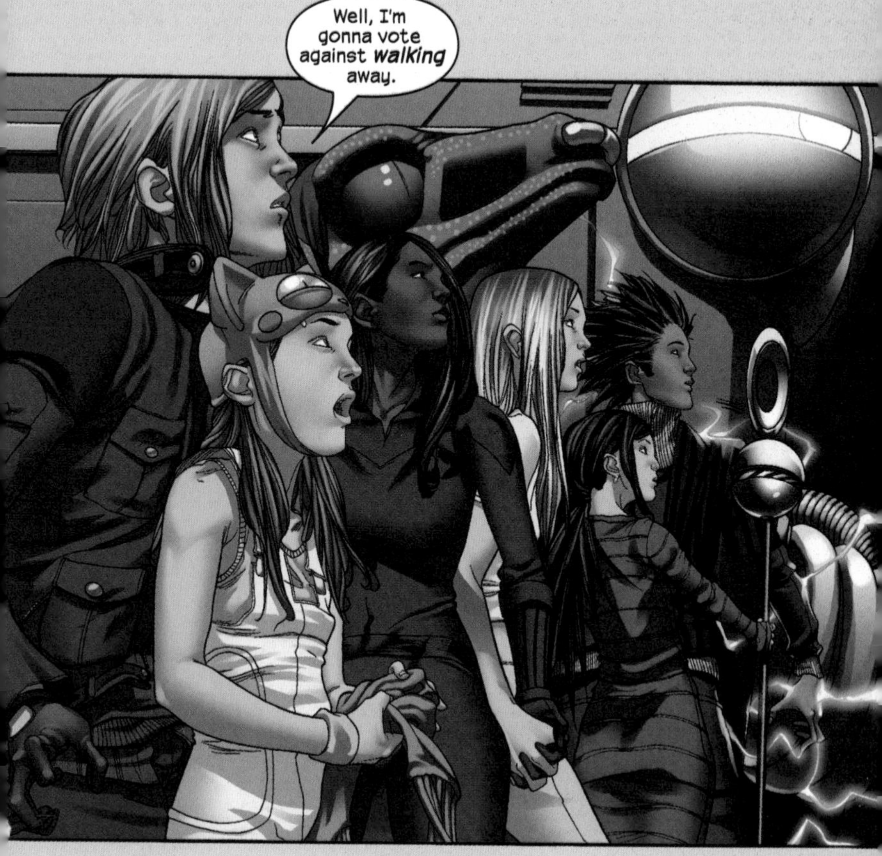
Well, I'm gonna vote against *walking* away.

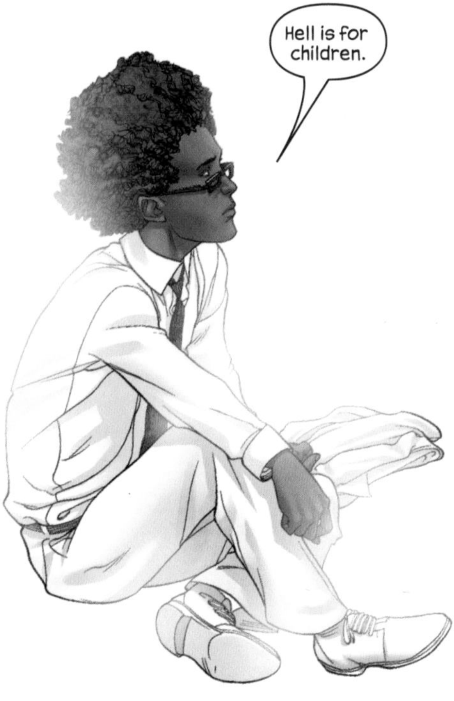
Hell is for children.

RUNAWAYS DESIGNS BY ADRIAN ALPHONA

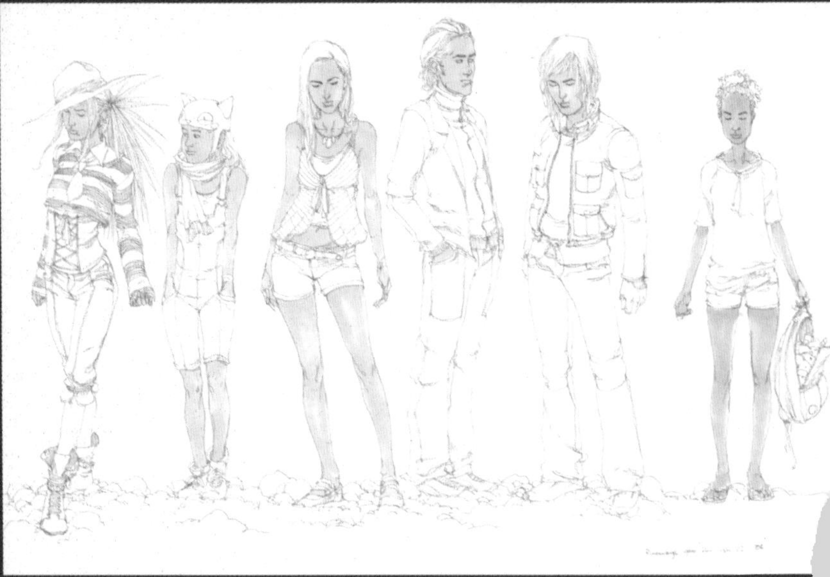

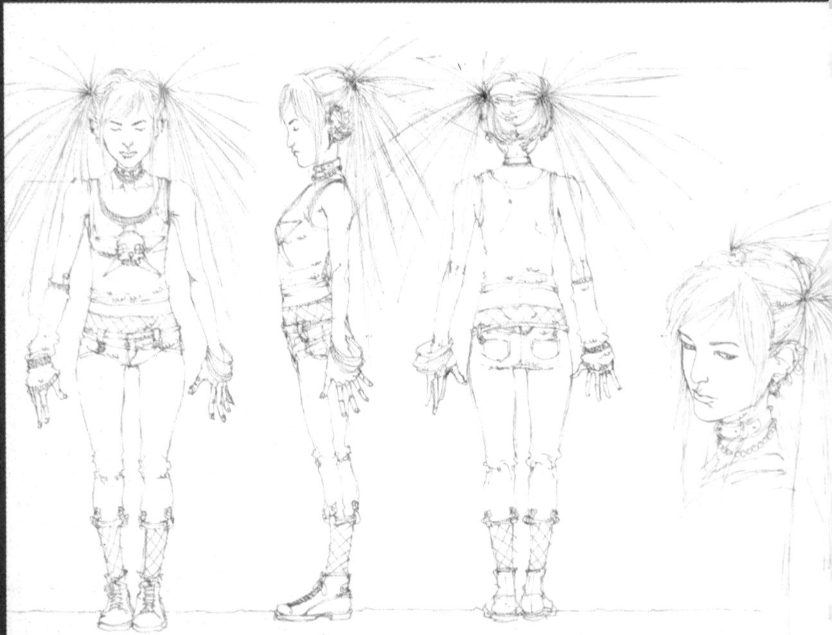